Culture Wars and Local Politics

STUDIES IN GOVERNMENT
AND PUBLIC POLICY

Culture Wars
and Local Politics

Edited by Elaine B. Sharp

University Press of Kansas

Published by the University Press of Kansas (Lawrence, Kansas 66049),
which was organized by the Kansas Board of Regents and is operated and
funded by Emporia State University, Fort Hays State University, Kansas State
University, Pittsburg State University, the University of Kansas, and Wichita
State University

Library of Congress Cataloging-in-Publication Data

Culture wars and local politics / edited by Elaine B. Sharp.
     p. cm. — (Studies in government and public policy)
   Includes bibliographical references and index.
   ISBN 0-7006-0935-0 (cloth : alk. paper). — ISBN 0-7006-0936-9
(pbk. : alk. paper)
    1. United States—Social policy—1980–1993. 2. United States—
Social policy—1993– 3. Culture—Political aspects—United States.
4. Social values—Political aspects—United States. 5. Local
government—United States. 6. Municipal government—United States.
I. Sharp, Elaine B. II. Series.
HN59.2.C83   1999
361.6'1'0973—dc21   98-45634

British Library Cataloguing in Publication Data is available.

Printed in the United States of America

10 9 8 7 6 5 4 3 2 1

Contents

1
Introduction

Elaine B. Sharp

In the summer of 1991, the city of Wichita was caught in the throes of controversy as Operation Rescue staged a major effort to blockade the city's abortion clinics. The event engulfed the community in controversy and chaos, strained the resources of local law enforcement, and galvanized forces in other communities. Pro-choice activists in Milwaukee, for example, organized a campaign in 1992 called "This Ain't Kansas Escorts" to keep their six abortion clinics open. With or without the looming presence of Operation Rescue, many communities in the United States have grappled with the potential for abortion clinic protest to turn violent—a potential that became all too real with the slaying of an abortion clinic doctor and a pro-abortion escort in Pensacola, Florida in 1993. In response to local governments' struggle to contain the violence with various policing and crowd-control strategies, the federal government in 1994 enacted the Freedom of Access to Clinic Entrances Act (FACE), providing severe penalties for those who use force, threat of force, or physical obstruction to interfere with or intimidate abortion clinic personnel or women attempting to obtain abortions. For a time, abortion clinic violence seemed to be muted. But the shooting of two abortion doctors in Brookline, Massachusetts in March 1996 underscored the continuing potential for violence and the continuing burden on local governments to maintain some semblance of security and social order despite the passionate protests that the abortion issue regularly evokes.

But the abortion issue is by no means the only matter that has engulfed communities and their local governments in heated controversy over matters of morality and conscience. In the spring of 1997, county commissioners in Mecklenberg County, North Carolina voted to suspend funding to the Arts and Science Council of Charlotte. The funding cutoff resulted from protests lodged by conservative groups who were offended by the presentation of *Angels in America: A Gay Fantasia on National Themes* at a theater subsidized with Arts and Science Council

1

funding. Charlotte is not the only city confronting controversy over arts funding and the sponsoring of artistic productions that offend the moral sensibilities of some taxpayers. In a pattern that parallels the pitched battles that have been fought at the federal level over the National Endowment for the Arts, cities such as Anchorage and Greensboro also have experienced heated fights over arts funding, sparked by projects deemed morally objectionable; and a number of other cities—such as Clearwater, Florida; San Antonio, Texas; and Santa Ana, California—have dealt with proposals either to withhold funds for the arts or to monitor closely how funds are to be used. In fact, one spokesperson for an arts advocacy organization calls the local level "the new battleground" in the war over artistic freedom, morally controversial projects, and tax dollars (Dobrzynski, 1997).

If local government is a new battleground in this war and an old battleground in the abortion wars, it is also an important venue for conflict over numerous other morality-based issues. For example, controversy erupted in New York City in 1993 over a multicultural school curriculum about gays and extensive condom distribution in the schools. Numerous school districts across the United States have become mired in controversy over curriculum reforms that introduce topics of sexual activity and homosexuality (Button et al., 1997), and efforts to create school-based health centers have been controversial endeavors for a number of counties, city governments, and school districts because of debates over condom distribution, fears that youth would receive information about abortion services, and similar issues (Marks and Marzke, 1993; Rienzo and Button, 1993).

Because local governments have led the way in enacting civil rights protections for homosexuals, clashes over gay rights are also evident at the municipal level. Although gay rights ordinances have sometimes been quietly adopted by localities, consideration of such measures frequently sparks heated exchanges over family values and the moral acceptability of homosexuality in the community. Once in place, gay rights ordinances can subsequently become the subject of community controversies when efforts are made to abolish such protections.

In still other communities, controversy has erupted over needle exchange programs designed to prevent the transmission of HIV infection that occurs when intravenous drug users share "dirty" needles. Such programs are controversial on moral grounds. In particular, opponents argue that such programs would encourage illegal drug use. Indeed, some African American leaders see needle exchange programs as a "pernicious attempt to avoid providing black drug users with adequate treatment" and as part of a genocidal agenda in which white America is pushing drugs on black Americans (Donovan, 1996:8).

Gambling, prostitution, and pornography are also the focus of passionate crusades and controversial local government policies. Cincinnati stands as the poster city for this generalization, with its national reputation as the site where Larry Flynt was convicted of obscenity charges in the late 1970s and where controversy erupted over an exhibition of art with homoerotic themes by Robert Mapplethorpe. In October 1997, Cincinnati officials sprang into action again in response to Larry Flynt's announcement that he would open a bookstore in the city to sell his magazine *Hustler* there for the first time in twenty years. In an emergency meeting, city council members considered changing the city's ordinance regulating adult business to require a special permit and special locational restriction on any business offering a significant proportion of adult-oriented merchandise.

Controversies like those described above are examples of what James Davison Hunter (1991, 1994) calls "culture wars" and Ken Meier (1994) calls "morality politics." They have a number of characteristics that distinguish them from "politics as usual" at the local level. First and foremost, they are disputes grounded in *moral* concerns. This is not to say that economic stakes are not involved at all. Conflicts over the regulation of X-rated video stores have material consequences for the targeted businesses, and homeowners are sometimes rallied to the cause of antipornography campaigns because of concerns about property values. Similarly, the providers of abortion services also have economic stakes in conflicts that threaten to affect women's access to abortion clinics. And fights over gay and lesbian rights protections sometimes involve health insurance or other benefits that constitute material stakes for gay and lesbian advocates and that have important economic consequences for the employers who would provide them. Despite their obvious economic implications, culture war controversies are distinctive because they are rooted in deep-seated moral values. In each of these controversies, at least one party to the conflict is mobilized largely because proposals or existing practices are viewed as an affront to religious belief or a violation of a fundamental moral code. In this respect, the phenomenon of culture wars corresponds with Tatalovich and Daynes's (1988:1) conceptualization of "social regulatory policy," which involves efforts by some individuals to impose "legal authority to modify or replace community values, moral practices, and norms of interpersonal conduct with new standards of behavior."

Because they derive from differences over fundamental values and moral concerns, culture wars are often extraordinarily passionate and strident. Following Ken Meier's treatment, scholars of morality policy typically note that debate over such policy involves uncompromising clashes over values, whereas nonmorality policy involves "conflicts between economic interests where compromise comes more easily" (Mooney and Lee, 1995:600). Others go even further, suggesting that the morality issues that are at the heart of culture war controversies give these disputes a strong potential for violence (Hunter, 1994). This is not to deny that citizens can become enraged over other matters, such as threats to their property values or high taxes. But activists in culture war issues are typically galvanized in ways that make compromise, coalition formation, and other elements of normal politics difficult.

In a related vein, Meier (1994:7) suggests that morality issues are highly salient to the general public because they touch on deeply held values and threats to those values. Furthermore, in contrast with many other aspects of local governance, the technical component of morality issues is relatively low. That is, morality issues can be presented in simple ways and can engage people who have no special expertise in the topical area. Thus, while the power of bureaucratic experts and other policy specialists is a common theme in studies of city service delivery, economic redevelopment, and other facets of local decision making, these experts and specialists are less crucial in culture wars, where the more distinctive characteristics are high levels of issue salience among the general public and occasional but extraordinarily high levels of mobilization of citizen groups.

Yet another distinctive feature of culture wars is the character of the citizen groups and institutions that are mobilized. Ordinarily, local politics involves citizens organized according to *territorial* interests, that is, neighborhood associations or similar residence-based groups; in many cities, racial and ethnic groups constitute another basis for the organization and mobilization of citizen interests at the local level. These interests are sometimes also represented in culture wars, but culture wars spark the involvement of an additional constellation of citizen groups and community institutions. Church leaders and religious organizations, for example, are not featured players in local politics as usual, but they are frequently and prominently involved in culture war controversies. In addition, culture wars frequently involve the activities of social movements, such as the pro-life movement, feminists, and the gay rights movement.

Finally, the actions of participants in culture wars frequently differ from the standard fare of political activism. As the following chapters will show, conventional political organizing, lobbying, and the like are to be found in the development of community politics surrounding culture war issues. But in addition, these issues frequently elicit nonconventional protest activities, including aggressive pro-life demonstrations outside abortion clinics or the homes of abortion providers, confrontational, antigay demonstrations at the funerals of individuals who have died of AIDS, and a host of other alternative forms of political agitation. Culture war controversies thus exemplify what Euchner (1996:20) calls "extraordinary politics": "Extraordinary politics aims to force the political establishment to address issues that it would rather ignore; operating outside formal institutions, extraordinary politics enjoys a latitude of movement and tactics not found in ordinary politics. But at the same time, extraordinary politics lacks the institutional structure and connections necessary for thorough deliberation." Euchner's comments about extraordinary politics, coupled with the work of scholars of morality policy and social regulatory policy, suggest that culture war issues are distinctive. That is, the character of politics in this arena is assumed to be different in important ways from politics as usual, different from the normal dynamics by which issues are raised, debated, and resolved at the local level. These differences presumably are reflected not only in the unusual activities of citizen groups but also in the actions of governing authorities dealing with culture war issues. To the extent that culture wars are different from politics as usual at the local level, there are important consequences for our ability to use existing theories of local politics to understand their development and resolution. But what roles do local government institutions play in culture wars?

LOCAL GOVERNMENT ROLES: A PRELIMINARY ASSESSMENT

Local governments play a variety of important roles in the development of culture wars at the community level. At first blush, it might seem that the explosive character of these controversies would mean that city, county, and school district officials would, if anything, be caught in the middle, and, as a result, play a role of trying to defuse the situation. Preliminary research (Sharp, 1996) focusing on a variety of case studies of such controversies shows that local officials do indeed play this role of *evasion.* That is, they attempt to defuse culture wars by delaying or deferring action on the demands of activists, making symbolic gestures to appease one side without activating the other, or otherwise diverting attention from what could be a heated and full-blown controversy.

That same research also shows that local officials sometimes play a number of quite different roles in such controversies. Some of these roles are overtly favorable to activists who are challenging the moral standards of the community or demanding policy changes that would give official imprimatur to behaviors or groups previously excluded from acceptability. In contrast with evasion, for example, officials sometimes bring these challenges and demands onto the formal agenda, deal with them through regular processes of deliberation, and ultimately enact policies consistent with challenger groups' demands. Such a role might be designated *responsive action.* There is also evidence of officials engaging in a somewhat different role of *hyperactively responsive action.* This role, gleaned from analysis of Downs' (1989) case studies of the development of unique antipornography ordinances in Indianapolis and Minneapolis, is characterized by more than simple responsiveness to culture war activists. It involves extraordinary responsiveness in the sense that decisions favorable to such activists are made in unusual haste, using processes that short-circuit the usual avenues for deliberation and cut off the voices of objecting parties. In addition to the use of nonstandard processes for decision making, hyperactive responsiveness often reveals officials taking a surprisingly cavalier approach to the potential that their actions will not hold up to judicial review, either in reckless disregard of First Amendment and other constitutional issues or out of a sense that local decisions favorable to culture war activists will give symbolic satisfaction, regardless of policy reversals when those decisions are reviewed by the courts.

Although responsiveness and hyperactive responsiveness both portray local government acting favorably toward activists who challenge the status quo, both roles are reactive. But local officials can play a more proactive role. In particular, public officials sometimes initiate attention to controversial, morality-based issues. Their motivations for doing so can involve a desire to gain visibility and political capital to enhance their electoral prospects or personal convictions relating to religious beliefs, morality concerns, and the like. The important point is that local government is not necessarily caught in the middle of culture wars because of conflicts brought to the doorstep of city hall by community activists. Public officials themselves sometimes serve as issue entrepreneurs, taking the lead in identifying morality-based discontent, propelling the issues onto the local agenda, and in the process, instigating these convulsive episodes of conflict. In short, the list of governmental roles in culture war controversies—evasion, responsiveness, and hyperactive responsiveness—must be extended to include *entrepreneurial instigation.*

The actions of local officials are not always favorable to culture-war activists, however. In fact, *repression* of culture war activists is a standard tool in the repertoire of local governments. Repression involves action by authorities to "either depress collective action or raise the cost of its two main preconditions— the organization and mobilization of opinion" (Tarrow, 1994:95). That is, officials may either directly discourage protest actions or make it more risky, expensive, or difficult for activists to organize and send messages to potentially sympathetic publics. Repressive actions can be harsh and obvious, as in the brutal police beatings of civil rights demonstrators in some Southern cities in the 1960s. Similarly, harsh and obvious forms of repression in the form of police actions against gays have been documented for some cities (D'Emilio, 1983). But repression can involve tools other than billy clubs. In many cities, governing bodies have attempted to deter disruptive protest activities by requiring financially burdensome insurance bonds before parade permits can be issued to demonstrators, and some communities have ordinances that restrict activists from demonstrating at certain locations, such as private residences. Other cities have thwarted disruptive protest by suing activist organizations for triple damages under the provisions of the RICO (Racketeer Influenced and Corrupt Organizations) statutes. More subtle forms of repression exist as well. Authorities can make official statements that characterize particular activist groups as outsiders or inappropriate agitators, thus legitimating a variety of informal measures by which private citizens intimidate those who would challenge the status quo (Sharp, 1996).

Each of these governmental roles—evasion, responsiveness, hyperactive responsiveness, entrepreneurial instigation, and repression—can be understood as a posture or set of strategic actions intentionally taken by governmental officials. But local officials may unintentionally play a role that is not of their choosing in such controversies. Repressive tactics can backfire, causing the mobilization of otherwise quiescent groups. Evasion can have the same results. From this perspective, an additional role of local government is the *unintentional instigation* of controversy over a culture war issue (Sharp, 1996:752–53).

ACCOUNTING FOR VARIATION IN LOCAL GOVERNMENT'S ROLE: SOME ASSEMBLY IS REQUIRED

The first task in understanding the local politics of culture wars is to determine whether the set of governmental roles outlined above (evasion, responsiveness, hyperactive responsiveness, entrepreneurial instigation, repression, and unintentional instigation) constitutes a comprehensive listing of governmental roles in such controversies and whether the conceptualization of any of the roles requires refinement. By exploring a variety of culture war issues in a large number of communities, the chapter authors for this volume contribute enormously to this task of scanning for overlooked roles and testing the limits of the initial conceptualization. In the process, they uncover some important conceptual issues. In part then, this volume is devoted to the task of the conceptual clarification that is absolutely critical to theory building. In light of the rich array of examples and depictions in the following chapters, the concluding chapter will assess the comprehensiveness of the typology of governmental roles and the clarifications needed to define the boundaries of each role.

But the volume aims at explanation as well as improved categorization. That local governments can and do play different roles in culture war controversies points to a crucial question: Under what circumstances should we expect to see local governments play one role rather than another? The answer requires a suitable theoretical framework for the study of local culture wars and use of the array of cases presented by the chapter contributors to take the first steps in establishing the plausibility of key hypotheses drawn from such a theoretical framework.

But, as noted earlier in this chapter, culture war controversies differ from politics as usual. Hence, there are good reasons for expecting that much of the theory that has been developed to account for urban political processes will not necessarily apply in a straightforward way.

In a sense, however, finding a place for the politics of culture wars in the larger realm of urban politics may not be an especially unique problem. Ever since Paul Peterson's classic treatment in *City Limits,* urban scholarship has encompassed the view that urban politics is not a unitary phenomenon. Inspired by Theodore Lowi's (1964) insights about the ways in which the type of policy at stake affects the structure of politics, and building deductively from a set of assumptions about the inherent competition among localities for the private sector investment that is necessary for economic vitality, Peterson depicts local governance as consisting of three different arenas—developmental, allocational and redistributional—each with its own distinctive stakes, players, and political dynamics. The *developmental* arena consists of decision making on issues that enhance the economic position of the city in the competition for private sector investment. The *allocational* arena deals with the distribution of traditional city services such as street plowing and sanitation, distributional activities that are "more or less neutral" in their economic effects" on the city (Peterson, 1981:41). The *redistributional* arena deals with policies that are targeted to low-income residents with consequent negative effects on the local economy.

Culture war issues do not comfortably fit within any of these arenas. Perhaps the closest fit is with the redistributional arena, in that culture war issues typically involve conflicts between the community's status quo with respect to the legitimacy of various ways of life or acceptable standards of behavior and the demands of challenging groups for a share of the community's stock of legitimacy. But in order to accommodate the values and morality standards of these new claimants, there would be encroachments on the values and morality standards of dominant groups. It takes a conceptual stretching to fit culture wars into Peterson's redistribution area, however, both because moral values rather than material resources are at stake and because negative repercussions for the city's economy are not as clear as they are in Peterson's discussion of the tax implications of targeted programs for the poor.

Culture wars therefore may be viewed more properly as constituting a distinctive, fourth arena of city politics. The key point of Peterson's work is not that his three arenas cover all possible aspects of city governance, but rather that the nature of politics in each arena is distinctive—driven by the character of the issues and the stakes for various groups and the city as a whole. Just as some staples of urban theory are therefore more applicable in some of his arenas than others (e.g., the relevance of fiscal capacity to understanding the redistributional arena, but not necessarily the developmental arena, or the greater relevance of pluralism in the allocational arena than in others), so also will we need to assemble an explanatory framework for the fourth arena of culture wars.

There are a variety of promising theoretical raw materials for use in that assembly, some adapted from general theories of urban policymaking, for example, and some drawn from the study of social movements more broadly. As the next section argues, however, all of these can be organized under a broader theoretical framework on the significance of culture in the study of politics.

CULTURE AND THEORY

Because we are interested in the functioning of urban governments in culture wars, an obvious starting point for assembling an explanatory framework is the concept of culture. Unfortunately, opening this door places us in a thicket of controversy, not only over cultural dynamics but over the very meaning of culture, for which "definitions . . . abound" (Johnston and Klandermans, 1995:3). At the most fundamental level, understanding what culture is revolves around two competing conceptualizations. One, emphasizing phenomena internal to the individual, focuses on ideas, values, beliefs, norms, and ideologies, and the impact of these internal phenomena on social action (Thompson et al., 1990; Swidler, 1995). From this perspective, "Ideas, developed and promoted by self-interested actors . . . come to have an independent influence on social action. People find themselves constrained by ideas that describe the world and specify what one can seek from it. Thus culture shapes action by defining what people want and how they imagine they can get it" (Swidler, 1995:25). The other conceptualization "sees culture as referring to the total way of life of a people, their interpersonal relations as well as their attitudes" (Thompson et al., 1990:1). This second conceptualization, with its view of culture as a "shared, collective product" emphasizes the way in which individual consciousness is shaped by culture (Swidler, 1995:26); that is, long-standing patterns of social interaction shape individual's beliefs and values. For our purposes, there is no need to resolve the competition between these two perspectives. Along with Thompson et al. (1990:1), we may instead view the two aspects of culture—internalized beliefs and the structure of social relations—as reciprocal and mutually reinforcing.

Controversies and Culture as Internalized Beliefs

Although there has been considerable debate over whether the contents of particular cultures are coherent (Smelser, 1992), it is widely acknowledged that there can be a relatively diverse mix of values, beliefs, norms, and other ideational elements represented in any culture. Meanwhile, older conceptions of culture as totally dominating individual action have given way to conceptions that emphasize human agency. Rather than being fully constrained by cultural ideas, individuals "energetically seek strategic advantage by using culturally encoded skills" and, in the process, "continually recreate culture" (Swidler, 1995:29). In Thompson et al.'s (1990:218) terms, culture "is a lively and responsive thing that is continually being renegotiated by individuals."

Taken together, these developments in cultural analysis suggest that the ideational content of a culture constitutes the raw material that activists can draw on as they attempt to build an advantageous position in a political conflict. Scholars of agenda setting have long acknowledged that the way in which claims, demands, and problem definitions are framed is crucially important (Schattschneider, 1960; Edleman, 1964; Iyengar, 1991; Kingdon, 1994). But a culturally based analysis suggests that not all frames are equally powerful or equally possible. Although cultural values are constantly being renegotiated, the strategic advantage at any particular moment presumably lies with those who can connect "political claims to deeply rooted cultural concerns" (Cobb and Ross, 1997:13).

Because cultures are complex constellations of diverse values rather than monolithically coherent structures, however, there can often be room for both sides in a political conflict to find important cultural grounding for their claims. In her contribution to this volume, Susan Clarke examines the unfolding of abortion conflict in Denver from just such a perspective, showing the competing yet culturally sanctioned "frames" offered by opposing sides in the conflict, the strategic introduction of new frames as the conflict unfolded, and the ways in which these frames both empowered and constrained governmental responses to the conflict.

Ultimately, the diverse and sometimes conflicting ideas, values, and norms that constitute a political culture are replicated at the individual level. In his contribution to this volume, Paul Schumaker explores the different principles or ideologies held by individual officials at the local level. Schumaker's study suggests that in the political culture of the United States, these cultural ideals add up to a widespread predisposition to avoid "legislating morality"—a cultural predisposition that can lead us to expect evasion of culture war issues as a prototypical course of action for school boards and city councils nationwide. By the same token, the political culture of the United States incorporates a variety of principles that can sometimes give local officials grounds for taking other sorts of actions in morality-based controversies. Some, such as "ensuring equal rights" or "preventing harm to others" are virtually universally held by local officials, suggesting that they are essential elements of the nation's political culture. Activists that can frame issues in such terms will have a privileged position in culture war conflicts. Other principles, such as "promoting moral standards of religion" or "promoting conformity to public opinion," are evoked by only a minority of local officials.

The variation in principles espoused by individual decision makers suggests the diversity of cultural ideals evident in the United States. More important, these differing principles are unlikely to be evenly distributed across the political geography of the nation. Although there is presumably an overarching cultural framework for the nation as a whole—one that incorporates a broad consensus on ideas and values such as individual freedom and equal rights—analysts of political culture have accepted the notion that the United States does not constitute a single political culture. Rather, it contains distinctive political subcultures. If this is the case, differences in how cities handle culture war issues might be traceable to differences in their political subcultures.

In order for this perspective to be maximally useful, it is important to identify different *types* of political subcultures, types that are theoretically grounded and hence theoretically linkable with the phenomena that we wish to explain. Otherwise, political culture is no more than a "residual variable," and cultural analysis degenerates into what some of its critics have described as "an explanation of last resort dragged in to fill the void when more conventional explanations fail" (Thompson et al., 1990:217). Thus, for example, it would not be particularly useful or enlightening to argue that Cincinnati officials have been entrepreneurial instigators of pornography-related culture wars simply because the culture of the community lends itself to such an approach, or to argue that officials in some other city repress abortion protest because of the character of the local political culture. We need to be more explicit about the key components of a local political culture, the ways in which those key components are synthesized into distinctive types, and the reasons for expecting city officials in particular types of cultures to be predisposed toward one rather than another role in culture war controversies.

At the simplest level, cultural differences across communities are frequently summarized as differences along the familiar liberal–conservative dimension, though the terms typically are intended to convey more than the distribution of beliefs about the role of government in society. They typically are used to convey information about the constellation of interest groups that are predominant in the community as well. In her contribution to this volume, for example, Woliver characterizes Greenville, South Carolina as more conservative than Columbia. This characterization stems not only from the pervasiveness of classic, limited-government conservatism in the community but also from the character and significance of religious institutions in the community and the relative salience of pro-life sentiments in the communities. And in their contribution to the volume, Haider-Markel and O'Brien explicitly consider the relative power of various interest groups with stakes in local hate crime ordinances.

By contrast, some scholars have attempted to devise typologies of political culture based on categorizations intended to differentiate more comprehensively the worldviews of various subcultures. Unfortunately, no paradigmatic typology of this kind exists. Instead, scholars have taken a variety of different approaches. In chapter eleven, for example, Paul Schumaker follows the lead of many scholars who have used Daniel Elazar's categorization of political cultures in the United States. Based on ethnic and religious group settlement patterns and the economic context facing those groups at key points in history, Elazar defines three political cultures: individualistic, traditionalistic, and moralistic. The *individualistic* political culture equates democracy with the marketplace and views government in utilitarian terms:

> According to this view, government need not have any direct concern with questions of the 'good society.' . . . Emphasizing the centrality of private concerns, the individualistic political culture places a premium on limiting community intervention—whether governmental or nongovernmental—into private activities, to the minimum degree necessary to keep the marketplace in proper working order. . . . The character of political participation in systems dominated by the individualistic political culture reflects the view that politics is just another means by which individuals may improve themselves socially and economically. In this sense politics is a 'business,' like any other that competes for talent (Elazar, 1994:230).

As with each of the other cultures defined by Elazar, the conceptualization of the individualistic culture incorporates expectations concerning the character of political participation. In particular, politics in an individualistic culture is viewed as a specialized activity for professionals rather than amateurs, party regularity is highly valued, and ideological concerns are dwarfed by a businesslike view of politics (Elazar, 1994:231).

By contrast, Elazar (1994:235) defines a *traditionalistic* political culture that is characterized by "paternalistic and elitist" conceptions that stem from an assumption of a hierarchically ordered society. In such a culture, "social and family ties are paramount," and "those who do not have a definite role to play in politics are not expected to be even minimally active as citizens." In a traditionalistic culture, government is accepted as having the role of "maintenance and encouragement of traditional patterns and, if necessary, their adjustment to changing conditions with the least possible upset" (Elazar, 1994:236).

In the *moralistic* political culture, politics is considered to be about "the search for the good society . . . an effort to exercise power for the betterment of the commonwealth" (Elazar, 1994:232). In contrast with the nonideological character of the politics in the individualistic culture,

> In the moralistic political culture, individualism is tempered by a general commitment to utilizing communal . . . power to intervene in the sphere of "private" activities when it is considered necessary to do so for the public good or the well-being of the community. Accordingly, issues have an important place in the moralistic style of politics, functioning to set the tone for political concern. Government is considered a positive instrument for political concern (Elazar, 1994:233).

Not surprisingly, then, the moralistic culture incorporates an expansive view of citizen involvement: "it embraces the notion that politics is ideally a matter of concern for all citizens, not just those who are professionally committed to political careers."

Elazar's categorization offers a wealth of possibilities for theorizing about how culture war issues are handled in different communities. Because activism by those who challenge the status quo on culture war issues is inconsistent with the cultural ethos of both traditionalistic and individualistic cultures, for example, repressive responses would presumably be more likely in those settings than in moralistic cultures, where open debate about what constitutes conduct conducive to the well-being of the community is considered a normal part of politics. Indeed, as Schumaker notes in his chapter, individuals in moralistic cultures are presumably more supportive of "legislating morality"; hence, we might expect entrepreneurial instigation of culture war issues to be more likely in those settings. Although evasion of culture war issues may be found in all kinds of communities, evasion might be expected to be an especially prevalent response in traditionalistic communities, where maintenance of the status quo and concerns for enforcement of traditional values are so crucial.

A different, and increasingly influential treatment of political culture derives from Robert Putnam's more recent work (1993, 1995a,b) on the concept of social capital. "By analogy with notions of physical capital and human capital—tools and training that enhance individual productivity—'social capital' refers to features of social organization such as networks, norms, and social trust that facilitate coordination and cooperation for mutual benefit" (Putnam, 1995a:67). From this point of view, political cultures can be distinguished from each other on the basis of their levels of social capital. Putnam, for example, characterized northern Italy as having a much higher level of social capital than southern Italy (1993). And in an assessment of the erosion of social capital in the United States, Putnam points to diminishing levels of churchgoing, labor union membership, participation in parent-teacher associations, and membership in fraternal and civic organizations (1995a:68–69), along with a decline in socializing with neighbors and in the extent to which Americans believe that most people can be trusted (1995a:73). But this post–World War II decline in associational membership, neighboring, and social trust, is presumably not uniform throughout the United States. Just as northern Italy is richer in social capital than southern Italy, so also might we characterize different communities within the United States in terms of their relative levels of social capital. Putnam's social capital concept suggests that the theoretically important distinctions in communities' political cultures are concerned with how participative and socially integrated they are (the aspect of culture involving the structure of social relations) and, consequently, how much mutual trust is developed (the aspect of culture involving internalized beliefs).

Putnam's social capital concept is part of a renaissance of attention to political culture in comparative politics (Jackman and Miller, 1996; see other contributors to that special issue). But, despite the obvious relevance for analysis of identity politics and culture wars, much of that scholarship is devoted to debate over its utility for predicting economic performance. Although research on varying levels of neighborhood activity and other forms of associational involvement have a relatively long history in urban scholarship in the United States, explicit attention to the concept of social capital has only recently begun to work its way into urban scholarship, particularly with reference to educational reform efforts (Schneider et al., 1997).

Approaching political culture through the lens of the social capital concept is nevertheless highly relevant for analysis of communities' handling of culture wars. Communities with high levels of social capital are characterized by "networks of civic engagement" that "foster sturdy norms of generalized reciprocity and encourage the emergence of social trust" (Putnam, 1995a:67). For these reasons, repression of activists on culture war issues should be less likely in communities with high social capital. High levels of social capital have other implications that are relevant for our analysis. The dense networks of civic engagement that characterize communities with high social capital "facilitate coordination and communication, amplify reputations, and thus allow dilemmas of collective action to be resolved. When economic and political negotiation is embedded in dense networks of social interaction, incentives for opportunism are reduced. At the same time, networks of civic engagement embody past success at collaboration, which can serve as a cultural template for future collaboration" (Putnam, 1995a:67). This suggests that, in communities with higher levels of social capital, there should be a lower propensity for entrepreneurial instigation of culture wars. The incentives for opportunism that are essential to entrepreneurial instigation are much lower in communities with high social capital.

Despite the relevance of a conceptualization of political culture based on social capital, the contributors to this volume do not *explicitly* incorporate such an approach in their explanations of city governments' handling of culture war controversies. However, the diverse cases that they present do provide evidence concerning culture wars in contexts that implicitly differ in terms of their levels of social capital. Woliver, for example, takes note of how rapid population growth transformed Greenville from a small community with a high level of social integration into a place where people with new ideas and lifestyles introduced rifts in the community. Rosenthal contrasts the highly participative climate in Rochester, New York with Albany's more ossified and socially unintegrated community setting. DeLeon's depiction of San Francisco suggests that city has extraordinarily high levels of social capital. Finally, the conclusion attempts more systematically to tease out these implicit differences in social capital across the case-study communities represented in the volume and to consider the implications for culture war controversies that are suggested by the case evidence.

CULTURE AS THE STRUCTURE OF SOCIAL RELATIONS: INSTITUTIONS AND REGIMES

Not all analysts are enthusiastic about cultural analysis of political phenomena. Some, like Jackman and Miller (1996), suggest that we study institutions instead of cultures. But, as noted above, the "structure of social relations" side of the definition of culture suggests that institutions are a part of culture. Culture is reflected in the values and ideals within individuals' heads; it is also reflected in the institutionalized arrangements that distinguish one way of life from another. Because these institutional arrangements shape and constrain action, we should also expect that they would affect the actions of both culture war activists and governing officials.

For the analysis of local governments' handling of culture wars, two kinds of institutions are particularly worthy of attention: specific, formal institutions of government (reformed vs. unreformed) and the more complex set of institutional arrangements, formal and informal, that constitute governing regimes. With respect to the formal institutions of government, there is a substantial line of inquiry in urban politics that investigates the impact of reformed institutions relative to unreformed institutions on various policymaking processes and outcomes (Lineberry and Fowler, 1967; Morgan and Hirlinger, 1993). Reform-style institutions, including at-large elections, nonpartisanship, and the council-manager form of government, are structural arrangements that theoretically "provide incentives for an emphasis on citywide issues and constituencies, advantages for those whose resources are not limited to a geographic or a partisan base, and constraints on politicization of administrative issues" (Sharp, 1997:263–64). Just as empirical research has shown that communities with reform-style institutions differ from unreformed communities with respect to minority representation (Karnig and Welch, 1981), intergovernmental service contracting (Morgan and Hirlinger, 1991), the adoption of progressive economic development policies (Elkins, 1995) and much more, so also might we expect that differences in their formal structures for governance would influence communities' handling of culture war issues. For example, entrepreneurial instigation is to be expected more in communities with unreformed structures because of the greater opportunities for neighborhood-based leadership and the enhanced politicization of issues in unreformed cities. On the other hand, the theoretical logic of these governing institutions suggests that repression would be less likely in unreformed than in reformed settings because the more extensive representation of diverse community interests in unreformed city councils maximizes the chance that there will be sympathetic figures within government to serve as guarantors against the oppression of culture war activists (Sharp, 1997:274–76).

These and other possibilities are explored in a variety of ways by the contributors to this volume. In his chapter, for example, Paul Schumaker investigates the possibility that officials' willingness to legislate morality is diminished in cities with reform-style council-manager forms of government, where the principles of businesslike governance and efficiency are paramount and the politicization of issues is frowned on. In their chapter, Haider-Markel and O'Brien consider whether the formal structure of local government institutions influences their handling of hate crime issues, while Button, Wald, and Rienzo do the same for their case-study communities' handling of gay rights legislation. In each of these chapters, multiple case-study cities that vary in their formal governing structures provide the opportunity to assess the impact of those differences on culture war issues. Other contributors to this volume focus on in-depth analysis of the way in which a single community (or pair of communities) handles a culture war controversy, as in Laura Woliver's examination of the repression of abortion protest in two South Carolina communities with reform-style structures; Susan Clarke's study of repression of abortion protest in Denver, a city with unreformed institutions; and Rick Musser's examination of efforts to repress a vitriolic antihomosexual activist in Topeka, a community with predominantly unreformed-style structures of government. These case studies provide the opportunity for comparative analysis of a single local governmental role—repression—in settings with contrasting formal institutions. That task is taken up in the concluding chapter.

The formal structures of local government constitute one set of institutional arrangements that can have a bearing on the handling of urban conflicts. But a substantial line of scholarship has now emerged around a broader conceptualization of the institutional arrangements that are important for the governance of American cities. That conceptualization is embodied in *regime theory*.

Essential to regime theory is an acknowledgment that the capacity to govern a city requires a combination of two distinctive types of resources: the authoritative legal powers of the state and the economic resources of the private sector. Regime theory depicts the *informal* arrangements by which governing coalitions are forged: coalitions that incorporate public power and private economic resources through voluntary, cooperative arrangements of political and economic elites (Stone, 1989).

Stone's articulation of this political economy perspective on urban regimes fits well with other theoretical treatments that distinguish different types of urban political economy, such as Stephen Elkin's (1987) distinction between pluralist political economies, federalist political economies, and entrepreneurial political economies. These distinctions hinge on the centrality of land interests in governing coalitions relative to other actors and institutions—such as federal grant programs and the professional city bureaucracy—that may be key players in a city's governing coalition. More generally, regime theory has served as a focusing concept for the development of a host of case studies exploring differing types of urban political regimes. Although regimes featuring a "close alliance between officials of the local state and land-based business people" are acknowledged as dominant (Imbroscio, 1997:6), numerous scholars have depicted other types. In particular, attention has focused on antigrowth regimes, in which officials develop important alliances with sectors of the community that are negatively impacted by growth (DiGaetano and Klemanski, 1991; Turner, 1992), and progressive regimes, in which the governing coalition reflects a relative emphasis on neighborhoods over downtown business interests and incorporates minority groups, low-income groups, and other populist elements (Swanstrom, 1985; DeLeon, 1992).

For purposes of analyzing culture wars, however, the problem with regime theory is that it is deeply rooted in political economy. That is, regime theory tends to place "disproportionate emphasis . . . on the activities and behavior of elites within the city" (Ferman, 1996:5) and, in particular, on political and economic elites. As a result, the "critical role of cultural and institutional factors in influencing political organization and decision making" (Ferman, 1996:4) tends to be overlooked, and the assumption is too easily made that the functioning and power of a particular regime, and particularly private business, is equally evident in all arenas of community decision making.

If culture war issues constitute a distinctive arena of local governance, it is important to acknowledge that the cultural values of a community, and the organizations and individuals that serve as gatekeepers for those values, comprise a third key resource for a governing regime (along with the legal powers of the state and the economic powers of private elites). The suggestion is that different regimes might reflect the cultural values of morality and identity in which they are embedded, not just the relative power of economic interests. The extent to which religious institutions or identity groups such as gays are incorporated in the governing coalition becomes central to the definition of regime types from this point of view.

Several contributors to this volume take just such an approach. Don Rosenthal distinguishes four different types of regimes according to the extent of their incorporation of gays in the governing coalition. Documenting how gay political organizing was, in differing ways, essential to the success of electoral coalitions in four New York state communities, Rosenthal dramatically illustrates that urban regimes are about much more than land-based or downtown business interests. Similarly, Rich DeLeon's chapter features San Francisco as a distinctive regime: one in which gays and other identity groups are firmly incorporated in a progressive regime that treats moral and cultural values as seriously as business interests and economic concerns. There is a longer tradition in urban scholarship of differentiating governing regimes on the basis of the extent of their incorporation of African Americans (Browning et al., 1984) or exploring the significance of regimes led by black mayors (Orr, 1990; Perry, 1990; Pinderhughes, 1990; Persons, 1993). To a large extent, that research also sustains a political economy emphasis, focusing on the distinctive handling of land-based and other business interests in minority-led cities and the consequences for developmental politics and the distribution of material benefits when racial minorities are installed in the governing coalition. However, the identity politics of race has important strands that are about morality. In their chapter, for example, Kirp and Bayer make clear that race is a "vital and volatile factor" in the politics of needle exchange programs. In some cities, such programs have been derailed or delayed by African Americans' moral abhorrence, at least until governing coalitions including credible black leadership have overcome the deep-seated feelings of the minority community.

The application of regime theory to culture war analysis may, therefore, require an extension of regime theory. Such an extension treats the moral values, identity groups, and religious institutions of communities as potential resources for assembling a stable governing regime and examines variations in how these resources are differentially incorporated in various types of regimes. There is, however, an alternative perspective on the relevance of regime theory to the analysis of culture war controversies. Consistent with the political economy framework that currently predominates in regime theory, this alternative perspective accepts that all types of political regimes typically have predominant interests in land use and development matters and a lack of engagement in culture war issues *unless and until* those issues impinge on the growth and development matters that are the core stakes for the regime. Under those circumstances, urban regimes would then be expected to mobilize for action on culture war issues in ways consistent with their predominant interests. In his chapter on the city of Topeka's handling of the flamboyant protests of an antihomosexual minister, for example, Rick Musser considers how the city's initial efforts to evade the controversy gave way to repressive measures when the minister's efforts threatened the city's national image and hence its economic development aspirations. In short, whether we adopt the predominant, political economy approach to regime theory or try to expand it to a new conceptualization of regimes based on moral values and cultural resources, there are points of connection between regime theory and the analysis of culture war controversies.

REFERENCES

Browning, Rufus P., Dale R. Marshall, and David H. Tabb. 1984. *Protest Is Not Enough.* Berkeley: University of California Press.

Button, James W., Barbara A. Rienzo, and Kenneth D. Wald. 1997. *Private Lives, Public Conflicts: Battles over Gay Rights in American Communities.* Washington, D.C.: Congressional Quarterly Press.

Cobb, Roger W., and Marc Howard Ross. 1997. "Agenda Setting and the Denial of Agenda Access: Key Concepts." In Roger W. Cobb and Marc Howard Ross, eds., *Cultural Strategies of Agenda Denial.* Lawrence: University Press of Kansas, pp. 3–24.

DeLeon, Richard E. 1992. *Left Coast City: Progressive Politics in San Francisco, 1975–1991.* Lawrence: University Press of Kansas.

D'Emilio, J. 1983. *Sexual Politics, Sexual Communities.* Chicago: University of Chicago Press.

DiGaetano, A., and J. Klemanski. 1991. "Restructuring the Suburbs: Political Economy of Economic Development in Auburn Hills, Michigan." *Journal of Urban Affairs* 13:137–58.

Dobrzynski, Judith H. 1997. "Battles Over Funds for Arts Felt at Local Level." *New York Times,* 14 August, p. A1(L).

Donovan, Mark C. 1996. "The Needle Exchange: AIDS, Drugs, and Political Competition." Paper prepared for delivery at the 1996 Annual Meeting of the American Political Science Association, 29 August–1 September, San Francisco.

Downs, Donald. 1989. *The New Politics of Pornography.* Chicago: University of Chicago Press.

Edelman, Murray. 1964. *The Symbolic Uses of Politics.* Urbana: University of Illinois Press.

Elazar, Daniel J. 1994. *The American Mosaic: The Impact of Space, Time, and Culture on American Politics.* Boulder, Colo.: Westview Press.

Elkin, Stephen L. 1987. *City and Regime in the American Republic.* Chicago: University of Chicago Press.

Elkins, David R. 1995. "Testing Competing Explanations for the Adoption of Type II Policies." *Urban Affairs Review* 30 (July): 809–39.

Euchner, Charles C. 1996. *Extraordinary Politics: How Protest and Dissent Are Changing American Democracy.* Boulder, Colo.: Westview Press.

Ferman, Barbara. 1996. *Challenging the Growth Machine.* Lawrence: University Press of Kansas.

Hunter, James Davison. 1991. *Culture Wars.* New York: Basic Books.

———. 1994. *Before the Shooting Begins: Searching for Democracy in America's Culture War.* New York: Free Press.

Imbroscio, David L. 1997. *Reconstructing City Politics.* Thousand Oaks, Calif.: Sage.

Iyengar, Shanto. 1991. *Is Anyone Responsible?* Chicago: University of Chicago Press.

Jackman, Robert W., and Ross A. Miller. 1996. "A Renaissance of Political Culture?" *American Journal of Political Science* 40 (August): 632–59.

Johnston, Hank, and Bert Klandermans. 1995. "The Cultural Analysis of Social Movements." In Hank Johnston and Bert Klandermans, eds., *Social Movements and Culture.* Minneapolis: University of Minnesota Press, pp. 3–24.

Karnig, Albert K., and Susan Welch. 1981. *Black Representation and Urban Policy.* Chicago: University of Chicago Press.

Kingdon, John. 1994. *Agendas, Alternatives, and Public Policies.* New York: HarperCollins.

Lineberry, Robert, and Edmund P. Fowler. 1967. "Reformism and Public Policies in American Cities." *American Political Science Review* 61 (September): 701–16.

Lowi, Theodore. 1964. "American Business, Public Policy, Case Studies, and Political Theory." *World Politics* 16:677–715.

Marks, Ellen L., and Carolyn H. Marzke. 1993. *Healthy Caring.* Princeton, N.J.: Mathtech, Inc.

Meier, Kenneth J. 1994. *The Politics of Sin: Drugs, Alcohol, and Public Policy.* Armonk, N.Y.: M. E. Sharpe.

Mooney, Christopher Z., and Mei-Hsien Lee. 1995. "Legislating Morality in the American States: The Case of Pre-*Roe* Abortion Regulation Reform." *American Journal of Political Science* 39 (August): 599–627.

Morgan, David R., and Michael W. Hirlinger. 1991. "Intergovernmental Service Contracts: A Multivariate Explanation." *Urban Affairs Quarterly* 27 (September): 128–44.

———. 1993. "The Dependent City and Intergovernmental Aid: The Impact of Recent Changes." *Urban Affairs Quarterly* 29 (December): 256–75.

Orr, Marion. 1990. "The Struggle for Black Empowerment in Baltimore: Electoral Control and Governing Coalitions." In Rufus P. Browning, Dale Rogers Marshall, and David H. Tabb, eds., *Racial Politics in American Cities.* New York: Longman, pp. 201–20.

Perry, Huey L. 1990. "The Evolution and Impact of Biracial Coalitions and Black Mayors in Birmingham and New Orleans." In Rufus P. Browning, Dale Rogers Marshall, and David H. Tabb, eds., *Racial Politics in American Cities.* New York: Longman, pp. 179–200.

Persons, Georgia A. 1993. "Black Mayoralties and the New Black Politics." In Georgia A. Persons, ed., *Dilemmas of Black Politics.* New York: HarperCollins, pp. 38–65.

Peterson, Paul. 1981. *City Limits.* Chicago: University of Chicago Press.

Pinderhughes, Dianne M. 1990. "An Examination of Chicago Politics for Evidence of Political Incorporation and Representation." In Rufus P. Browning, Dale Rogers Marshall, and David H. Tabb, eds., *Racial Politics in American Cities.* New York: Longman, pp. 117–36.

Putnam, Robert. 1993. *Making Democracy Work.* Princeton, N.J.: Princeton University Press.

———. 1995a. "Bowling Alone: America's Declining Social Capital." *Journal of Democracy* 6 (January): 65–78.

———. 1995b. "Tuning In, Tuning Out: The Strange Disappearance of Social Capital in America." *PS: Political Science and Politics* 28 (December): 664–83.

Rienzo, Barbara A., and James W. Button. 1993. "The Politics of School-Based Clinics: A Community-Level Analysis." *Journal of School Health* 63 (August): 266–72.

Schattschneider, E. E. 1960. *The Semi-Sovereign People.* New York: Holt.

Schneider, Mark, Paul Teske, Melissa Marschall, Michael Mintrom, and Christine Roch. 1997. "Institutional Arrangements and the Creation of Social Capital: The Effects of School Choice." *American Political Science Review* 91:82–93.

Sharp, Elaine B. 1996. "Culture Wars and City Politics: Local Government's Role in Social Conflict." *Urban Affairs Review* 31 (July): 738–58.

―――. 1997. "A Comparative Anatomy of Urban Social Conflict." *Political Research Quarterly* 50 (June): 261–80.

Smelser, Neil J. 1992. "Culture: Coherent or Incoherent." In Richard Munch and Neil J. Smelser, eds., *Theory of Culture.* Berkeley: University of California Press, pp. 3–28.

Stone, Clarence. 1989. *Regime Politics: Governing Atlanta, 1946–1988.* Lawrence: University Press of Kansas.

Swanstrom, Todd. 1985. *The Crisis of Growth Politics.* Philadelphia: Temple University Press.

Swidler, Ann. 1995. "Cultural Power and Social Movements." In Hank Johnston and Bert Klandermans, eds., *Social Movements and Culture.* Minneapolis: University of Minnesota Press, pp. 25–40.

Tarrow, Sidney. 1994. *Power in Movement.* Cambridge: Cambridge University Press.

Tatalovich, Raymond, and Byron W. Daynes, eds. 1988. *Social Regulatory Policy: Moral Controversies in American Politics.* Boulder, Colo.: Westview Press.

Thompson, Michael, Richard Ellis, and Aaron Wildavsky. 1990. *Cultural Theory.* Boulder, Colo.: Westview Press.

Turner, Robyn. 1992. "Growth Politics and Downtown Development: The Economic Imperative in Sunbelt Cities." *Urban Affairs Quarterly* 28:3–21.

2
Abortion Conflicts and City Governments: Negotiating Coexistence in South Carolina

Laura R. Woliver

Whether a woman can choose a legal abortion depends on access.[1] Because abortion facilities are most often in cities, highly contentious conflicts concerning abortion often occur within the regulatory jurisdictions and powers of local governments, pulling city officials into "the eye of a firestorm" (Sharp, 1996:738; see also Tatalovich and Daynes, 1988). The uncompromising nature of abortion politics guarantees its role as fodder in urban culture wars.

The United States Supreme Court decision *Webster v. Reproductive Health Services, Inc.* (1989, 104 S.Ct. 3040) permitted state-level restrictions on abortion services, heightening the potential political power of grassroots mobilization over state and local abortion legislation. Indeed, some assert that *Webster* refederalized abortion politics by returning the primary focus of abortion policymaking to the states (see Segers and Byrnes, 1995:5–12). Antiabortion groups have succeeded in targeting state legislatures for restrictions on abortion providers, services, and procedures, to name a few (Halva-Neubauer, 1993; O'Connor, 1996:62–65). State and local policies, cultures, and practices, therefore, will be very important in determining future access to legal abortions.

In addition, mobilizing grassroots activists in order to bring pressure to bear on the national government is a time-honored and powerful group and movement tactic (see, e.g., Garrow, 1978; Woliver, 1996b, 1998; Gimpel, 1998). To maximize these pressures, pro-life groups attempt to shut down local (usually urban) clinics, intimidate doctors from offering legal abortions, and create hostile local atmospheres to discourage clinics and practitioners from offering these services. How city officials handle the reproductive politics aspects of modern culture wars will shape abortion access and the politics of those cities tremendously. Abortion politics clearly involves communication, pressure tactics, and political resources from nationwide social movements (pro-life, pro-choice, feminist, antifeminist) flowing to state and then to local venues, and a reverse flow from local activists to state pressure and to national movement attentions.

Grassroots mobilizing is facilitated by fluid social movements: preexisting networks, coalitions, and organizations that reshape themselves to incorporate a new, local issue. As Friedman and McAdam (1992:162) explain, "Successful movements usually do not create attractive collective identities from scratch; rather, they redefine existing roles within established organizations as the basis of an emerging activist identity." Abortion politics displays this as religious, conservative, progressive, and liberal groups and networks reorient their goals and attentions and overlap in their involvement with abortion issues.

This chapter examines how theories and literature on social movements, grassroots dissent, and governmental responses to dissent can help us understand abortion-related politics at the subnational level. In particular, the chapter relies on a theoretical framework that treats activism and government response as paired collective-action problems (Lichbach, 1995). That is, just as citizen activists must overcome costs (in the form of inertia and resource constraints) that hinder political mobilization, so also does government find it costly to control citizen activism. Gaining consensus among political elites about what should be done, assembling the legal and financial resources that might be required to manage contentious conflicts, and avoiding a loss of political legitimacy when harsh measures are used are all challenges for governments as they respond to protest movements. In the drive to outmaneuver each other in solving the collective action problem, both local activists and local governments have reached out to extralocal institutions to try to tip the balance of resources in their favor. Similarly, both local activists and local governments exhibit social learning processes, that is, strategic use of information to develop adaptations in their approach to the collective-action problem. Because of the parallel way in which both local activists and governing officials have effectively utilized extralocal resources and social learning, neither side has prevailed. Local officials have contained but not successfully repressed the groups engaged in abortion conflict in South Carolina; and those groups continue their activism and therefore continue to generate community controversy, even though the state has a political culture hostile to such displays of conflict and local officials have engaged in repressive efforts.

The chapter is informed by dozens of interviews conducted since 1991 with lobbyists, amicus-brief writers, interest-group leaders, and spokespeople in both pro-life and pro-choice camps at the national level and in South Carolina. In Columbia and Greenville, South Carolina, additional interviews were conducted with retired and active city, police, and court officials. Correspondence, personal interviews, and direct observations of both pro-life and pro-choice speakers, protests, church gatherings, and legislative hearings over the years in South Carolina are also discussed in this chapter. The intent is to explore the impact of large, fluid social movements on abortion activists at the state and local levels, thus fueling local culture wars.

CONSTRAINTS ON ABORTION-RELATED ACTIVISM

For a number of important reasons, conflict over abortion would be expected to be very muted in communities in South Carolina. First, elements of the state's political and social culture mitigate against the mobilization of group conflict. The state maintains a highly traditionalistic political culture, with low citizen participation in politics and institutions that often blunt citizen reform attempts. The traditionalist culture "emphasizes social hierarchy with an economic, social, and political elite at the top to which ordinary citizens routinely defer" (Graham and Moore, 1994:3–4). A recent county-by-county analysis of many aspects of local political cultures continues to support the general proposition that South Carolina has a traditionalistic heritage and orientation (Lieske, 1993). In fact, "Despite encouragement and pressures from historical circumstances, South Carolinians have taken only timid departures from past traditions and customs" (Graham and Moore, 1994:45; see also Botsch, 1992).

Two ideas regarding political activism and conflict are deep-seated in South Carolina's history and political culture: "First, internal division was unnatural and dangerous, and second, political opposition was external and undesirable" (Graham and Moore, 1994:46). Open warfare over moral issues goes against the grain in South Carolina, violating the norms of quietly pretending that everyone agrees on moral issues and standards.

In fact, there is not a consensus about abortion in South Carolina. South Carolinians' abortion opinions are similar to national abortion opinion, according to a 1989 survey by the Survey Research Laboratory in the Institute of Public Affairs at the University of South Carolina (USC). The USC poll found a majority of South Carolinians (59.4 percent) feel that abortion should be legal only under certain circumstances, whereas 22.9 percent believe abortion should be legal under any circumstances, and 17.8 percent believe abortion should be illegal in all circumstances (Oldendick, 1990:11–12). The complexity of abortion attitudes in the mass public and the increasingly partisan distinctions on the issue (Dugger, 1991; Adams, 1997; Conway et al., 1997) are echoed in South Carolina.

Despite these opinion differences among the mass public, the abovementioned norms of conflict avoidance might be expected to mute activism over the abortion issue, especially because modern pro-business sentiments reinforce an emphasis on "civilities": (Chafe, 1980) not tolerating overt dissent and above all maintaining the status quo (Graham and Moore, 1994:100). In recent South Carolina politics, one dominant cultural theme is a pro-business one emphasizing the aggressive courting of economic development prospects (see also Eisinger, 1988; Cobb, 1993). Political Action Committee contributions to South Carolina politicians display a dominant pro-business presence and an almost invisible union effort (Botsch, 1992; see also Schneider and Teske, 1993). Even traditionally hallowed, religiously based laws, such as the "blue laws" that restricted commerce and liquor sales on Sundays, have recently been reformed in the face of such strong business interests concerned with tourism and industrial and resort development.

In addition to these features of the social context, one might expect abortion-related conflict to be minimized in South Carolina because of the strength of conservative political forces in the state. Translated into a policy stance that strongly favors the pro-life side of the abortion debate, such a context might be expected to deter the mobilization of activists on the issue: Pro-choice forces would be intimidated by the strength of the state's support for the pro-life side, and pro-life forces would have less of a perceived need to mobilize.

Indeed, the state is very conservative, tending to be strongly Republican in both national and state elections (see Barone and Ujifusa, 1997:1266–90). Republican Party leaders nationwide have increasingly taken staunch pro-life positions (Adams, 1997). South Carolina Republican Party leaders are similarly staunchly antiabortion choice (Mooreland and Steed, 1998). Recent policy developments at the state level underscore the relative power of pro-life interests in the state. In 1995–1996, an important battle was waged over licensing regulations being written by the South Carolina Department of Health and Environmental Control (DHEC) for any clinic where five or more abortions are performed per month (Woliver, 1996c). Pro-choice groups saw these proposed new regulations as raising the financial costs for clinics and patients, and raising the psychic cost to patients who fear their names could slip into public records (Planned Parenthood of Central South Carolina, 1996; Scoppe, 1996). Pro-life forces saw these regulations as protecting health and safety, another incremental victory in their long march to close all abortion clinics (Woliver interviews).

The strength of pro-life interests in South Carolina is also evident in the recent ban on late-term abortions. After President Clinton's 1996 veto of the partial-birth-abortion ban, the National Right to Life Committee (NRLC) sent copies of the federal bill to their state affiliates. The South Carolina affiliate of the NRLC quickly passed a copy of the federal bill to an ally in the South Carolina legislature. The bill passed the South Carolina Assembly by a vote of 105 to 4, with no amendments. In the South Carolina Senate, the bill moved through in a record nine days and was passed without amendment or opposition. The Senate had a voice vote on the bill and no "nays" were heard (Woliver interviews; see also Scoppe, 1997a,b). The only exception to the ban is when the abortion is the *only* documented way to save the mother's life. Governor David Beasley happily signed the bill. National and local pro-life activists have stated that these bans are just the start of their piece-by-piece efforts to scare doctors away from offering abortions and to establish precedents for state protection of the fetus as human life.

These state policy developments illustrate the relative power of pro-life forces in South Carolina and reinforce expectations that antiabortion activism would be minimal in the state, and, in particular, that violent clashes over abortion would be rare. Theories of violence for political causes posit that frustration at the lack of progress for one's side can increase the chances for violent acts of dissent. An analysis of abortion clinic bombings of the late 1970s and early 1980s found that, controlling for other factors, states where the legislature passed resolutions calling for bans on legal abortion had less likelihood of antiabortion violence, "a pattern which suggests that the legislative resolutions may provide abortion opponents with a sense of government responsiveness which makes resorting to violence seem less necessary" (Nice, 1988:187). The sustained pro-life responsiveness by South Carolina *state* officials thus functions as another constraint on abortion-related activism for pro-life groups and presumably intimidates would-be mobilizers of pro-choice groups.

FACTORS FAVORING MOBILIZATION OF ACTIVISM

Although local political engagement can be difficult for people who challenge authority (Haeberle, 1989; Woliver, 1993, 1996a; Mohr, 1995:406), religious commitment (Genovese, 1976; Morris, 1984; Holsworth, 1989; Harris, 1994), a sense of community (Bellah et al., 1985; Woliver, 1993; Herbst, 1994; Lendler, 1997), a cognitive structuring of the perceived injustice (Snow et al., 1986), and an individual's sense of moral outrage can sometimes overcome the reasons why people often do not dissent (Boyte, 1980; Evans and Boyte, 1986). The South Carolina context provides many of these resources for overcoming barriers to mobilization of abortion activists.

For example, South Carolina has many politically active churches. Close identity to a community helps citizens to mobilize, according to theories of collective action (Chong, 1991; Lichbach, 1994:15–16). With abortion, the dissenting community is often tied to churches such as those exhibiting political strength in South Carolina history and politics. The power and activism of conservative churches and religiously based organizations, law firms, and think tanks has played an important role in abortion politics nationally and at the local level (Guth, 1995; Green, et al., 1996; Ivers, 1998). Indeed, in South Carolina, "after twenty years of religious reshuffling, the GOP has become the party of united conservative Protestantism, attracting fundamentalists, charismatics, pentecostals, and conservative Southern Baptists in a powerful alignment, adding these elements to its traditional mainline Protestant base" (Guth, 1995:142; see also Smith, 1997). The antiabortion movement has been able to tap into deeply felt religious beliefs and disgust with mainstream modern American society, politics, and values (Himmelstein, 1990; Blanchard, 1994; Aho, 1996; Simonds, 1996; Williams and Blackburn, 1996).

Fluid social movements that change perceptions of social and political boundaries and possibilities also shape grassroots abortion mobilization (Gusfield, 1981; see also Mueller, 1994). Social learning (McCann, 1994:230) occurs in local abortion politics as antiabortion activists flex their might to try to close down clinics, and on the opposite side of the issue, as the clinics and their adherents fight to stay open. Social movements also provide a language to describe and name an injustice. "One of the residues" of social movements, Gusfield wrote, "is the existence of a vocabulary and an opening of ideas and actions which in the past was either unknown or unthinkable" (1981:325). The rhetoric and images used by pro-life and pro-choice interests at the grassroots level display the "framing contests" (McAdam et al., 1996:17) being waged at the national level in the larger social movements involved in formulating state and local abortion policies (Woliver, 1996b, 1998). The theatrics and rhetoric of movements, in turn, are important ways to disseminate the meanings actors give to events (Edelman, 1989).

Developing a sense of moral outrage about abortion has been an important tactic for mobilization of antiabortion activism. In South Carolina, the legal status of abortion rights and any governmental responses that reinforce those rights help to forge that sense of moral outrage, especially in the context of the state's traditional culture and norms of maintaining a veneer of consensus. One theme in the memoirs of gay people who grew up in the south in places like South Carolina, for instance, is how everyone pretended that they were not gay and kept up the "act" for the sake of harmony and appearances (Sears, 1991). Where you got into trouble was wanting people to admit that you were gay and accept you for what you really were. Current abortion politics reflects similar outrage when practices and behaviors long known to have occurred are brought out into the open, with governmental acknowledgment if not protection. As Blanchard says about antiabortion activists, "Their primary concern is not the *occurrence* of abortion but its *legalization,* which gives it the stamp of legal and, more important, moral approval" (1994:107). As many scholars have documented, abortions have always occurred, with selective enforcement of the police powers to stop them in states that officially outlawed the procedure (Mohr, 1978; Graber, 1996). South Carolina's pre-*Roe* history and practices are no different.

As Luker found, pro-life and pro-choice abortion activists have alternative world views, in which the moral status of the embryo is an implicit statement about the role of children and women in modern American society (Luker, 1984; see also Rhode and Lawson, 1993:4). Abortion activists display the link between status movements and identity issues: "Here the grievances are actuated by perceived threats to how one defines oneself, such as the way that the popularization of abortion threatens, for some women, traditional conceptions of motherhood. Status movements take action about 'other people's business' because that business often poses a threat to how the mobilizing group defines itself" (Johnston et al., 1994:22). These identity issues about individual status, worth, and rights, can become mobilizing factors for new social movements whose adherents bring their culture wars to cities. Activists mobilized by moral stances concerning abortion see victories in their constant "witnessing for the unborn" (Woliver interviews), their ceaseless monitoring and questioning of every angle of city officials' accommodation to legalized abortion, and their presence, which tries to make a statement that abortion is immoral.

Mobilization of abortion-related activism has also been facilitated by the resources brought to South Carolina by national social movement influences. Indeed, the line between national and local interests and political passions increasingly fades as national groups frequently use grassroots mobilizations for their causes (Nownes and Freeman, 1998:93). Many of the groups active in abortion issues at the local level are "repeat players" with all the advantages of experience, connections, networks, and seasoned staff (Galanter, 1974; see also Staggenborg, 1991, 1996; O'Connor, 1996, 1998:282). Pro-choice interests are connected to national offices of pro-choice groups, have commitments and coalitions that are feminist, and are staffed by activists who are identified as feminist (Woliver interviews). Both Greenville and Columbia have chapters of the National Organization for Women (NOW). In Greenville, the local NOW chapter is instrumental in organizing clinic escorts when needed, and chapter leaders are frequently relied on by the local press for statements on abortion disputes. The pro-life activists are also tied to national groups who lobby for the pro-life point of view. In addition, pro-life interests in South Carolina can tap into a network besides prolife coalitions: conservative church activists, who provide an easily mobilizable, co-optable network of potential participants.

In South Carolina, there are fascinating and powerful ad hoc issue coalitions regarding abortion involving fundamentalist, conservative Christian congregations; the South Carolina Baptist Convention; and the South Carolina Catholic Church and Presbyterians of South Carolina. As pointed out in several interviews, these religious groups would not agree on many culture war issues but are united on abortion politics. Adding to the power of the antiabortion groups is the relative silence in South Carolina politics of other religious voices, groups, or coalitions.

Local, state, and national abortion groups and activists also engage in niche positioning. Niche positioning occurs when, because of competition for resources within a policy domain, interest groups specialize, or partition off, tactics, activism, orientation, and fund-raising. Gray and Lowery found niche positioning in their study of interest-group ecologies in six states: "This suggests that interest group niches—and thus the structure of interest group communities—are more strongly determined by the internal needs of organized interests than by their patterns of interface with government." (Gray and Lowery, 1996:108.)

Niche positioning is evident in South Carolina abortion politics, where Planned Parenthood takes the role of monitoring legislation that would inhibit the ability of well-funded clinics to conduct business; and the state ACLU argues the bigger, more politically based points regarding privacy rights, First Amendment freedoms, and broader issues of women's rights (Woliver interviews). Pro-life groups also have niches. Columbia Sidewalk Counseling and Greenville's Pastors for Life engage in face-to-face debates with clinic staff, patients, and supporters on more than a weekly basis, while South Carolina Citizens for Life (the state National Right to Life affiliate) does more traditional lobbying and grassroots organizing

(Woliver interviews). Overlying all of this is the lobbying by conservative Christian groups concerned with family values, morality, and parental rights.

The partitioning of roles by abortion interests shapes the impact that radical groups have on more moderate ones. Pro-life spokespeople consistently denounce pro-life activists who engage in civil disobedience and destructive acts, including the killing of abortion clinic personnel (Woliver interviews). Yet the outrageousness of those people makes the behavior of more moderate pro-life groups seem comparatively understandable. This "radical flank effect" redounds to the benefit of other, perhaps more reasonable, groups within a larger movement (McAdam et al., 1996:14), and plays a role in the fluid nature of social movements.

A NATIONAL CONFLAGRATION NEGOTIATED LOCALLY, ONE DAY AT A TIME

It is impossible to say how much abortion-related activism and conflict there would be in South Carolina if not for the constraints on activism that have been noted—constraints stemming from the state's traditional culture, political conservatism, state-level responsiveness to pro-life forces, and pro-business emphasis. These complicate the collective-action problem for would-be activists. But, as the foregoing section explains, there are a number of countervailing considerations that facilitate abortion activists' mobilizing efforts, considerations having to do with the development of a dense network of local and extralocal organizations that bring distinctive resources to the mobilizing effort.

Hence, despite the constraints, conflict and the mobilization of activists on abortion has occurred at the local level, where South Carolina has a number of openly operating clinics providing abortion services and a fairly healthy and well-supported Planned Parenthood affiliate that offers a range of health-care options for women, including abortion. The remainder of this chapter focuses on abortion-related activism and governmental responses in two South Carolina cities—Greenville and Columbia—which illustrate nicely how local governments have also drawn on extralocal resources to overcome their corresponding collective-action problems. The two cases also illustrate the dynamics of local activism and local government response, with each side engaging in strategic adaptation.

Greenville has had more antiabortion activity than any other place in the state. In contrast, Columbia, with similar numbers of openly running clinics, has had fewer confrontations and arrests. Operation Rescue targeted Greenville in 1989 resulting in many arrests (Epes, 1989; Fleischer, 1989; Moore, 1989a,b,c; Moore and Piazza, 1989). Between 1989 and 1993, there were repeated arrests of protesters at the clinics in Greenville (*Greenville (S.C.) News,* 1992; Greczyn, 1992; Lore, 1992; Moore, 1992; Moore and Schwarz, 1992; Scoppe, 1992). In a five-week period in 1993, Greenville police arrested more than nine hundred people at clinic blockades (Allison, 1993; Carnett, 1993; Dumiak, 1993a,b; Ellison-Rider,

1993a,b; *Greenville (S.C.) News,* 1993; Koziatek, 1993; Perry, 1993; Schultz, 1993; Wood, 1993).

Although the political culture of South Carolina might lead one to expect repression because of the strong norms against open conflict over moral issues and standards, the state political context might lead one to expect evasion rather than repression because abortion-related conflict at local clinics has been sparked by pro-life forces that are politically more dominant. This circumstance exemplifies Lichbach's (1995) notion that, just as protest groups must overcome collective-action costs (the "rebel's dilemma"), so also does the control of protest groups constitute a collective-action problem for the state (the "state's dilemma") involving the costliness of repressive strategies. As the following case information will show, local governments respond to this by adopting a distinctive mixture of repressive and evasive strategies that allow them to take advantage of the constraints on political activism that are embedded in the state's political and social culture; but contextual factors at the local level mean that this strategy is more successful for some local governments than others. For their part, social movement activists, especially on the pro-life side, have attempted to overcome their collective-action dilemma by developing new tactics that simultaneously impose enhanced costs on local government and abortion clinics.

Greenville and Columbia: The Local Context

Columbia and Greenville, South Carolina, have council-manager forms of government (Sherrill and Stoudemire, 1950; Easterwood, 1984; Graham and Moore, 1994:206) with relatively weak mayors. Columbia's 4–2–1 election system (four from council districts, two elected at-large, and one mayor at-large) for city council is seen by a few officials as allowing a more diverse and open-minded collection of people to be elected to the council. The Greenville city council also has four single-member districts and two members elected at large. These mixed city council election systems were viewed by interviewees as a responsible way to represent the city, especially in contrast to the contentiousness on their respective county councils.

Although similar in terms of their governing institutions, Columbia and Greenville differ in terms of their political cultures. Greenville, home to conservative Bob Jones University (yet also Furman University) is relatively more conservative than Columbia. Although the Bob Jones community seems to set the tone for the city, their influence is indirect on abortion wars because "Theologically, Bob Jones has maintained a separatist philosophy—in short, its stance against ecumenism has hampered its work with other groups who share a pro-life philosophy, but come from different religious traditions. Finally, the University does not have a strong tradition of social activism. The community looks inward for spiritual renewal and generally stays out of community affairs. While that tradition has been broken with its involvement in Republican party politics, it has not reached into broader policy concerns such as abortion" (Halva-Neubauer et al., 1993:22; Woliver interviews). However, the influence of Bob Jones University faculty, staff, students, and alumni in Greenville politics is widely acknowledged. In 1996, the Greenville County Council passed an antigay ordinance, which resulted in the Olympic Torch being shrouded as it passed through Greenville County on the way to Atlanta (the torch was uncovered in the city of Greenville itself). The bad publicity this caused for Greenville was universally lamented by interviewees and was linked in their assessments to local antiabortion activism (Woliver interviews; see also Wyman, 1996a,b). With culture war issues, city officials worry that publicity over antigay county ordinances or strident and conflictual showdowns at places like the women's clinics would harm the area's business prospects.

Columbia, as the capital city, and the site of the University of South Carolina (and five other smaller colleges), is not as conservative as the rest of the area or many parts of the state. For instance, Richland County, where Columbia is located, votes Democratic. Columbia is also more racially diverse than Greenville.

Both cities have experienced rapid population growth in the last ten years. The Greenville-Spartanburg area, in particular, has boomed with growth and economic development (the BMW automobile manufacturing plant and many others have located to the area). As one city official proudly pointed out, the Greenville-Spartanburg area now has almost a million people, making the area forty-sixth in national media markets (New Orleans, by comparison, is forty-seventh). Rapid and dramatic growth, this official also postulated, helped cause some of the political friction in the area as the old guard who previously had handled everything quietly is now challenged by new people with new ideas and lifestyles, who do not as a matter of course accept the old order.

Attractions and Limits of Repression

A repressive governmental response can be triggered by culture wars involving abortion clinics because "it [repression] occurs when authorities feel loss of control because of the disruption and violence potential" (Sharp, 1997). Local officials interviewed for this chapter feel especially vulnerable about becoming a locus for another "Wichita [Kans.]," a reference to a community that received national attention when it was convulsed by conflict during an Operation Rescue-sponsored blockade. Although expressing faith that "homegrown" demonstrators on both sides of the issue, with whom they have been routinely dealing for years, would not resort to violence, many officials recounted their fears of "an outside nut case" coming through. The safety of the doctors at the clinics was of particular concern to them. The specter of outside groups deciding that their city would be a good target for a sustained, highly media-genic protest, or the nightmares caused by a single nut case driving to their town with loaded guns makes these officials face the random nature of how an issue like abortion could play out locally. These comments highlight the fear of violence and need for control that are important motivators of a repressive response. A few months after many of these interviews were conducted, the tragic reality of these officials' concerns was demonstrated when a deadly bomb exploded in front of a clinic in Birmingham, Alabama.

City officials' awareness of the randomness of these events and their vulnerability to them is acknowledged within collective-action theories that admit "aggregate levels and particular outbreaks of collective dissent are unpredictable" because there are so many contexts for rebellion (Lichbach, 1994:28). What beleaguered city officials do in such circumstances depends on the context and on intergovernmental dynamics, and is motivated by a desire to minimize the combustible potential of these moral conflicts. Above all, local officials' responses suggest that, despite fears of loss of control, repression is not an action that they undertake readily or in full-blown fashion. More typically, there are efforts to head off the need for a repressive response or to minimize the amount of repression that must be used to maintain order.

The strategic use of information is crucial in this regard. For example, both Greenville and Columbia officials note that watching what happened when Operation Rescue besieged Wichita, Kansas and other highly sustained demonstration locations nationwide helped them prepare for the eventuality of similar events. Because Greenville's massive demonstrations and arrests took place before any serious blockades in Columbia, Columbia city officials felt even more advantaged because they could learn from the experiences of officials in Greenville. As one city of Columbia person stated, "we had the luxury of learning from them, and we planned ahead." The importance of such sequencing in comparing behavior of interest groups over time, where tactics and strategies are adjusted in light of others' experiences (DeGregori and Rossatti, 1995:231–32) is expanded here to help explain the behavior of city officials responding to impassioned interest groups. DeLeon (chap. 7) makes a similar theoretical contribution within this volume when he highlights sequential learning across cities on gay rights issues, with San Francisco in the leadership vanguard.

In both South Carolina cities, officials related that they almost always had prior notice from abortion protest leaders about a planned confrontation. Officials strategically used that information in ways that constitute low-level repression, exercised in order to avert the need for more forceful forms of repression. Police and city officials would meet ahead of time with the blockade or picketing group leaders, and separately with the clinic directors, and remind them of all the pertinent city ordinances and the city's intent to keep the peace and uphold the laws. Such quiet reminders of police powers raise the costs of becoming a dissident for citizens contemplating rebellion (Lichbach, 1994:22; see also Gamson, 1975) and hence qualify as repression. But, if such low-level repression is successful, local government is relieved of the more costly forms of repression that would be exercised if they lost control of protesters.

In addition to these initial efforts to avert the need for extreme forms of repression, local officials attempted to avoid the appearance of repression, even when they were engaging in it, by operating under the rubric of federal court decisions, injunctions, and legislation. In January 1993, the U.S. Supreme Court in *National Organization of Women v. Scheidler* upheld use of the Racketeer Influenced and Corrupt Organization Act (RICO) against abortion clinic protesters. The 1994 Freedom of Access to Clinic Entrances Act (FACE) makes violence at abortion clinics a federal offense, provides for stiff jail sentences and fines and potentially (depending on a President's abortion stance and directions to his/her Attorney General) strong enforcement through the huge resources of the United States Justice Department. Potential use of both RICO and FACE—with their stiff fines, jail terms, and Justice Department involvement—along with a 1994 U.S. Supreme Court ruling *(Madsen v. Women's Health Center)* that a thirty-six-foot buffer zone between protesters and clinic entrances and driveways was not a violation of First Amendment free speech freedoms, has hampered some aggressive local antiabortion protest (Woliver interviews; see also Kelly, 1995:207). These rules lead to highly scripted, almost choreographed, routines of protest outside clinics, and protective counterresponses by clinic supporters.

Officials in Columbia and Greenville (no matter what their views on abortion) expressed gratitude for the relief that federal court orders and FACE provide them in trying to negotiate and contain clinic confrontations. These structures give local officials authority to regulate the free speech rights of the protesters and the free access rights for the clinics while allowing them to avoid the wrath of local activists by claiming they are merely implementing federal laws and orders.

These federal laws are also used as instruments of evasion for local officials concerned about inadvertent instigation of further dissent or too much responsiveness. "When emotional, culture-war-style issues are at stake . . . public officials can sometimes be overwhelmed by intense, special interest minorities or themselves committed to moral crusades. The resulting rush to policy, in processes that override procedural safeguards, squelch dissent, and ignore constitutional viability, can be problematic" (Sharp, 1996:754). Although guidelines from on high, such as FACE or the federal courts' decision concerning the use of RICO statutes against protesters, may be groused about as "the Feds' mandate," they actually help structure the local officials' responses and deflect criticism from city authorities trying to negotiate some kind of day-by-day coexistence. In almost every interview conducted for this study, city officials stated some version of the position that *Roe v. Wade* was the law of the land, and their role was simply to keep the peace and not make abortion policy. In short, local officials mask repression with evasion by invoking their policymaking powerlessness and directing outraged citizens to state and federal authorities.

Arrests and prosecution of abortion protesters are, of course, tools for repression of dissidents, and they have been used as such in the case-study communities. One derivative of the conservative political climate in South Carolina is an intolerance of vociferous dissent, and a steely law-and-order orientation. In both Greenville and Columbia, the willingness of law enforcement to arrest abortion protesters and prosecute them was well publicized before announced or rumored blockades and, for the most part, implemented (Woliver interviews; see also Halva-Neubauer et al., 1993:20). Officials plan for and focus on what they can at least partly control: train police officers in how to handle the large numbers of civilly disobedient blockaders and how to remove protesters from the scene while not violating their rights, while always remaining cognizant that the media's cameras are rolling. At the same time, reopen the clinics, and allow the patients and staff to enter and exit the facilities safely. One city official said, "We have been lucky thus far. But it could all change in an instant." However, the federal court injunctions, the RICO threat, and the FACE Act are credited with a recent downturn in arrests and violently disruptive confrontations at the clinics (see also Segers, 1995:237).

Activists' Adaptations to Local Government Responses

Antiabortion forces have adapted in several ways to local governments' combination of repression and evasion. On the one hand, they have tapped into broader networks of activism of people opposed to infanticide, euthanasia, and assisted suicide (Kelly, 1995:207). More importantly for our purposes, pro-life forces have adopted new tactics in their fight against abortion clinics. Recently, antiabortion activists in Greenville have shifted to a strategy of constant questions to city officials about zoning ordinances, public health requirements, traffic safety, and so forth—questions that take an inordinate amount of local officials' time. In Greenville, this minute monitoring (to some people, "harassing") of whether clinics have violated any ordinance, code, or health policy, was made easier when Pastors for Life purchased the building adjacent to one of the main Greenville clinics. The two buildings "share" a driveway. Disputes concerning the driveway and much else (the tall fence, zoning ordinance violations, the traffic in and out) has continuously been brought to city officials. "One side always wants the other side to be whipped into shape by the City," one experienced hand reported and continued, "So our involvement [the City of Greenville's] doesn't relate to the critical issue of whether a woman should be able to choose freely to carry a fetus or whether this is a human being who should be protected; this is the concern of those advocates. But, they [abortion activists] articulate their issue within the city administrative framework of zoning, safety, and having the police enforce a city's court injunction" (Woliver interviews).

Often clinic personnel, antiabortion protesters, and police officers develop standard routines surrounding their efforts (Woliver interviews; see also Hertz, 1991; Simonds, 1996). Currently one of the Greenville clinics is open only on Friday and Saturday, and on those days demonstrators are at the site trying to hand out leaflets and discourage patients from entering the facility. In Columbia, one clinic was constantly picketed by a devoted few from Columbia Sidewalk Counseling. That particular clinic was recently closed after the doctor who owned it died in a car accident. Since then, Columbia Sidewalk Counseling has been picketing outside the offices of the local Planned Parenthood clinic. In both cities, the pickets and the clinic staff know the routines and are watchful for any violations of the basic outlines of permissible antiabortion speech rights or free and safe clinic-access issues.

A new tactic by pro-life activists in Greenville and Columbia, as well as other locations across the country, is occasional picketing outside high schools, while displaying big posters of aborted bloody fetuses and handing out graphic leaflets to the students on their way into school (see Columbia Sidewalk Counseling, 1997). City officials have had to handle complaints from irate parents about the propriety of this. In the Greenville area, the issue was complicated because a few middle and elementary schools were adjacent to the high schools where the huge placards were displayed. City officials strictly enforce sign codes and sidewalk picketing ordinances in these and other situations. Given the volatile nature of disputes like this, city and police officials are especially careful to try to be evenhanded. One high-ranking city politician reflected on how difficult this is, "People who are very focused on these kinds of issues, their prism is the issue. A city or local government is focused on its mission, to enforce the law. However, what you do can be misconstrued, but it is just your job, not aimed at any one side. Zoning enforcement is routine and done all the time, yet the groups see it as enforcement which is aimed at them. It is always a powder keg, and you have to be careful."

As this city official confirms, the local authorities are "fulcrums" (Tarrow, 1994:6) for the larger goals of the morality based pro-life and pro-choice national social movements. City officials assert that this is not really what local governments, city workers, police, and local officials are trained, hired, and elected to do. As one high-ranking official sighed, "What you need is a good kindergarten teacher." And every good kindergarten teacher knows the importance of consistency in the application of sanctions and rewards in order to keep down rebellions. Similarly, it has been theorized that even more rebellious protest can follow when "regimes incoherently mix reform (accommodation) and reaction (repression), and pursue these policies in fits and starts, thereby weakening the regime and facilitating revolution" (Lichbach, 1987:287). Intuitively grasping this, local officials in South Carolina attempt to evade abortion controversy as best they can through straightforward administration of local land-use, health, and traffic regulations coupled with repression of protesters that violate FACE.

CONCLUSION: MANAGING LOCAL ABORTION CONFLICTS

People engage in grassroots politics for a variety of reasons. Some have short-term, immediate concerns that they want redressed. Others come to grassroots actions with a longer-term perspective, not expecting immediate justice but "measures of justice" (Woliver, 1993), and believe they can make a small impact on a long journey for social and political justice. Even groups that seem to fail have an impact. The power in movement is "cumulative" (Tarrow, 1994:191), helping explain movement adherents' willingness to work for state legislation, city ordinances, or local court decisions that they know will most likely be overturned by higher federal courts. Even when they fail to meet their self-designated objectives, citizen mobilization usually leaves "residues of reform" (Tarrow, 1994:186; see also Skocpol et al., 1993). The knowledge and perspectives emerging from new social movements, and the social learning of politically active citizens even in transitory mobilizations, influence and help shape future grassroots groups and movements. In the cases examined here, this social learning is exhibited in the development of ever more creative tactics to use local government as a fulcrum for advancing movement goals.

In addition to the dynamics of social movement learning and strategic adaptation, this chapter shows the importance of extralocal forces in understanding local activism. With city-level abortion issues, we find not only a fluid network of social movement forces (including conservatism, family values, women's health advocates, and feminists) but substantial and complex interactions between local, state, and national elements of these social movements. For this reason, local politicians can quickly and easily find themselves in the middle of national movement contagions. Evaluations of grassroots successes and failures therefore need to be judged within a community context that is permeated by national and state forces.

But the same observations can be made about local government, which is confronting dilemmas of collective action that parallel those of social movement activists. The successes and failures of governing regimes need to be judged within a community context shaped by developments at the state and national levels. Local antiabortion activists try to bring to bear city ordinances, zoning issues, and heightened public awareness of the locations and business of the abortion clinics to keep up the pressure at the local level, while others clamp down on the clinics through state legislation. Pro-choice interests counter with the imprimatur of *Roe,* RICO, FACE, and other related court decisions to make city officials keep the peace at clinics and permit them to conduct their business without undue hindrances.

Maxims from theories of rebellion remind us that neither regimes nor opposition groups are monolithic (Lichbach, 1987:273; 1995). Given the constraints on local regimes and the costliness of overtly repressive strategies, repression and evasion are rational responses for city policymakers dealing with intractable culture war issues such as abortion clinic disputes. More particularly, repression coupled with a special form of evasion is the response of choice for local governments in South Carolina. Local officials manage conflict by using federal and state laws and court orders as tools for repression while evading full responsibility for taking an authoritative local stand on the core of the abortion issue.

But if external institutions provide resources that both local activists and local governments use in abortion conflicts, it is important to acknowledge a special, external constraint on local government action. That constraint is evident once we acknowledge how the economic development context shapes the character of abortion politics at the local level. In both of the case-study cities, and indeed in many southern cities, there are strong beliefs in the importance of projecting an "image" (Pagano and Bowman, 1997:44) of a modern, pro-business, "New South." Religiously based rebellion, replete with photogenic "rescues" and massive resistance to national policies at local abortion clinics, is seen as counterproductive to this business image. But the concerns about image serve as more substantial constraints on governing officials than on abortion activists, who operate outside the value structure of the business regimes and are often not swayed by reminders that their behavior could hurt the area's business image. Contrary to assumptions of many regime theories, while city officials might be anticipating the desires of business for a stable, noncontroversial pro-business climate, morality-based groups demand accountability to values that are not driven by business concerns. The dominant economic development orientation of many cities, such as the two studied here, mean that the powers that be often see these moral rebels as behaving "irrationally" (from the heart, outside the norms of finance and accounting), where it is best to placate, minimize, and not further instigate their passions.

Just as social movement activists exhibit social learning—strategic adaptation based on information—so also do local governments exhibit social learning in culture wars. However, some communities are more advantaged than others in this regard. Greenville and Columbia have a lot in common, yet have experienced different intensities of abortion conflict. Greenville's choice as a target for Operation Rescue forced local officials there to deal with a giant culture war conflagration. Columbia's relative lack of protest is partly based on the area's slightly less conservative culture and local support for Planned Parenthood and the clinic they operate. But in addition, because the massive arrests and turmoil occurred in Greenville first, Columbia prosecutors and other officials were able to learn from Greenville's experience. They were particularly vigilant about trying to prevent similar massive disruptions in Columbia.

The big protests and screaming confrontations might have died down for now, while a quieter, procedural, institutional approach by abortion opponents in South Carolina has whittled down abortion choices through state legislation. At the same time, in cities like Greenville, the size, spacing, and placements of pro-life placards, driveway accessibility for warring neighbors, and many more such issues keep the culture war heated up at the city level in this intractable moral and political dispute.

ACKNOWLEDGMENTS

I would like to thank Erin Kahaney, Rachel Kraus, and Angela Ledford for their research assistance. Special thanks to Glen Halva-Neubauer of Furman University for his advice and shared expertise. Although I have not cited them by name because of the contentiousness of the issues, I express my special appreciation to the many politicians, activists, journalists, and medical personnel who graciously provided time in their busy lives for my interviews.

REFERENCES

Adams, Greg D. 1997. "Abortion: Evidence of an Issue Evolution." *American Journal of Political Science* 41(3): 718–37.
Aho, James. 1996. "Popular Christianity and Political Extremism." In Christian Smith, ed., *Disruptive Religion: the Force of Faith in Social Movement Activism.* New York: Routledge, pp. 189–204.
Allison, Wes. 1993. "Federal Judge Refuses to Block Arrests of Abortion Protesters." *Greenville (S.C.) News,* 5 February, p. 1a.
Barone, Michael, and Grant Ujifusa. 1997. *The Almanac of American Politics 1998.* Washington, D.C.: National Journal.
Bellah, R. N., R. Madsen, W. M. Sullivan, A. Swidler, and S. M. Tipton. 1985. *Habits of the Heart: Individualism and Commitment in American Life.* Berkeley: University of California Press.
Blanchard, Dallas A. 1994. *The Anti-Abortion Movement and the Rise of the Religious Right: From Polite to Fiery Protest.* New York: Twayne Publishers.
Botsch, Robert E. 1992. "South Carolina: The Rise of the New South." In Ronald J. Hrebenar and Clive S. Thomas, eds., *Interest Group Politics in the Southern States.* Tuscaloosa: University of Alabama Press, pp. 209–30.
Boyte, H. C. 1980. *The Backyard Revolution: Understanding the New Citizen Movement.* Philadelphia: Temple University Press.
Carnett, Sheila. 1993. "450 Anti-Abortion Activists Ticketed." *Greenville (S.C.) News,* 31 January, p. 1a.
Chafe, William H. 1980. *Civilities and Civil Rights: Greensboro, North Carolina, and the Black Struggle for Freedom.* New York: Oxford University Press.
Chong, D. 1991. *Collective Action and the Civil Rights Movement.* Chicago: University of Chicago Press.
Cobb, James C. 1993. *The Selling of the South.* Urbana: University of Illinois Press.
Columbia Sidewalk Counseling. "God Is Going Back to School." 1997. Press Release, 2 September.
Conway, M. Margaret, Gertrude A. Steuernagel, and David W. Ahern. 1997. *Women and Political Participation: Cultural Change in the Political Arena.* Washington, D.C.: Congressional Quarterly Press.
DeGregorio, Christine, and Jack E. Rossotti. 1995. "Campaigning for the Court: Interest Group Participation in the Bork and Thomas Confirmation Processes." In Allan J. Cigler and Burdett Loomis, eds., *Interest Group Politics,* 4th ed. Washington, D.C.: Congressional Quarterly Press, pp. 215–38.
DeLeon, Richard. 1999. "San Francisco and Domestic Partners: New Fields of Battle." In Elaine B. Sharp, ed., *Culture Wars and Local Politics.* Lawrence: University Press of Kansas.
Dugger, Karen. 1991. "Race Differences in the Determinants of Support for Legalized Abortion." *Social Science Quarterly* 72(3): 570–87.

Dumiak, Michael. 1993a. "50 Anti-Abortion Protesters Arrested by Greenville Police." *Greenville (S.C.) News*, 21 February, p. 1B.

————. 1993b. "51 Arrested in anti-Abortion Campaign: 864 People Have Been Ticketed in the Past Five Weeks," *Greenville (S.C.) News*, 28 February, p. 1a.

Easterwood, Michael. 1984. "The Municipality and South Carolina Government," In Charlie B. Tyer and Cole Blease Graham, Jr., eds., *Local Government in South Carolina*. Columbia: Bureau of Governmental Research and Service, University of South Carolina, pp. 9–49.

Edelman, Murray. 1989. *Constructing the Political Spectacle*. Chicago: University of Chicago Press.

Eisinger, Peter K. 1988. *The Rise of the Entrepreneurial State: State and Local Economic Development in the United States*. Madison: University of Wisconsin Press.

Ellison-Rider, Elaine. 1993a. "Anti-Abortion Protest Chilled by Stiff Wind." *Greenville (S.C.) News*, 14 February, p. 1b.

————. 1993b. "Police Arrest 37 Outside Clinic." *Greenville (S.C.) News*, 7 March, p. 2b.

Epes, James. 1989. "Pro-Life Group Prepares for 2nd 'Rescue' Operation." *Greenville (S.C.) Piedmont*, 28 April, p. 2c.

Evans, S. M., and H. C. Boyte. 1986. *Free Spaces: The Sources of Democratic Change in America*. New York: Harper & Row.

Fleischer, Jo. 1989. "31 Charged Protesting Abortion." *Greenville (S.C.) News*, 9 July, p. 1b.

Friedman, D., and D. McAdam. 1992. "Collective Identity and Activism: Networks, Choices, and the Life of a Social Movement." In A. D. Morris and C. McC. Mueller, eds., *Frontiers in Social Movement Theory*. New Haven, Conn.: Yale University Press, pp. 156–73.

Galanter, Marc. 1974. "Why the 'Haves' Come Out Ahead: Speculations on the Limits of Legal Change." *Law & Society Review* 9:95–106.

Gamson, William A. 1975. *The Strategy of Social Protest*. Homewood, Ill.: Dorsey.

Garrow, David J. 1978. *Protest at Selma: Martin Luther King, Jr. and the Voting Rights Act of 1965*. New Haven, Conn.: Yale University Press.

Genovese, E. D. 1976. *Roll, Jordan, Roll: The World the Slaves Made*. New York: Vintage Books.

Gimpel, James G. 1998. "Grassroots Organizations and Equilibrium Cycles in Group Mobilization and Access." In Paul S. Herrnson, Ronald G. Shaiko, and Clyde Wilcox, eds., *The Interest Group Connection: Electioneering, Lobbying, and Policymaking in Washington*. Chatham, N.J.: Chatham House Publishers, pp. 100–115.

Graber, Mark A. 1996. *Rethinking Abortion: Equal Choice, the Constitution, and Reproductive Politics*. Princeton, N.J.: Princeton University Press.

Graham, Cole Blease, Jr., and William V. Moore. 1994. *South Carolina Politics and Government*. Lincoln: University of Nebraska Press.

Gray, Virginia, and David Lowery. 1996. "A Niche Theory of Interest Representation." *Journal of Politics* 58 (1, February): 91–111.

Greczyn, Mary. 1992. "21 Clergymen Arrested Outside Abortion Clinic." *Greenville (S.C.) News*, 6 December, p. 1a.

Green, John C., James L. Goth, Corwin E. Smidt, and Lyman A. Kellstedt. 1996. *Religion and the Culture Wars: Dispatches from the Front*. Lanham, Md.: Rowman and Littlefield.

Greenville (S.C.) News. 1992. "Abortion Protest Expected." 21 March, p. 2a.

———. 1993. "Police Almost Outnumber Few Activists at Clinic." 4 April, p. 2b.

Gusfield, J. R. 1981. "Social Movements and Social Change: Perspectives of Linearity and Fluidity." In L. Kriesberg, ed., *Research in Social Movements, Conflict, and Change.* Greenwich, Conn.: JAI Press, pp. 317–39.

Guth, James L. 1995. "South Carolina: The Christian Right Wins One." In Mark J. Rozell and Clyde Wilcox, eds., *God at the Grass Roots: The Christian Right in the 1994 Elections.* Lanham, Md.: Rowman and Littlefield, pp. 133–45.

Halva-Neubauer, Glen A. 1993. "The States After *Roe*—No 'Paper Tigers.'" In Malcolm L. Goggin, ed., *Understanding the New Politics of Abortion.* Newbury Park, Calif.: Sage.

Halva-Neubauer, Glen A., Raymond Tatalovich, and Byron W. Daynes. 1993. "Locating Abortion Clinics: Aggregate Data and Case Study Approaches to the Implementation Process." Paper presented at the 1993 Annual Meeting of the American Political Science Association, Washington, D.C.

Haeberle, Steven H. 1989. *Planting the Grass Roots: Structuring Citizen Participation.* New York: Praeger.

Harris, F. 1994. "Something Within: Religion as a Mobilizer of African-American Political Activism." *Journal of Politics* 56(1): 42–68.

Herbst, S. 1994. *Politics at the Margin: Historical Studies of Public Expression Outside the Mainstream.* Cambridge: Cambridge University Press.

Hertz, Sue. 1991. *Caught in the Crossfire: A Year on Abortion's Front Line.* New York: Prentice Hall.

Himmelstein, Jerome L. 1990. *To the Right: The Transformation of American Conservatism.* Berkeley: University of California Press.

Holsworth, R. D. 1989. *Let Your Life Speak: A Study of Politics, Religion, and Antinuclear Weapons Activism.* Madison: University of Wisconsin Press.

Ivers, Gregg. 1998. "Please God, Save this Honorable Court: The Emergence of the Conservative Religious Bar." In Paul S. Herrnson, Ronald G. Shaiko, and Clyde Wilcox, eds., *The Interest Group Connection: Electioneering, Lobbying, and Policymaking in Washington.* Chatham, N.J.: Chatham House Publishers, pp. 289–301.

Johnston, Hank, Enrique Larana, and Joseph R. Gusfield. 1994. "Identities, Grievances, and New Social Movements," In Enrique Larana, Hank Johnston, and Joseph R. Gusfield, eds., *New Social Movements: From Ideology to Identity.* Philadelphia: Temple University Press, pp. 3–35.

Kelly, James R. 1995. "Beyond Compromise: *Casey,* Common Ground, and the Pro-Life Movement," In Mary C. Segers and Timothy A. Byrnes, eds., *Abortion Politics in American States.* Armonk, N.Y.: M. E. Sharpe, pp. 205–24.

Koziatek, Mike. 1993. "Anti-Abortion Rally Leads to 318 Arrests." *Greenville (S.C.) News,* 7 February, p. 1a.

Lendler, Marc. 1997. *Crisis and Political Beliefs: The Case of the Colt Firearms Strike.* New Haven, Conn.: Yale University Press.

Lichbach, Mark I. 1987. "Deterrence or Escalation? The Puzzle of Aggregate Studies of Repression and Dissent." *Journal of Conflict Resolution* 31(2): 266–97.

———. 1994. "Rethinking Rationality and Rebellion." *Rationality and Society* 6(1): 8–39.

———. 1995. *The Rebel's Dilemma.* Ann Arbor: University of Michigan Press.

Lieske, Joel. 1993. "Regional Subcultures of the United States." *Journal of Politics* 55(4): 888–913.

Lore, Diane. 1992. "Abortion Protest Moves to Upstate." *The (Columbia, S.C.) State,* 22 March, p. 1a.

Luker, Kristin. 1984. *Abortion and the Politics of Motherhood.* Berkeley: University of California Press.

McAdam, Doug, John D. McCarthy, and Mayer N. Zald. 1996. "Introduction: Opportunities, Mobilizing Structures, and Framing Processes—Toward a Synthetic, Comparative Perspective on Social Movements." In Doug McAdam, John D. McCarthy, and Mayer N. Zald, eds., *Comparative Perspectives on Social Movements.* Cambridge: Cambridge University Press, pp. 1–20.

McCann, M. W. 1994. *Rights at Work: Pay Equity Reform and the Politics of Legal Mobilization.* Chicago: University of Chicago Press.

Mohr, James C. 1978. *Abortion in America: The Origins and Evolution of National Policy, 1800–1900.* New York: Oxford University Press.

Mohr, Richard D. 1995. "Anti-Gay Stereotypes." In Paula Rothenberg, ed., *Race, Class, and Gender in the U.S.* New York: St. Martin's Press, pp. 402–7.

Moore, Toby. 1989a. "New Style of Abortion Protest Sparks Debate: Operation Rescue Plans to Come to Upstate Next Month." *Greenville (S.C.) News,* 22 January, p. 1e.

———. 1989b. "28 Pro-Life Activists Arrested in Greenville: Similar Protests Planned Saturday." *Greenville (S.C.) News,* 28 April, p. 1a.

———. (1989c). "64 Arrested at Third Rescue: Some Say Officers Were Rough." *Greenville (S.C.) News,* 30 April, p. 1a.

———. 1992. "'Rescue' Anti-Abortion Demonstration Might Be Held Over Weekend." *Greenville (S.C.) News,* 18 March.

Moore, Toby, and Bob Piazza. 1989. "57 People Arrested at Abortion Protest: No Injuries in State's 1st 'Operation Rescue.'" *Greenville (S.C.) News,* 18 February, p. 1a.

Moore, Toby, and Christopher Schwarz. 1992. "65 Arrested at Abortion Clinic 'Rescue.'" *Greenville (S.C.) News,* 22 March, p. 1a.

Mooreland, Laurence W., and Robert P. Steed. 1998. "The Abortion Issue among South Carolina Republican Party Activists and the Potential for Party Fracturing." Paper presented at the South Carolina Political Science Convention, Columbia College, 28 February.

Morris, A. D. 1984. *The Origins of the Civil Rights Movement: Black Communities Organizing for Change.* New York: Free Press.

Mueller, Carol. 1994. "Conflict Networks and the Origins of Women's Liberation," In Enrique Larana, Hank Johnston, and Joseph R. Gusfield, eds., *New Social Movements: From Ideology to Identity.* Philadelphia: Temple University Press, pp. 234–63.

Nice, David C. 1988. "Abortion Clinic Bombings as Political Violence." *American Journal of Political Science* 32(1): 178–95.

Nownes, Anthony J., and Patricia Freeman. 1998. "Interest Group Activity in the States." *Journal of Politics* 60(1): 86–112.

O'Connor, Karen. 1996. *No Neutral Ground? Abortion Politics in an Age of Absolutes.* Boulder, Colo.: Westview Press.

———. 1998. "Lobbying the Justices or Lobbying for Justice?" In Paul S. Herrnson, Ronald G. Shaiko, and Clyde Wilcox, eds., *The Interest Group Connection: Electioneering, Lobbying, and Policymaking in Washington.* Chatham, N.J.: Chatham House Publishers, pp. 267–88.

Oldendick, Robert. 1990. "Abortion: How South Carolinians View the Issue." *South Carolina Forum* 1(2): 11–15.

Pagano, Michael A., and Ann O'M. Bowman. 1997. *Cityscapes and Capital.* Baltimore: Johns Hopkins University Press.

Perry, Dale. 1993. "Police Gear Up For Anti-Abortion Protest." *Greenville (S.C.) Piedmont,* 29 January, p. 1a.

Planned Parenthood of Central South Carolina and Planned Parenthood of the Low Country. 1996. *State of the State* (Newsletter) February–March.

Rhode, Deborah L., and Annette Lawson. 1993. "Introduction." In Annette Lawson and Deborah L. Rhode, eds., *The Politics of Pregnancy: Adolescent Sexuality and Public Policy.* New Haven, Conn.: Yale University Press, pp. 1–19.

Schneider, Mark, and Paul Teske. 1993. "The Antigrowth Entrepreneur: Challenging the 'Equilibrium' of the Growth Machine." *Journal of Politics* 55 (August): 720–36.

Scoppe, Cindi Ross. 1992. "Operation Rescue Plans S.C. Blockades." *The (Columbia, S.C.) State,* 16 February, p. 1b.

————. 1996. "Abortion Rules Face Rewrite: Opponents Don't Want DHEC to Get Medical Records Access." *The (Columbia, S.C.) State,* 22 March, p. B6.

————. 1997a. "House Rejects 'Partial-Birth' Abortion: Ban Procedure in S.C., Lawmakers Say," *The (Columbia, S.C.) State,* 28 February, pp. 1, 10 A.

————. 1997b. "'Partial-birth' ban Passes in Senate: S.C. 6th in Outlawing Abortion Procedure." *The Columbia (S.C.) State,* 14 March, pp. 1, 6 A.

Schultz, Steven. 1993. "500 Arrested at Prayer Vigil Outside Clinic." *Spartanburg (S.C.) Herald-Journal,* 31 January, p. 1a.

Sears, James. 1991. *Growing Up Gay in the South.* New York: Haworth Press.

Segers, Mary C. 1995. "The Pro-Choice Movement Post-*Casey:* Preserving Access," In Mary C. Segers and Timothy A. Byrnes, eds., *Abortion Politics in American States.* Armonk, N.Y.: M. E. Sharpe, pp. 225–45.

Segers, Mary C., and Timothy A. Byrnes. 1995. "Introduction: Abortion Politics in American States." In Mary C. Segers and Timothy A. Byrnes, eds., *Abortion Politics in American States.* Armonk, N.Y.: M. E. Sharpe, pp. 1–15.

Sharp, Elaine. 1996. "Culture Wars and City Politics: Local Government's Role in Social Conflict." *Urban Affairs Review* 31(6), pp. 738–58.

————. 1997. "A Comparative Anatomy of Urban Social Conflict." *Political Research Quarterly* 50 (June): 261–80.

Sherrill, George R., and Robert H. Stoudemire. 1950. *Municipal Government in South Carolina.* Columbia: University of South Carolina Press.

Simonds, Wendy. 1996. *Abortion at Work: Ideology and Practice in a Feminist Clinic.* New Brunswick, N.J.: Rutgers University Press.

Skocpol, T., M. Abend-Wein, C. Howard, and S. G. Lehmann. 1993. "Women's Associations and the Enactment of Mothers' Pensions in the United States." *American Political Science Review* 87(3): 686–701.

Smith, Oran P. 1997. *The Rise of Baptist Republicanism.* New York: New York University Press.

Snow, D. A., E. B. Rochford, Jr., S. K. Worden, and R. D. Benford. 1986. "Frame Alignment Processes, Micromobilization, and Movement Participation." *American Sociological Review* 51(4): 464–81.

Staggenborg, Suzanne. 1991. *The Pro-Choice Movement: Organization and Activism in the Abortion Conflict.* New York: Oxford University Press.

———. 1996. "The Survival of the Women's Movement: Turnover and Continuity in Bloomington, Indiana." *Mobilization: An International Journal* 1(2): 143–58.

Tarrow, Sidney. 1994. *Power in Movement.* Cambridge: Cambridge University Press.

Tatalovich, Raymond, and Bryan Daynes. 1988. *Social Regulatory Policy: Moral Controversies in American Politics.* Boulder, Colo.: Westview.

Williams, Rhys H., and Jeffrey Blackburn. 1996. "Many Are Called but Few Obey: Ideological Commitment and Activism in Operation Rescue." In Christian Smith, ed., *Disruptive Religion: The Force of Faith in Social Movement Activism.* New York: Routledge, pp. 167–85.

Woliver, Laura R. 1993. *From Outrage to Action: The Politics of Grass-Roots Dissent.* Urbana: University of Illinois Press.

———. 1993. "Representation and Abortion Politics in the American Medical Profession." Paper presented at the 1993 American Political Science Association Convention, Washington, D.C.

———. 1996a. "Mobilizing and Sustaining Grassroots Dissent." *Journal of Social Issues* 52(spring): 139–51.

———. 1996b. "Rhetoric and Symbols in American Abortion Politics." In Marianne Githens and Dorothy McBride Stetson, eds., *Abortion Politics: Public Policy in Cross-Cultural Perspective.* New York: Routledge, pp. 5–28.

———. 1996c. "Local Diligence: The Impact of Fluid Social Movements on Abortion Politics." Paper presented at the 1996 Midwest Political Science Convention, Chicago.

———. 1997. "Grass-Roots Coalitions and Abortion Politics." Paper presented at the 1997 Midwest Political Science Convention, Chicago.

———. 1998. "Social Movements and Abortion Law." In Anne N. Costain and Andrew S. McFarland, eds., *Social Movements and American Political Institutions.* Lanham, Md.: Rowman and Littlefield.

Wood, Mark. 1993. "Abortion Foes Keep Up Vigil; 318 Arrested." *Spartanburg (S.C.) Herald-Journal,* 7 February, p. 1a.

Wyman, Scott. 1996a. "Suburbs Won't See Olympic Flame: Run Organizers Will Keep Torch Out of View from Greenville County Line to City Limits in Response to Anti-Gay Resolution." *Greenville (S.C.) News,* 25 June, p. 1a.

———. 1996b. "Greenville County's Image Tested by Olympic Rebuke." *Greenville (S.C.) News,* 26 June, p. 1a.

3
Ideas, Interests, and Institutions Shaping Abortion Politics in Denver

Susan E. Clarke

Local conflicts over abortion issues can best be understood in terms of the triangle of institutions, ideas, and interests shaping the policy process: how institutions mold the ideas prevailing in debates and how ideas and institutions shape the way people understand their interests. This broader perspective is useful because moral controversies do not primarily reflect the material stakes or coalition-building strategies featured in interest-group perspectives (Sharp, 1996; Cobb and Ross, 1997). Rather, these conflicts center on competing ideas—deeply held beliefs about religious values, individual rights, and constitutional principles—and the institutional contexts shaping policy responses.

This chapter analyzes the strategic choices available to local officials in responding to disruptive abortion conflicts and the factors conditioning their choices. Tarrow (1994:92) argues that state responses to movements primarily entail repression and facilitation. That is, local officials' choices range from facilitating challengers by lowering the cost of collective action and increasing the likelihood of agenda status for their concerns to repressing challengers' disruptive acts and raising the costs of collective action (Tarrow, 1994:92). By presenting these options as a continuum, Tarrow underscores the strategic choices facing local officials.[1] Cobb and Ross's (1997) typology of high-, medium-, and low-cost strategies of agenda denial further differentiates the range of repressive local responses to conflict. High-cost strategies signify the types of repressive acts that public officials use to increase the cost of collective action for protesters and deny them agenda status (Tarrow, 1994; Cobb and Ross, 1997; Sharp 1997).

In democratic settings, directly repressive state acts must be justified as legitimate and necessary responses. For justification, local governments draw on ideas or issue frames blaming abortion conflicts on the acts of protesters and prescribing high-cost repressive policy responses as solutions. These frames and strategies are molded by the institutional context in which local officials act: this context enables them to employ rules (such as legal ordinances) to raise the costs of protest but also potentially limits repression because nonselective repression can harm allies as well as challengers. These institutional constraints on repression, along with incentives to accommodate competing values of public order and civil liberties in abortion conflicts, encourage local officials to mix repressive strategies with efforts to normalize protest through less obtrusive (and less costly) forms of regulation. In pursuing these dual strategies—repression and normalization—local officials structure the opportunities available to pro-choice and pro-life activist groups.

These intersecting aspects of ideas, interests, and institutions are illustrated by the conflict over abortion issues in Denver from 1989 to 1996. The interests, ideas, and institutional context are reconstructed using a computerized file of local newspaper accounts of abortion issues; these newspaper texts then are analyzed using NUD*IST software, which allows the sorting of different statements by, for example, pro-choice and pro-life organizations and the issue framing presented by each group.[2] Denver is a particularly good case for examining the importance of ideas and institutions because polls and public statements consistently indicated that a majority of local officials and citizens shared pro-choice sentiments. According to an interest-group perspective, pro-choice coalitions would drive policy decisions and deny agenda access to the antiabortion minority. Instead, we find a range of strategic policy choices over time.

Briefly, this analysis reveals three linked processes: Denver justified repression by socially constructing disruptive challengers such as Operation Rescue as negative, outside groups harming all residents of the city and deserving the costly penalties imposed on them. The city eventually limited expansion of repressive strategies in the face of city council concerns that more repressive tactics would unduly constrain local electoral constituencies. To explain and gain support for these complex responses, local officials constructed frames that allowed them to repress disruptive conflicts but also safeguard positions of local constituencies and antiabortion protesters willing to forego disruptive conflicts. Finally, these high-cost repressive strategies were accompanied by efforts to normalize disruptive abortion conflicts. That is, local officials acted to bring these value conflicts within the boundaries of accepted political exchange—and to lower the costs to the city—by creating rules of the game that would normalize collective action in the abortion arena (Piven and Cloward, 1992).

INTERESTS, INSTITUTIONS, AND IDEAS: AN OVERVIEW OF ABORTION POLITICS IN DENVER

Interests

Denver's progressive history of reproductive rights stretches back to the 1900s when Margaret Sanger visited Denver as part of a national tour to draw attention to birth control issues. The first birth control clinic in Colorado opened in Denver in 1926, providing diaphragms to married women interested in spacing their children. But giving birth control advice remained a violation of the state's obscenity law until 1961; an abortion underground operated in Denver through the 1960s until passage of state legislation legalizing abortion in 1967.[3] Abortion services were first legally provided in Denver in 1973 with the passage of *Roe v. Wade* (1973, 410 U.S. 113).

Colorado's pro-choice legislative legacy includes the first state provision legalizing abortion (1967) and the first statewide abortion-access bill, the "bubble law" (1993), creating an eight-foot buffer zone around anyone entering or leaving a clinic.[4] To some, these landmark provisions are less a reflection of pro-choice sentiment than of the libertarian leanings of a state often reluctant to intervene in privacy issues such as motorcycle helmet laws and smoking (Gavin, 1992). Nevertheless, state legislators see the voting population as pro-choice and are reluctant to bring the abortion issue onto the legislature floor; a survey of 1989 legislators showed that sixty-nine of the one hundred legislators would vote against any attempt to make abortion illegal (Gavin, 1992).

Relative to other states, Colorado ranks relatively high in availability of abortion services at the county level: 86 percent of women live in a county with a provider of abortion services available compared to a national rate of 70 percent in 1992 (Henshaw and VanVort, 1994). As in other states, abortions are performed primarily in metropolitan areas: eleven of the twelve Title X clinics in Colorado are in Denver; the abortion rates in Denver historically are higher than the state rates, although there has been a convergence in these trends since 1990. The increase in the number of abortions reported in Colorado that began in 1967 peaked in 1980; after 1984, the numbers declined, reaching a twenty-year low of 9,384 in 1995 (State of Colorado, 1997:113). In Denver, the struggle over abortion occurred, therefore, in a state context of declining abortion rates.[5]

The abortion conflict in Denver is played out in a multiethnic setting. Although still a minority population, the Latino community there is growing. The majority of Latinos are Catholics, but there are splits over abortion issues within the Latino community and within the Catholic church in Denver. The Archbishop remained "neutral" on antiabortion protests in the late 1980s, instructing Catholics to follow their conscience. By the mid-1990s, however, he argued that policymakers must put priority on their religious beliefs in responding to abortion conflicts.

Institutional Context

Increasingly, the institutional context for abortion conflicts is local. Supreme Court decisions devolving regulation of access to abortion services to state and local governments account for this localization trend. In July 1989, the Supreme Court's decision (*Webster v. Reproductive Health Services,* 109 S.Ct. 3040) giving states broad new authority to regulate abortions spurred increased mobilization of pro-choice and antiabortion groups nationwide. Similarly, the June 1992 Supreme

Court decision (*Planned Parenthood of Southeastern Pennsylvania v. Casey*, 60 USLW 4795) upholding Pennsylvania's restrictive abortion laws was seen as limiting federal judges' ability to intervene in clinic blockades and other disruptive efforts. This persuaded many Colorado activists that *Roe v. Wade* was vulnerable to being overturned and that struggles over abortion rights would be won or lost in the state legislatures and local conflicts over access.

Anticipation of the demise of *Roe v. Wade* shifted the institutional venues for both pro-choice and antiabortion activists in Colorado to state and local arenas. This prompted local conflicts over clinic access, increased involvement in state electoral campaigns and legislative activities, greater reliance on the courts and, for pro-life activists, use of Colorado's liberal initiative provisions to push initiatives with restrictive abortion conditions onto the state ballot.[6] As Operation Rescue embarked on its local clinic blockade campaign, groups such as Planned Parenthood were pushed into defensive postures; one Denver leader confessed, "This is not our battlefield. Our battle will be in the legislatures and in Congress" (Simpson, 1989).

The incoming Clinton administration and its rapid reversal of many policies set in the Reagan-Bush administrations altered the tone and intensity of local abortion conflicts. Both antiabortion and pro-choice activists cite Clinton's election as changing the tenor of local activism: One described Clinton's election as "a wake-up call" that upped the antiabortion movement ante, while a Planned Parenthood leader agreed that the election "was a real turning point. I think that this is when you saw some very different people joining this group. People who are angry with Clinton or some other turn of events find this a cause now. How much concern they have about the issues is a real question" (Harrington 1995).

As communities become battlefields for abortion conflicts, local officials face a quandary: They have no substantive power to resolve these conflicts, only to police them. They are motivated to act when conflicts over first principles become disruptive; disruptive protest by challengers to existing laws not only threatens public order, but also raises real concerns about the fiscal and image costs to the city. How local officials choose to exercise their police powers is conditioned by the institutional context. Because this institutional context varies across American cities, we can anticipate distinctive but not necessarily singular trajectories of cultural conflicts and policy responses.

In Denver, as in other American cities, the institutional setting is fragmented and penetrated by other governmental authorities. It includes, for example, federal court decisions, executive orders, and congressional restrictions on use of federal funds; the state legislature and citizen initiatives; the mayor and city council (thirteen members, elected by both district and at-large procedures); the local district attorney's office responsible for enforcing city ordinances; the county courts hearing ordinance cases; the unionized police force; a range of federally funded clinics and private hospitals and clinics; and the Catholic church. These diverse institutions interact with one another but with little formal coordination. This interaction and fragmentation provide multiple decision points where stakeholders can block actions that adversely affect their interests. Typically, such stalemates are overcome, and consensus is achieved through logrolling and distributive policies; but in cultural conflicts, such tactics generally are not possible because of the value conflicts involved.

In Colorado, decisions made beyond the city limits continually reshaped the menu of policy choices available to local officials and reconfigured groups' incentives and disincentives to adopt particular strategies. The Colorado state legislature and the county, state, and federal courts upheld and reinforced Denver's efforts to suppress antiabortion activities with some consistency. Noting concerns that the Supreme Court might overturn *Roe v. Wade,* Governor Romer proclaimed in 1992 that "if a woman's privacy is not protected by the Supreme Court, then we need state laws in Colorado to protect them" (Culver, 1992). The city thus was enabled and emboldened to continue to increase the costs of collective action for those challenging the status quo.

Nested in this intergovernmental setting, local institutions provide specific incentives: Fulfill responsibilities to protect public order; avoid votes on issues where competing values are at stake; rely on use of police powers; use nonlegislative arenas making decisions based on law; push conflictual issues to higher decision arenas; persuade local voters that some disruptive protesters deserve repressive responses; seek lower-cost means of denying challengers; and channel unconventional activities into conventional political processes.

Ideas

The role of ideas and stories is critical to understanding abortion conflicts. In abortion conflicts, the role of ideas is more than residual explanations or worldviews of key actors; ideas are constitutive of meaning—of how groups interpret their interests—and the possibilities for action (Hall, 1997:185). In this cognitive perspective, the struggles over "naming/blaming/ claiming" (Felstiner et al., 1980–81) in abortion conflicts can be seen as framing processes. In these struggles, groups are attempting to create issue frames that name the problem, attribute blame, and mobilize followers through metaphors and symbols (Snow and Benford, 1992). As Woliver (1996:6) notes, this frame rhetoric is "an important representation of a group's interests" with consequential implications for policymaking.

Frames "package" the abortion issue; they help citizens interpret ambiguous and confusing elements in the debate by stringing them together in a story line about abortion. This not only permits citizens to interpret their interests and situate themselves in the abortion debate, it also provides activists with a means of getting the attention of policymakers. Contending groups frame "the abortion problem" for local decision makers: Their stories attribute blame to certain aspects of the situation, they resonate with other values and beliefs important to citizens and decision makers, and they privilege some solutions over others (Snow and Benford, 1992). These stories or frames allow decision makers to select certain dimensions of the situation, or context, for attention and to direct problem-solving efforts to particular definitions of "the problem" of abortion conflicts.

Competing ideas about abortion—frames of reproductive rights, public order, free speech, and morality—are central to understanding the intensity of abortion conflicts as well as the nature of local policy responses. In the years leading up to the Supreme Court decisions of the late 1980s, the rhetoric of abortion conflicts in Denver featured differences in cultural and religious values and beliefs about women's reproductive lives and the status of the fetus. In a very broad sense, pro-choice activists sought to rename religious and cultural differences as questions of reproductive rights and rights to personal privacy. They defined the uneven access to abortion as unjust to women and promoted legislation removing barriers to abortion as a matter of reproductive rights. To pro-life activists, permitting or publicly supporting abortion is a question of morality, albeit backed by claims of rationality and scientific evidence on the viability of the fetus (Woliver, 1996). They blame this immoral situation on public policymakers and prescribe and legitimate a range of challenges to these political authorities, including disruptive tactics. The *Casey* and *Webster* decisions devolving abortion access issues to state and local communities set off intense local conflicts over these questions. In the wake of these decisions and subsequent local conflicts, competing frames of free speech and public order emerged. Pro-choice groups continued to emphasize women's reproductive rights in these conflicts, but local officials were understandably chary of siding with any strong position, whatever their personal beliefs. As a result, pro-choice groups and local government officials increasingly focused on the threat to public order and the costs to all local taxpayers caused by disruptive protest. As the leader of Colorado Republicans for Choice put it, "We are not afraid of words, pamphlets or signs—we are afraid for our safety" (Gavin 1993).

The morality frame was amplified by a free speech frame arguing first principles and the precedence of First Amendment rights to free speech. Independent of the substantive nature of the issue, this perspective emphasizes individuals' rights to express themselves through picketing and protesting. These procedural guarantees are core values for other groups such as labor unions, environmentalists, and gays and lesbians. Although pro-choice groups also referred to free speech, they emphasized the city's right to regulate the expression of free speech in the face of conflicting values. In Denver, local officials struggled to find policy responses that were feasible, given their institutional constraints, and responsive to these competing values of public order and free speech.

ABORTION CONFLICTS AND LOCAL GOVERNMENT RESPONSES

Denver has been the scene of some of the most protracted and violent abortion protests in the country, thanks to targeting by national groups such as Operation Rescue and the recent mobilization of local fundamentalist Christian groups. Although many local groups have been involved in struggles over abortion, including weekly picketing of abortion clinics from the late 1980s into the 1990s, the "spikes" in disruptive activity are linked with the periodic entry of Operation Rescue. Abortion conflicts in Denver rose in response to Operation Rescue's targeting of Denver in its clinic blockade campaign and the Pope's visit during World Youth Day. These events triggered repressive responses from local government officials as well as continual efforts to normalize disruptive protest in order to lower the costs of social control and avoid harm to other electoral constituencies.

Overall Patterns of Abortion Protest Activities

Mentions in the *Denver Post* of abortion conflict activities by pro-life and pro-choice groups in Denver from 1989 to 1996 portray a distinctive rise in activity in the early 1990s and then a plateau or leveling off after 1993. This parallels national patterns showing abortion protest activities, particularly those sponsored by Operation Rescue, peaking in 1992–93.[7]

Operation Rescue in Denver

Operation Rescue began a national campaign of clinic blockades in 1988. In spring 1989 its announcement that Denver was a target city for these blockades spurred an April rally sponsored by the local NARAL organization; over twelve hundred attended, including city council members and state legislators who personally pledged dollar donations to NARAL for every antiabortion protester at clinic blockades. On July 8, a violent Operation Rescue blockade at an east Denver Planned Parenthood clinic left both sides shaken. A rush on police lines by three hundred antiabortion protesters and assaults on clients brought a strong police response, including Metro SWAT teams and canine and horse patrols. Amid charges of police brutality, sixty arrests were made, but protesters were released on their own recognizance.

Abortion conflict escalated in 1993 in Colorado with the Pope's visit to Denver for World Youth Day, August 11–15. This triggered intense mobilizations of local and nonlocal pro-choice and pro-life activists. Pro-life activists scheduled a national conference in Denver to coincide with the Pope's visit; Operation Rescue threatened to stop abortions in Denver during the Pope's visit. In response, twelve of the thirteen city council members signed a statement asking antiabortion activists to keep their protests peaceful. Local police canceled all vacations and days off in order to prepare. Planned Parenthood successfully filed a lawsuit in Denver District Court for a temporary restraining order keeping protesters across the street from clinics during the Pope's visit. Pro-choice activists also began "clinic defense" training in preparation for World Youth Day; ultimately, they outnumbered antiabortionist activists at clinics three to one during the Pope's visit. The strong local police and judicial responses to the July 1989 clinic blockades and the local countermobilizations during World Youth Day in 1993 stymied Operation Rescue's Colorado forays.[8] As the dynamic interactions of state authority and pro-choice and pro-life activists unfolded in Denver, the state often seemed to be a fulcrum for attacking other groups rather than a target in itself (Tarrow, 1994:62; see also Meyer and Staggenborg, 1996). The countermobilization prowess of the pro-choice groups, particularly the aggressive leadership and resources of Planned Parenthood, overwhelmed the ability of antiabortion activists to sustain disruptive protests at Denver clinics.

Persistent Repressive Policy Responses to Disruptive Abortion Protests

Mayor Pena and his successor, Wellington Webb, emphasized repressive (Tarrow, 1994; Sharp, 1996) responses to disruptive challenges: They jailed protesters, and levied fines and fees for police services on national groups such as Operation Rescue. Denver adopted this repressive response to antiabortion protesters, particularly Operation Rescue, from the beginning and refused to negotiate on penalties. During a 1990 clinic blockade, the city rejected an offer to end the demonstration and avoid further arrests in exchange for freeing two arrestees and dropping charges. The Assistant City Attorney at the blockade, who had the authority to dismiss the charges, declared "They chose the action. It was not appropriate to ignore it. . . . We could save money and time if we dropped all the tickets we write" (Grelen, 1990). Operation Rescue organizers claimed this showed that city officials "seem to be in sympathy with the abortion providers. It seems the only people treated by the letter of the law are anti-abortion people. The City wants our people prosecuted. They don't want to see our people treated fairly" (Grelen, 1970). On the other hand, city police believed that Operation Rescue had targeted Denver and intended to "tie up the system," being particularly angry with the Police Department "because it has been less cooperative" than other police departments (Pankratz, 1990c). The Police Chief saw the police as in the middle, attempting to defend the rights of the demonstrators while assuring legal rights to abortion; their role meant protecting the rights of both sides in the conflicts (*Denver Post,* 1989). Denver County Judge Jacqueline St. Joan heard many of the abortion arrest cases; antiabortion activists perceived her as "throwing the book at abortion protesters" with heavy fines, maximum jail time, and procedural tactics, while pro-choice activists lauded her courage.

In one of the sentencing hearings, Judge St. Joan declared "I want you to decide as a group how you are going to proceed in this city—whether you are going to act within the law and make your points known as best you can or continue your self-righteousness in a manner that not only breaks the law but also costs the city money" (Pankratz, 1990a). As St. Joan continued to increase the costs of disruptive tactics with heavy fines and maximum sentences (often suspended if no other violations occurred), Operation Rescue leaders admitted this strategy may have succeeded in persuading some Operation Rescue participants to stop their protests (Pankratz, 1990a.). After she received death threats in 1993, armed deputies were placed in Judge St. Joan's courtroom until she stepped down in July 1994.

Over time, the city modified some of its arrest strategies, using a wheelchair to arrest protesters, for example, rather than dragging away limp bodies. But they also escalated the costs of protesting. In 1990, the city refused to waive cash bonds and release demonstrators on their own recognizance; the sheriff's department described this as a change in policy and stated that personal-recognizance bonds would not be granted to those participating in mass arrests. To Operation Rescue, this escalation targeted their group's disruptive tactics; as one leader noted, "I would say this is just another example of organized opposition to Operation Rescue. How many mass arrests do you have in Denver? And it happened within four weeks of the last arraignment" (Fulcher, 1990). Pro-life protesters also claimed that if they did not enter guilty or no-contest pleas, the city threatened to add conspiracy charges (Pankratz, 1990b).

ACCOUNTING FOR PERSISTENT REPRESSIVE POLICY RESPONSES

As Sharp (1996) notes, intensive protests and policy response incur high costs in terms of lost lives, property damage, departmental budgets, and more intangible areas such as city image and business climate. These high costs of direct repression led Cobb and Ross (1997) to anticipate that policymakers would prefer low-cost strategies for rejecting agenda challengers. Instead, they found a U-shaped pattern of responses in their case studies of agenda denial: There are fewer instances of high- and low-cost strategies than anticipated and more reliance on medium-cost strategies such as linking protesters with unpopular groups ("hate crimes"), blaming the group for the problem, and raising the fears of the general public. They interpret this pattern as reflecting the national mood of the 1990s: Violent protest and repressive responses are less frequent than in other periods, and negotiation and compromise on technical, complex issues appear to dominate the national agenda.

Are these same patterns likely in local culture wars? With the exception of Jackman's (1997) account of high-cost strategies to deny agenda access to RU

486, a pharmaceutical method of early abortion, Cobb and Ross's cases do not include more contentious cultural conflict issues. And, with one exception, their cases are all at the national level. Because many of the conflictual issues on the national agenda in earlier years now have devolved to subnational agendas, the national political calm may mask an increasingly volatile local politics. Furthermore, the local political arena allows real distinctions between "insiders" and "outsiders"; this removes one of the constraints on higher-cost strategies if protesting groups can be labeled as "outsiders" with little group legitimacy in the local community even if there are local supporters of their position. In addition, the abortion issue creates a potentially large affected group of women who would be disadvantaged by a change in the status quo of abortion rights. From Cobb and Ross's perspective, this should increase the likelihood of mobilization and intense response from such affected groups, even if local policymakers are seeking more moderate measures. Yet there is every reason to expect local officials to prefer lower-cost strategies. The institutional constraints noted above encourage such choices. Local policymakers want to address immediate public order needs, but they also need to conserve their resources and avoid the risks of excessive reactions—"too much responsiveness," as Sharp puts it. The fewer resources—political, material, symbolic, and otherwise—expended on cultural conflicts, the more available for other issues. Cultural conflict issues are not amenable to the negotiation and compromise processes characteristic of other local policy issues. There are no divisible benefits or "small opportunities" attendant to these conflicts that might provide the "glue" for coalitions nor are other groups willing to cooperate in order to ensure future cooperation on other issues (Stone, 1989:193). The Junior League, for example, declined to take a pro-choice stand in 1990 for fear of the potentially divisive impact on their membership. Their concerns were not only potentially alienating ethnic and religious minorities in the membership but also affecting over one thousand inactive, sustaining members who pay membership dues (George, 1990).

The nature of local cultural conflict issues, therefore, leads us to expect that cities may initially respond with high-cost repressive strategies but will seek lower-cost responses. But the policy response in Denver remained repressive through the mid-1990s: Officials arrested, fined, and jailed pro-life protesters; used "pain compliance" tactics to subdue protesters; refused to release them on their own recognizance; brought suit against organized pro-life groups; threatened maximum penalties for recidivist offenders; put liens on the houses of protesters and garnisheed their wages; charged pro-life groups and activists the costs of extra police services; evicted protesters from jail; and insisted they pay fines instead of serve jail sentences. There is no real evidence of an effort to let up on these high-cost strategies until the mid-1990s, perhaps because Denver was targeted by Operation Rescue for disruptive protest activities throughout this period and essentially operated in a state of siege. How could the city legitimate persistent, high-cost, repressive responses?

Congruence with Public Opinion

Public opinion polls through the 1980s revealed that most Coloradans supported abortion rights; most local candidates and state legislators also claimed to be pro-choice. In rallies and protests, supporters of abortion rights consistently outnumbered pro-life groups. Mayor Pena and Mayor Wellington Webb's repressive strategies were congruent with the sentiments of the majority, particularly with the better organized groups with strong local electoral ties, such as Planned Parenthood and NARAL. Both mayors consistently spoke out for women's reproductive rights, drawing on the support of the city council and the local media. In June 1992, for example, Mayor Webb spoke to a pro-choice gathering at the state capitol "Now is the time to speak out and defend the right to a safe abortion. We are the majority and not the minority."

Social Construction of Target Groups: Operation Rescue

The city legitimated the continued use of repressive responses by social construction processes depicting Operation Rescue as the weak, negative element of pro-life politics, deserving of the negative penalties local officials heaped on it. The thin, weak resources of Operation Rescue and their outsider status allowed the city and pro-choice activists to attack their legitimacy and paint themselves as the victim of violent harassment. The *Denver Post* (1992a) described them as "Denver's unwanted guests from Operation Rescue. These folks come into town to break our laws, then get morally indignant at our police for arresting them. When arrested they refuse to cooperate, then whine 'police brutality' when weary officers haul them off to the hoosegow against their will." The groups mobilized by Operation Rescue for World Youth Day were described as "self-righteous gangs" and denounced as practicing "homegrown terrorism" (*Denver Post,* 1993). As targets of Operation Rescue protests, Planned Parenthood activists were especially vehement: Antiabortionists were charged as being "just as terroristic as the people who bombed the World Trade Center" (Gottlieb 1993), and as practicing "anti-choice terrorism" (Obmascik and Cortez 1995). One Planned Parenthood leader described them as "agitators" (Culver 1993a) using "illegal antics."

As Operation Rescue continued to protest, disobey police orders, harass patients and doctors at abortion clinics, and block entry to clinics, local leaders sought to portray them as a "municipal nuisance," indirectly targeting all Denver citizens, not just the pro-choice activists on the front line (*Denver Post,* 1992b). By emphasizing the proximity of the abortion problem, even to those not directly engaged in the conflicts, in terms of the city's costs of dealing with such actions, policymakers increased its salience for all residents (Snow and Benford, 1992; Rochefort and Cobb, 1994). "The public at large" bears the burden of police overtime bills and crowded court systems, as a *Post* editorial put it (*Denver Post,* 1993). Furthermore, devoting police resources to pro-life activities meant police would not be able to protect "law-abiding" citizens (*Denver Post,* 1993). By labeling the disruptive activists in negative terms, policymakers legitimated crafting of a broader, more coherent city response. As the *Post* editorial emphasized, "the police and municipal judges simply can't solve the problem on their own." (*Denver Post,* 1992b); the editorial urged the council to consider assessing Operation Rescue for the costs of the protest activities.

In contrast, local groups who might support pro-life positions but eschewed these strategies were greeted with tolerance and little police intervention. Local pro-life groups such as the Pro-Family Coalition and Colorado Right to Life Committee refused to join in Operation Rescue's early forays into Colorado; one local activist said demonstrations carry "some pretty high risks. . . . Our purpose is not to take the chance of jail, fines or lawsuits. That would not be accomplishing our goal." Even though some of these groups participated in picketing and clinic "counseling," they disavowed adopting more disruptive tactics.

A Rocky Mountain Planned Parenthood leader distinguished among these anti-abortion strategies: "They have a right to their opinions. . . . Where the difference is, those people are trying to influence other people. They're trying to do it politically, which is a legitimate forum. But they're also trying to do it by intimidation and threat" (Lipsher, 1993a). In the face of daily picketing of clinics in the early 1990s, Planned Parenthood declared they were not against peaceful picketing, "We are very much in favor of their First Amendment rights" (Pankratz, 1990a). This free speech procedural theme was reinforced in media accounts and commentary. According to one *Denver Post* columnist, "That's all anyone asks, that the Operation Rescue troublemakers stop breaking the law. They can make their anti-abortion views known in any peaceful, civil, law-abiding way. It is their right."

Media Frames

The media promoted the public order frame almost exclusively and backed the city's repressive responses. *Denver Post* editorials consistently supported aggressive responses to disruptive tactics; columnists were more strident, claiming "Jail or get-serious fines, that can get the job done. Making Operation Rescue troublemakers—not you and me—pay for the police and courts costs they cause, that can get the job done" (Gavin, 1990). The punitive and deterrent intent of Judge St. Joan's decisions was lauded as simply sentencing "defendants within the limits of the law, presumably with the specific intent of discouraging recurrences of the criminal activity. Isn't that the idea?" (Simpson, 1990). To local pro-life organization leaders, "the media have never helped us at all. They've either ignored or smeared us" (Culver, 1993b).

The media and pro-choice activists distinguished between local pro-life groups and the newly arrived Operation Rescue groups. As the *Post* put it, "some of the peaceful protesters have been replaced by activists with police records and guns." After the violent July 1989 encounter raised charges of police brutality, one police officer noted, "It's kind of a strange situation. They come into a city; they tell you they're going to break the laws" (Fulcher, 1989). To local NARAL leaders, "what used to be committed people protesting as part of their religious belief system has in the last few years become people gone over the edge into fanaticism" (Harrington, 1995). In response, Operation Rescue leaders claimed their protesters were trained in nonviolence but that less-disciplined outsiders sometimes joined in (Robinson, 1989).

Curbing Further Repressive Strategies

Nevertheless, the city did resist more extreme repressive strategies. By the early 1990s, the city council began to split on ordinances restricting picketing of clinics and doctors' homes by abortion foes. Although similar laws have been adopted in other cities such as Sunnyvale, California; Concord, New Hampshire; Washington, D.C.; San Jose, California; and New York City—and Denver adopted a shield law protecting access to clinics in 1990—the council and the local media balked at this more repressive measure. In August 1992, the city council voted against the picketing bill, 8–5.[9] Opponents criticized Operation Rescue but voiced concerns about how such ordinances might affect other electoral constituencies important to council members. Councilwoman Mary DeGroot, author of Denver's "bubble law," expressed her concern that the bill would make it impossible for people to picket lawfully the governor's mansion, slumlords, or crack houses. As she pointed out, "my concern is that this will be used in instances that none of us ever envisioned" (Eddy, 1992b). Although consistently pro-choice editorially, the *Denver Post* backed the defeat of this bill because of possible infringement on free speech and peaceable assembly protections and implementation problems.[10] The defeat of the picketing bill was not in response to pressures from pro-life activists; rather it was closer to a self-corrective response as council members recognized the perceived risks to other electoral constituencies associated with more repressive strategies.

Risks to Electoral Constituencies

As Councilwoman DeGroot argued, the disturbing the peace and trespass charges frequently lodged against abortion protesters could be easily turned on local organized groups voicing their concerns on other issues. She illustrated her concerns by giving the example of a neighborhood in her district where residents put a crack house out of business by picketing it and forcing potential customers to go elsewhere (Eddy, 1992a). Preserving the protest modes available to these groups—such as labor unions, renters, environmentalists—became a significant issue for some council members independent of their views on abortion. Similarly, in addition to the concerns about robbing organized groups of means of voicing their views on nonabortion issues, local officials were also concerned with losing the future support of local groups. This included potential alienation of local Catholic voters possibly sympathetic to the position of pro-life activists if not their strategies.

In the siege mentality prompted by the continuous targeting of Denver for antiabortion protests, the city's role in the 1980s clearly can be characterized as repressive measures taken in response to perceived threats to the city's social order and image. But a growing sensitivity to constitutional issues and broader electoral constituencies led to curbs on stronger repressive policies. This strategy of selective repression emphasizing procedures and political process was legitimated by portraying Operation Rescue as an outsider group practicing terroristic tactics rather than reasonable political discourse. It was facilitated by rhetorical frames allowing local government to ensure free speech—for local, nondisruptive groups and other constituencies occasionally using disruptive tactics—while repressing it for those associated with Operation Rescue's disruptive tactics. The public order frame became increasingly salient as the public costs of disruptive tactics mounted; yet in the face of competing frames and values, expansion of repressive strategies was limited.

This moderating shift cannot be attributed to shifting interest configurations: The disruptive tactics of pro-life protesters did not lead to coalitions or alliances that would have enhanced their political influence and gained concessions from the city. Rather, it reflects the institutional incentives ensuring that city council members consider the effects of nonselective repression on their constituencies and their reelection chances. But the tempering of repressive responses required the construction of rhetorical frames legitimating selective repressive policy responses. Rather than policy choices shifting along the continuum from high- to lower-cost strategies, the Denver case suggests a layering of strategies: stabilizing high-cost repressive strategies while searching for lower-cost strategies that not only suppress disruptive protest but structure the rules of the game in this volatile arena.

NORMALIZING ABORTION CONFLICT

In the absence of cooperation, the city sought routine. Local culture wars over abortion in Denver spurred efforts to normalize local abortion conflicts. Along with targeting repressive strategies to outsiders such as Operation Rescue, the city simultaneously tried to structure conflicts by establishing rules of the game that would increase certainty and lower costs and risks for all stakeholders. As Tarrow notes (1994:96), these efforts to legitimate and institutionalize collective action often prove to be more effective means of social control than direct repression. To local governments, they offer a less costly option, avoiding the perceived risks of more repressive tactics—particularly the effects of ordinances and precedents on other electoral constituencies and alienation of local voters whose support would be needed on other issues. The stabilization of activity in the mid-1990s, therefore, reflects a routinization of abortion politics deliberately pursued by local and state officials. This routinization occurred through portrayal of Operation Rescue as destructive outsiders even as the city made continual offers to consult with peaceful protesters on procedures that would allow them to express their views at a lower cost to the city.

This local stabilization involved strong local law enforcement of three existing ordinances: trespassing, disobedience to a lawful order, and loitering. For example, local officials vigorously enforced trespass laws prior to the 1993 statewide abortion-access "bubble law." Even before the state law was in place, an antiabortion protester complained "we couldn't get within eight feet if we wanted to," and a clinic escort admitted that "there's been a lot of testing of the laws. They know what they can get away with. It really is pretty well established now" (Lipsher, 1993a). In addition to enforcing existing regulations, local police actively sought communication with protest groups prior to demonstrations to establish procedures for the activities. One of Mayor Pena's aides claimed that "Even before the Operation Rescue incident earlier this year (July 1989), the police invited Planned Parenthood and pro-life people to sit down and agree on certain ground rules. The pro-life organizers later broke those rules" (Sinisi, 1989). The Denver Police Chief's letter to Operation Rescue of Colorado asserted that "If the experience in other cities is repeated here, criminal charges will put a heavy burden on the Denver Sheriff's Department and on the court system. This could cost the citizens of Denver a great deal of money and hinder the handling of other criminal cases which must be dealt with. We sincerely hope, therefore, that no illegal activity will occur" (Briggs, 1989).

These hopes were dashed in the violent confrontation at a Planned Parenthood clinic July 8, 1989. Police claimed there had been an agreement to picket the clinic without blocking its entrances, but Operation Rescue's police liaison believed the police violated an agreement to keep the groups separated when police assisted patients attempting to reach the clinic. Despite the resulting atmosphere of mutual distrust, police subsequently asked representatives of Operation Rescue and Planned Parenthood to participate in a closed-meeting review of police performance during the July 8 protest. They asked these groups to "tell us what they thought we did right and what could be improved upon" (Robinson, 1989) and sought better liaison with pro-life activists in order to avoid future clashes. Similarly, during the Pope's 1993 visit, the city set aside official "protest sites" near the location of the official Mass.

Normalization also occurred through group efforts. By late 1993, a group of fourteen to sixteen pro-choice and antiabortion activists began to meet informally to address the conditions leading to abortions. In 1995, they announced the existence of The Common Ground Network for Life and Choice and identified their common ground as the belief that there were too many abortions. As one participant stated, "Abortions occur on life's ragged edges. My vision is that we could harness the energy we use in opposing each other and address the root causes of unwanted pregnancies" (Culver, 1995).

With these normalization and issue-containment strategies, protests became routinized over time. As one reporter described it, "the struggle over abortion rights in Colorado rages on in a symbolic battle of protest and fortification. The players in the weekly display of guerrilla theater remain the same. The arguments remain the same. The tactics remain the same" (Lipsher 1993a). The media were especially sensitive to this loss of novelty (Rochefort and Cobb, 1994): "The street theater has grown so tiresome, the crossfire of video cameras so routine, that the hard-core veterans on both sides have come to recognize each other from previous events, not unlike itinerant fans of the Grateful Dead. . . . For all the high-stakes issues involved, the abortion debate has sunk to the level of tired gamesmanship" (Simpson 1993).

CONCLUSION

From 1989 to 1996, local officials in Denver were embroiled in local culture wars over abortion. They faced mobilization and countermobilization of local groups triggered by national and state decisions on abortion restrictions and targeted disruptive protest organized by Operation Rescue. In response, they pursued three linked policy responses: *repression* justified by socially constructing disruptive challengers such as Operation Rescue as negative, outside groups; *curbing the expansion of repressive strategies* in the face of city council concerns that more repressive tactics would unduly constrain local electoral constituencies; and efforts to *normalize* disruptive abortion conflicts by bringing these value conflicts within the boundaries of accepted political exchange. By 1993, legal mechanisms were in place at the state, county, and local levels regulating the time, manner, and place for the exercise of free speech in the abortion debate; the city was adept at using its police powers, particularly the "bubble law" and permitting procedures to modify the disruptive protests of antiabortion activists; and some degree of normalization of abortion conflicts had been achieved.[11]

This account of abortion conflicts in Denver suggests that local culture wars embroil local officials in efforts to alter the costs of collective action in their community. Their strategic choices among the repertoire of possible repression and normalization tactics are influenced by the acts of the protesters themselves as well as by other political actors at different levels, the framing of the issues, and the institutional incentives that privilege some solutions over others. In Denver, the city's framing of abortion conflicts in ways that accommodated public order and free speech issues provided procedural grounds for local officials to continue to support pro-choice positions and suppress disruptive activities but safeguard other constituencies. This underscores the constitutive role of ideas: Frame construction was critical to shaping city council members' understanding of their interests in abortion conflicts and guiding their sense of possible policy choices; the frames also responded directly to the institutional incentives, sanctions, and resources available to key stakeholders in the conflict.

NOTES

1. Piven and Cloward (1992) are critical of approaches that blur "the distinction between normative and nonnormative forms of collective action" (p. 301) as well as those normalizing the "political impact of collective protest" (p. 302). They recognize the broad patterning of collective action by institutions but argue that the differences in both protest and response are understated by this perspective.

2. NUD*IST (Non-numerical Unstructured Data-Indexing, Searching, & Theorizing) is a software program (Sage) designed for indexing, searching, and theorizing with qualitative data. It preserves the context of the data, the text, while allowing classification and analysis.

3. Former (1975–86) Governor Dick Lamm sponsored the 1967 bill as a freshmen representative; he enlisted nearly half the legislators as co-sponsors, but the bill still faced significant opposition, particularly from Catholics in legislative leadership positions. The bill permitted abortions with the approval of a three-physician hospital panel, when a child was likely to be born with a serious disability; when the pregnancy was the result of rape, incest, or statutory rape; or when the woman was in danger of physical or mental harm from bearing a child (Anderson, 1992).

4. State Representative Diana DeGette (D-Denver) introduced HB1209 establishing a buffer zone around clinics and forbidding leafleting unless patients request information. DeGette "hoped the measure would decrease tensions on both sides of the abortion debate and that few people would actually be prosecuted under the law" (Lipsher 1993b).

5. Indeed, some attribute this decline in abortion rates to the loss of providers due to clinic violence; Colorado has lost fourteen providers since 1982 (Lamm, 1995).

6. Colorado voters supported an initiative in 1985 barring use of Medicaid funds for most abortions; a petition to repeal this failed at the polls in 1988. Petitions for initiatives supporting Parental Notification failed to get on the ballot in 1990; a similar ballot initiative failed in 1994, as did a Parental Responsibility initiative in 1996.

7. Nationally, violent incidents against abortion providers peaked in 1984–86, declined in 1987–91, then escalated to a high of 434 violent incidents reported in 1993. Incidents of nonviolent disruption—picketing, harassing phone calls, and hate mail—doubled from 1995 to 1996, although there was a 21 percent decline in violent incidents in that same period. This is attributed in part to the deterrent effects of the 1994 FACE act; the conservative state legislative agendas offering an alternative venue in many states; greater expenditures on security; programs and staff training by abortion providers; and the increased utilization of legal tools such as injunctions, buffer zones, and restraining orders (National Abortion Federation, 1997).

8. Similar patterns emerged at the national level. Although the national right-to-life movement had moved beyond its challenger status to become accepted, regular participants in political decision processes, the breakaway Operation Rescue group remained an outsider challenger pursuing disruptive tactics (Lo, 1992:232). Violent incidents continued, including the murders of abortion doctors in 1994, but Operation Rescue appeared

less able to recruit and mobilize new members for protest activities; by the late 1990s, some of its leaders were redirecting their grassroots organizations to electoral politics (Shin, 1997).

9. In the initial vote one month earlier, the picketing bill was supported, 10–2, with Councilwoman Mary DeGroot and Councilwoman (and President) Ramona Martinez in opposition.

10. In July 1993, the 10th U.S. Circuit Court of Appeals reinstated a 1989 federal civil rights suit brought against the city and some police officers for arrests for picketing a Planned Parenthood clinic with signs saying "The Killing Place." The Appeals court held these were not "fighting words" and that the protesters had a constitutional right to be picketing on the sidewalk. On September 30, the city agreed in a consent order to refrain from arresting protestors carrying such signs outside clinics and settled the 1989 lawsuit by paying the plaintiffs $5,000 each.

11. Nevertheless, Colorado ranked as one of the twelve states with the highest levels of antiabortion violence in 1995: These incidents included vandalism, bomb threats, home picketing, stalking, FACE violations, and death threats (Feminist Majority Foundation, 1997). These reports are from a sample of eight Colorado clinics in the Foundation's 1996 Clinic Violence Survey.

REFERENCES

Anderson, Eric. 1992. "Colorado's Pioneering Abortion Law 25 Years Old." *Denver Post*, 26 April, p. 1A.
Briggs, Bill. 1989. "Denver Police Braced to Guard Clinic During Abortion Protests Next Week." *Denver Post*, 22 April, p. 1B.
Cobb, Roger W., and Marc H. Ross. 1997. *Cultural Strategies of Agenda Denial*. Lawrence: University Press of Kansas.
Culver, Virginia. 1992. "Romer Defends Women's Right to Choose At Pro-Choice Rally." *Denver Post*, 24 January, p. 1B.
———. 1993a. "Abortion Battle Lines Drawn; Pro-Choice Groups Train to Meet Protests During Pope's Visit." *Denver Post*, 21 July, p. 4B.
———. 1993b. "Abortion Foes Plan WYD Strategy; Thousands to Protest During Pope's Visit." *Denver Post*, 27 July, p. 1B.
———. 1995. "Abortion Foes Find Common Ground." *Denver Post*, 13 January, p. 1B.
Denver Post. 1989. Editorial: "Abortion Foes Broke the Law." July, p. 7B.
———. 1992a. Editorial: "Operation Chutzpah." 16 March, p. 6B.
———. 1992b. Editorial: "Picketing Ban Rightly Killed." 12 August, p. 6B.
———. 1993. Editorial: "Pope Should Disown Radical Anti-Abortionists." 12 August, p. 10B.
Eddy, Mark. 1992a. "Picketing Outside Homes Targeted Operation Rescue Protests in Neighborhood Spur Council." *Denver Post*, 22 May, p. 2B.
———. 1992b. "Operation Rescue Target of New Law." *Denver Post*, 2 June, p. 1B.
Felstiner, W. L. R., R. I. Abel, and A. Sarat. 1980–81. "The Emergence and Transformation of Disputes: Naming, Blaming, Claiming." *Law & Society Review* 15:631–53.
Feminist Majority Foundation. 1997. *1996 Clinic Violence Survey Report*. www.feminist. org/research/cvsurveys/1996/cvsurvey14.html

Fulcher, Michelle P. 1989. "Arrested 'Rescuers' May File Suit." *Denver Post,* 10 July, p. 1B.

———. 1990. "24 Deny Guilt in Abortion Protest." *Denver Post,* 12 March, p. 1B.

Gavin, Jennifer. 1992. "Colorado Legal-Abortion Legacy Should Stand, Analysts Say." *Denver Post,* 2 February, p. 9A.

———. 1993. "Abortion Clinics' Zone OK." *Denver Post,* 4 March, p. 4B.

Gavin, Tom. 1990. "One Point of Light." *Denver Post,* 11 March, p. 3H.

George, Mary. 1990. "Junior League Considers Reproductive Rights Stand." *Denver Post,* 30 January, p. 1A.

Gottlieb, Alan. 1993. "Agency Chief: Pope's Stands Aid Rescue Group's Agenda." *Denver Post,* 5 August, p. 1B.

Grelen, Jay. 1990. "24 Arrested at Anti-Abortion Blockade." *Denver Post,* 11 March, p. 1C.

Hall, Peter A. 1997. "The Role of Interests, Institutions, and Ideas in the Comparative Political Economy of the Industrialized Nations." In Mark I. Lichbach and Alan S. Zuckerman, eds., *Comparative Politics: Rationality, Culture, and Structure.* Cambridge: Cambridge University Press, pp. 174–207.

Harrington, Maureen. 1995. "Protest Shifts Gears; Abortion Debate Becomes Battle." *Denver Post,* 24 January, p. 1B.

Henshaw, Stanley K., and Jennifer Van Vort. 1994. "Abortion Services in the United States, 1991 and 1992." *Family Planning Perspectives* 26:100–112.

Jackman, Jennifer L. 1997. "Blue Smoke, Mirrors, and Mediators: The Symbolic Context over RU 486." In Roger W. Cobb and Marc H. Ross, eds., *Cultural Strategies of Agenda Denial.* Lawrence: University Press of Kansas, pp. 112–38.

Lamm, Dottie. 1995. "Abortion Can Avert Violence." *Denver Post,* 5 February, p. 4D.

Lipsher, Steve. 1993a. "Anti-Abortion Groups Decry 'Bubble Law'; Tactics Likely to Stay the Same." *Denver Post,* 30 March, p. 1B.

———. 1993b. "Romer Signs Abortion Clinics 'Bubble Bill.'" *Denver Post,* 20 April, p. 4B.

Lo, Clarence Y. H. 1992. "Communities of Challengers in Social Movement Theory." In Aldon D. Morris and Carol McClurg Mueller, eds., *Frontiers in Social Movement Theory.* New Haven, Conn.: Yale University Press, pp. 224–47.

Meyer, David, and Suzanne Staggenborg. 1996. "Movements, Countermovements, and the Structure of Political Opportunity." *American Journal of Sociology* 101:1628–60.

National Abortion Federation. 1997. "Abortion Providers Release 1996 Report on Anti-Choice Violence." January 16: www.cais.com/naf/violence/stats.htm

Obmascik, Mark, and Angela Cortez. 1995. "Vandals Do $25,000 in Damage During Attacks on Two Clinics." *Denver Post,* 19 March, p. 5C.

Pankratz, Howard. 1990a. "6 Abortion Protesters Get Maximum." *Denver Post,* 20 March, p. 1B.

———. 1990b. "2 Abortion Protesters Jailed 1 Day for Failure to Pay Fine." *Denver Post,* 22 March, p. 1A.

———. 1990c. "17 Abortion Protesters Choose Jail over Fines." *Denver Post,* 30 March, p. 1A.

Piven, Frances Fox, and Richard Cloward. 1992. "Normalizing Collective Protest." In Aldon D. Morris and Carol McClurg Mueller, eds., *Frontiers in Social Movement Theory.* New Haven, Conn.: Yale University Press, pp. 301–25.

Robinson, Marilyn. 1989. "Handling of Anti-Abortion Protest Gets High Marks." *Denver Post,* 12 July, p. 1B.

Rochefort, D., and Roger W. Cobb. 1994. "Problem Definition: An Emerging Perspective." In D. Rochefort and Roger W. Cobb, eds., *The Politics of Problem Definition.* Lawrence: University Press of Kansas, pp. 1–31.

Sharp, Elaine B. 1996. "Culture Wars and City Politics." *Urban Affairs Review* 31: 738–58.

———. 1997. "A Comparative Anatomy of Urban Social Conflict." *Political Research Quarterly* 50 (June): 261–80.

Shin, Annys. 1997. "New Marching Orders." *National Journal,* 23 August, p. 1696.

Simpson, Kevin. 1989. "Face-Off Turns Violent in Denver." *Denver Post,* 9 July, p. 1A.

———. 1990. "Rescue Folks Turn Up Heat on St. Joan." *Denver Post,* 15 March, p. 1B.

———. 1993. "Pope's Visit Revives Same, Tiresome Abortion Street Theater." *Denver Post,* 12 August, p. 1B.

Sinisi, J. Sebastian. 1989. "Abortion Foes Picket Police Station." *Denver Post,* 18 September, p. B5.

Snow, David A., and Robert D. Benford. 1992. " Master Frames and Cycles of Protest." In Aldon D. Morris and Carol McClurg Mueller, eds., *Frontiers in Social Movement Theory.* New Haven, Conn.: Yale University Press, pp. 133–55.

State of Colorado. 1997. *Colorado Vital Statistics, 1995.* Denver, Colo.: Department of Public Health and Statistics, Health Statistics and Vital Records Division, Health Statistics Section, April.

Stone, Clarence. 1989. *Regime Politics.* Lawrence: University Press of Kansas.

Tarrow, Sidney. 1994. *Power in Movement.* Cambridge: Cambridge University Press.

Woliver, Laura R. 1996. "Rhetoric and Symbols in American Abortion Politics." In Marianne Githens and Dorothy McBride Stetson, eds., *Abortion Politics: Public Policy in Cross-Cultural Perspective.* New York: Routledge, pp. 5–28.

4
Regime Change
and Gay and Lesbian Politics
in Four New York Cities

Donald B. Rosenthal

This chapter examines the changing behaviors of four local political regimes in upstate New York (Albany, Buffalo, Rochester, and Syracuse) toward lesbians and gay men over the past two decades. It acknowledges that major socioeconomic and cultural changes in American society have permitted the civil rights of gays and lesbians to become a legitimate subject for discussion and for favorable actions by some local regimes and that these changes have been associated with the increasing political mobilization of local lesbian and gay populations. It emphasizes, however, that local political elites have served as mediators of incorporation or defenders of exclusion, depending on two contending considerations: their personal values and experiences and their calculations of the relative political benefits or costs of accommodating the claims of lesbians and gay men. Thus, the cultural and political changes visible in varying degrees in all four cities by 1997 did not come about because of the political mobilization of lesbians and gay men alone, or because of societal changes that had an impact at the local level. Rather, they required the mediation of local political regimes.[1]

SOCIAL AND POLITICAL CONTEXTS

Changes in the American economy and social structure—such as rising levels of education and urbanization; the greater employment of women outside the home; and the opening of local value systems to more cosmopolitan cultural sources via radio, television, and movies—have contributed to altering attitudes toward homosexuals since the 1950s (Adam 1987; Cruickshank 1992). The responses of other culture-defining institutions like churches to these alterations in society have been uneven, with more liberal denominations seeking to accommodate them and more conservative churches upholding messages of resistance to change.[2]

Meanwhile, in the wake of the civil rights movement among African Americans and the revitalized women's movement of the 1960s, a noncentralized lesbian and gay rights movement emerged (Marotta 1981; D'Emilio 1983; Adam 1987; Cruickshank 1992). Early manifestations of this activism appeared first in places like San Francisco and New York shortly after World War II (Shilts 1982; D'Emilio 1983), but it was not until after the 1969 Stonewall riots in New York City that a more visible national political movement began to surface focused on assuring civil rights protections to gay men and lesbians. This movement has succeeded in passing local ordinances extending protections in employment, housing, and public accommodations in more than 160 communities (Button et al., 1997) and, more recently, has generated responses to other policy demands, including health and related benefits for same-gender partners of public employees. In addition, eleven states have now passed civil rights laws protecting gays and lesbians.

For the most part, gay and lesbian activists in this chapter's four case-study communities have pursued what Cohen (1997) has characterized as an "ethnic model of inclusion"—one that focuses on a politics of "recognition" and civil rights protections rather than developing a substantive issues agenda that addresses larger social and economic inequities. Some material rewards do flow to a relatively small group of middle-class, mainly white, lesbians and gay men who are active in local politics, but few substantive benefits have gone to those who are not politically well placed. Nonetheless, for many gays and lesbians, the symbolic and psychological rewards, including those that come even from the co-optation of group leaders, are sufficient to enhance satisfaction with local regimes.

Lesbians and gay men became engaged in national Democratic Party politics relatively early in the development of the post-Stonewall movement and have continued to focus part of their political energies on strengthening those connections. In New York state, particularly under the leadership of Governor Mario Cuomo (1983–95), the relationship became especially close. Although Cuomo had demonstrated little concern for gays and lesbians during his rise to power, shortly after his inauguration in 1983, he issued an executive order protecting state employees against discrimination based on sexual orientation.[3] Indeed, by the time of his unsuccessful campaign for re-election in 1994, he had emerged as something of a champion of lesbian and gay rights in state politics. Equally important, during his twelve years in office, he so intertwined the state party organization and his own campaigns for re-election with gay-friendly policies that local party officials tended to treat the two as inseparable. Those connections had consequences for the way local conflicts over gay and lesbian rights ordinances were fought out in Albany and Syracuse in the early 1990s.

POLITICAL REGIMES IN THE FOUR CITIES

This section looks at the changes the four local regimes have made in response to the political claims of lesbians and gay men since the 1970s. By 1997, not only did three of the cities (all but Syracuse) have a lesbian or gay member of their city councils, but all those councils had also passed pro-gay legislation at some point, and gays and lesbians were a political group of growing importance, at least within local Democratic Party circles.

This analysis builds on the work of David Easton (1965:192) who defined "regime" as a set of constraints "that are generally accepted . . . by rulers and ruled alike and that give at least broad indications of what are or are not permissible goals, practices, and structures in the system." Clarence Stone (1989:6) broadens that perspective by including in his conceptualization of regime, "the informal arrangements by which public bodies and private interests function together in order to be able to make and carry out governing decisions."[4]

In order to trace the way regimes have treated lesbians and gay men over the past two decades, I have proposed (Rosenthal 1996a) a model of political incorporation that has moved regimes through four stages: repression, exclusion, symbolic incorporation, and substantive incorporation. In some of its features, particularly in its first two phases, this model parallels the governmental roles treated by Sharp (1996, 1997).[5] Unlike the present work, however, Sharp's concerns are less with the content and character of particular cultural movements and the differences among local regimes than with the choices made by local government officials in responding to the challenges and opportunities represented by the issues associated with "culture wars."

For my purposes, *repression* means using the instrumentalities of a local regime (especially the police but also, where cooperative, the media and churches) to deny legitimacy to the social aspirations of gays and lesbians, thereby forcing members of that population to operate—if they operate at all—in an underground of sporadically monitored bars and (for gay men) "cruising areas," where police raids and acts of entrapment form part of the gay community's experience with the regime. Reductions in repression in New York State's localities had much to do with judicial rulings that accompanied mobilization of gay and lesbian populations and preceded measures taken voluntarily by most local regimes.[6]

Sharp follows Tarrow (1994:95) in treating repression as a choice made by regimes in order to "either depress collective action or raise the cost of its main preconditions—the organization and mobilization of opinion" (Sharp, 1996:748) after local cultural values have been challenged. My argument, as it applies specifically to the gay and lesbian experience, is that repression is essentially a reflection of long-standing cultural traditions embedded in local regimes and that, once overcome, it is very difficult to reimpose similar forms of control without sustaining substantial costs. Those costs are likely to be particularly high when the climate of opinion in national and state politics and society have shifted against local repression. That does not mean that regimes cannot continue to take actions unfavorable to the interests of lesbians and gay men. It does mean that the actions regimes take are increasingly open to challenges from gays and lesbians and their allies, challenges that are treated with an increasing measure of legitimacy.

Nor does a reduction in levels of repression automatically lead a regime to embrace gays and lesbians. It may lead, instead, to what Sharp (1996:747) describes as "evasion," or what I refer to as "exclusion." Sharp sees *evasion* as a method local regimes employ to avoid dealing with issues, though she complicates her definition by conflating evasion with "symbolic politics and other low-key efforts to maintain the status quo," a usage that appears to overlap with her notion of "responsiveness."

From my perspective, *exclusion* refers to a phase of regime relationships with lesbians and gay men in which the regime no longer actively denies a legitimate voice in public affairs to gay men and lesbians but also makes no effort to protect those discriminated against from the behaviors of the regime's agents (sometimes acting on their own) or of private parties.

By *symbolic incorporation,* I mean the willingness of a regime (including local party and government officials, as well as other legitimacy-granting social and cultural institutions) to extend the emblems of legitimacy to gays and lesbians. In its most common form, this may involve issuing proclamations celebrating gay pride events, participating in those events, and favorable media coverage of these or other activities.

At some point, a group may achieve *substantive incorporation* when leaders of the regime recognize members of the group not only as legitimate recipients of the symbolic rewards of political participation but as full-fledged participants whose individual and collective ambitions deserve ongoing consideration. That attention may take a variety of forms ranging from nominations to office to policy decisions that respond to the concerns of members of the group.[7]

In the following sections, we examine how the four regimes responded to the challenges represented by the presence of lesbians and gay men.

Rochester: Incorporation into a Pluralist Regime

Rochester's political regime has long promoted culturally pluralist political values. In the nineteenth century, the city's middle-class population, urged on by Frederick Douglass, was prominently associated with the abolitionist movement. Rochester was also the home of Susan B. Anthony and a center of the early women's movement.[8] The city's political culture also made it a natural haven for "liberal Republicanism," particularly during the years that Nelson Rockefeller was governor of the state (1959–74). Indeed, during some of that period (1964–70), Republicans held a majority in the city council.

More than the other three cities, Rochester's dominant political culture is linked to a set of homegrown industries (Eastman Kodak; Xerox; Bausch and Lomb) with advanced technologies that attracted a significant number of professionals and technocrats to the metropolitan area.[9] They helped support institutions (University of Rochester; Rochester Institute of Technology; Eastman School of Music) which allowed their exployees considerable freedom in pursuing their own intellectual and personal interests.

In this open environment, Rochester was one of the first generation of non-coastal middle-sized cities to serve as an outpost of national gay and lesbian activism in the nation. With relatively little opposition from the regime, the movement took root in October 1970 when about a hundred people met on the campus of the University of Rochester to form what became in 1973 the Gay Alliance of the Genesee Valley (GAGV), an interorganizational network drawing together a variety of affinity groups.

About the same time, political activists organized the Rochester Gay Task Force (later the Lesbian and Gay Political Caucus), which became involved in local elections by supporting Democratic candidates for municipal office. With gay and lesbian support, the election of 1973 saw Democrats win control of the city council and begin to build an overwhelming majority that has essentially turned Rochester into a one-party Democratic city, but one in which the party organization itself has become rather weak. As a result, it was relatively easy for lesbians and gay men to win seats on Democratic Party committees and to become a recognized part of the party infrastructure in the city.

In the late 1970s, the gay and lesbian community's increasing influence was recognized by the creation of a formal liaison from the Rochester police department, a position that is still in place. About the same time, the community received its first substantive public benefit from the regime in the form of a CETA grant, channeled through the local United Way, for assistance with organizational development. GAGV's grant proposal had been vehemently attacked by the sole remaining Republican on the city council, who was supported in his opposition by religious fundamentalists outside the government. Nonetheless, the majority of the council voted to support the two-year award, which was used by GAGV to hire staff and put the organization on a stronger administrative footing.

There was occasional discord during the incorporation process. In 1982, for example, the Rochester Chamber of Commerce (which received some funding from the city), refused to honor a request from GAGV to use a Chamber-owned hall for a dinner and awards ceremony. Despite protests supported by some members of the city council and others in the city, the Chamber refused to change its position. This represented a symbolic defeat for GAGV, but it also mobilized the gay and lesbian community. Members of the city council were reluctant to use their governmental leverage against the Chamber, but they did pass a largely symbolic municipal ordinance extending employment protections to gay and lesbian municipal employees.[10] When lesbians and gay men also sought to have a broader antidiscrimination ordinance passed by the county government, however, that proposal never received a serious hearing.

In 1985, one of the leaders of the Lesbian and Gay Political Caucus, Tim Mains, ran for the city council. Even though he did not receive the endorsement of the party organization in the Democratic primary, he won a narrow victory for an at-large seat and went on to win easily in the general election, thereby becoming the first openly gay elected official in New York state. (He was elected to his fourth term in 1997.)

Indicative of the continuing responsiveness of the regime to gay and lesbian issues, the Rochester city council passed an ordinance in April 1994 that extended health benefits to domestic partners of city employees (by a vote of 7 to 2) and established a register of domestic partners for all city residents (by a vote of 5 to 4).

In an otherwise friendly political environment, lesbians and gay men continue to engage in occasional conflicts with the regime. Thus, GAGV struggled for three years with the city administration to gain a property tax exemption for the community center it opened in 1990. When the organization applied for an exemption in January 1991, the city's assessor denied the request on the grounds that the center was not a true "educational" institution within the terms of the law granting such exemptions because the material it distributed did not qualify as "objective" or "neutral."[11] The issue was then taken to the state courts. At the district level, the presiding judge ruled in April 1993 that the city had discriminated against the center "on the basis of the character of its membership and the content of its speech, clear denials of constitutional rights" (Jordan, 1993:1). The lame-duck mayor supported his assessor by backing an appeal to the appellate court, which also ruled in favor of the exemption in February 1994. The incoming mayor had indicated his support for the exemption during the campaign and chose not to pursue the suit to the highest appellate level.

Albany: Machine Politics and Cultural Accommodations

For much of the twentieth century, Albany was governed by one of the most famous political machines in American history (Robinson 1977; Swanstrom and Ward 1987; Erie 1988). That machine drew its principal support from conservative working-class and lower-middle-class Irish Catholics. It made only grudging efforts to cultivate new bases of support, though as the African American population grew, it filled a few positions with reliable African Americans. Few women held elected or appointed offices.

A more cosmopolitan subculture began to emerge in the 1970s as middle-class migrants came to Albany lured by a rapid growth in state employment and by the expansion of the State University of New York at Albany. These dissident forces began to come together politically in the mid-1970s at the neighborhood level, where block clubs were developed in a couple of gentrifying neighborhoods. Later, this progressive coalition reached out to African Americans who resented the exclusionary treatment they were receiving. A small number of politically active gays and lesbians also joined these early efforts.

The machine largely ignored this coalition well into the 1980s. In the case of lesbians and gay men, there were occasional repressive acts such as a police raid that shut down the city's only gay bathhouse in the late 1970s. For most of the time, as one prominent gay leader remarked, "The machine wasn't particularly hostile but they didn't have any interest in improving the condition of relations with the lesbian and gay community" (Jim Perry, interview by author, 26 May 1989).

In the face of exclusion and sporadic repression, a few lesbian and gay activists came together in 1983 to form an independent political organization, the Eleanor Roosevelt Democratic Club (ERDC). Much of its support came from a gentrifying neighborhood where many lesbians and gay men lived. ERDC worked with other neighborhood groups to support independent candidacies in the 1985 municipal elections and managed to elect two members to the fifteen-member city council: a neighborhood activist and an African American from a poor ward of the city.

The death in office in 1983 of long-time mayor Erastus Corning had initiated a period of jockeying for ascendancy in the machine. At first, machine candidates continued to maintain unchallenged control of the mayor's office and seats on the city council. Thus, in March 1988, when newly elected councilwoman Nancy Burton proposed an amendment to a pending civil rights ordinance that would have added protections based on sexual orientation, her amendment was voted down by a 12 to 2 margin.[12] This occurred despite the amendment's support from more than sixty religious and community organizations and the endorsements of Governor Cuomo and the state's attorney general. Indeed, the mayor was reputed to have said, rather dismissively, "Albany isn't ready for a gay rights ordinance" (*Community* 1988a:1).

In the municipal elections of 1989, the ERDC endorsed four candidates who indicated support for gay and lesbian rights. Three went on to win, among them Keith St. John, who became the first gay African American elected to office in the United States. The progressive caucus brought the gay rights amendment to a vote in January 1991 and was again defeated, but this time by a vote of 10 to 5.

The mayor, who was a contestant for party leadership, chose to respond to the direction events were taking by reaching out to the lesbian and gay community in his January 1992 "state of the city" address when he expressed his support for a slightly revised ordinance by declaring, "I believe Albany is ready for this ordinance" (Conti, 1992:1). Negotiations ensued over whether religious institutions should be exempted from the ordinance's provisions. When St. John agreed to that provision, a public hearing was held. Although the proposal attracted heated opposition from religious conservatives, the ordinance passed in December 1992 by a vote of 8 to 6.[13]

The final nail was driven in the coffin of the old machine in 1993 when the incumbent mayor was denied support for re-election by the party. The resulting contest for mayor pitted two long-time party people against each other: one, Gerald Jennings, was a dissident machine Democrat who had run successfully as an independent in 1989 for a seat on the city council with strong ERDC involvement. In 1993, both mayoral candidates sought lesbian and gay backing, but the ERDC gave it to Jennings. He was elected easily, along with nine city council candidates endorsed by ERDC. The group also backed the winning candidates for city comptroller (Nancy Burton) and city council president. In the only seat where a candidate endorsed by ERDC lost, all three candidates had indicated their support for the gay rights ordinance.

By the municipal elections of 1997, ERDC had become part of the governing regime, though they did not press for substantive benefits. Instead, they were active in the spring of 1996 in promoting the city council's 11 to 2 passage (with one abstention) of a measure that established a domestic partnership register for city residents. This symbolic legislation did little more than confirm the electoral clout that lesbian and gay activists already had.[14]

By this point, ERDC had so identified itself with Jennings' political organization that it had begun to lose some of its standing with its long-time coalition partners, as well as some lesbian and gay activists. Nonetheless, Jennings won re-election easily in 1997, and a gay leader of ERDC was elected to the city council.[15]

Buffalo's Caretaker Regime and the Politics of Stagnation

For the last twenty years, city politics in Buffalo has been marked by conflicts among three fragments within the local Democratic Party: political activists who were centrist-to-liberal in their economic and social outlooks; conservative neighborhood-based politicians rooted in ethnic communities and loosely tied together by a shared conservative outlook on social issues; and a group of African American activists led by Arthur Eve, an influential member of the state assembly.

The centrists controlled the machinery of the Democratic Party in Buffalo and Erie County and usually held a majority in the Buffalo city council. From 1977 to 1993, however, the mayor was Jimmy Griffin, a former state senate member, whose base lay among the conservative ethnics. His appeal was that of a populist fighting the party organization on behalf of the "little" (white) man. Griffin expounded a low-tax and low-expenditure policy popular with his working-class base and social values consistent with a local political culture where racism was barely disguised and contempt for gay men and lesbians was outspoken.

Eve and the African American faction felt they were not being accorded sufficient influence within the party. Consequently, they selectively withheld electoral support from candidates backed by the Democratic Party, or they supported candidates of their own. As a result, Griffin regularly won re-election with only a plurality of votes.

This political infighting took place against the background of enormous losses in the industrial base of the metropolitan area beginning in the 1970s and the out-migration of many younger people. Given these desperate economic conditions, municipal government took on a "caretaker" character in which political conflicts often centered on the material rewards that could be won by each faction from their connections to the state or federal government.[16] In this environment, challenges to existing social policy were rare, but when they did break out, as they did over abortion, they could be quite bitter.

The public face of the party organization throughout much of the 1980s was one of indifference to issues affecting gays and lesbians. A few party and government officials were personally in contact with lesbian and gay activists and drew on their financial contributions to run campaigns, but there was little public acknowledgment of this association.

Even before Stonewall, Buffalo had been home to a chapter of the Mattachine Society, an organization created as a forum for community-building activities outside the bars and bathhouses. By the late 1970s, however, that organization was in a weakened condition, and there was no immediate successor. Even so, members of the community were mobilized on an ad hoc basis on several occasions during the Griffin years to protest one of the mayor's verbal attacks or to challenge the behaviors of his police department, which launched occasional crackdowns on gay men and conducted heavy-handed surveillance of gay bars.

During much of the 1980s, the president of the city council was George Arthur, an African American associated with the county party. As the result of occasional conversations with a few closeted members of the gay and lesbian community, Arthur shepherded a resolution through the council in 1983 that provided anti-discrimination protections for gay and lesbian city employees. Passage of the ordinance was managed by Arthur without consulting the party leadership. Rather, he dealt directly with individual members of the council, promising them that he would "take the heat" if controversy resulted.[17] Neither the lesbian and gay community, given its weakened condition organizationally, nor cultural conservatives and religious fundamentalists mobilized on the issue, and there was little media coverage. In any case, Mayor Griffin vetoed the measure, but the ordinance was passed 9–2 (with two abstentions) over his veto. The measure proved ineffective, however, because Griffin refused to implement it.

Arthur's behavior constitutes entrepreneurial instigation, but not in the sense used by Sharp (1996:750) of attempting to "mobilize the public on symbolic or morals issues," because there was no real effort to mobilize the public. Arthur's behavior was entrepreneurial in a different way because it may have been designed in part to mobilize support by lesbians and gay men for Arthur's candidacy for mayor against Griffin in 1985. Yet in reality, the gay and lesbian vote counted for little in the political equation of the time because it was difficult to target. Arthur defeated Griffin in the Democratic primary, but went on to lose to him in the general election, where Griffin had the endorsement of the Republican Party and of a small state Conservative Party. The Eve forces pointedly abstained.

However, passage of the ordinance may have heralded a minor adjustment in the treatment of gays and lesbians. In 1989, William Hoyt was the Democratic Party's nominee for mayor. Even more than Arthur, Hoyt was personally close to members of the lesbian and gay community and outspoken on issues of concern to them.[18] He received both money and campaign support from them, but, again, opposition to Griffin was divided between white moderates and an independent candidate supported by the Eve group. Griffin was easily reelected.

The mayor's homophobia was only marginally chastened by his minority political status. In the midst of a press conference called to deal with a major scandal in the city's parks department early in 1990, he was questioned about police harassment of men in the parks and proceeded to inveigh against gay men's public behaviors. It was the same parks department scandal, however, that contributed to Griffin's decision early in 1993 not to run again for mayor.

Griffin was succeeded by Anthony Masiello, a state senator, who was supported by the leadership of the Democratic Party and ultimately by the Eve faction. Masiello could have won without courting lesbian and gay support, but he went out of his way during the campaign to seek that support as part of an effort to reach out to various minority communities previously excluded from political influence by Griffin.

Once in office, Masiello was reluctant to undertake policy initiatives that reflected the concerns of gay men and lesbians. He did, however, take a few tentative steps toward softening regime relations with the community, notably selecting a new police commissioner from outside of Buffalo and higher-level police staff prepared to consult members of the community as issues arose. Most of the actions Masiello took were of a symbolic nature. He issued gay pride proclamations and had supportive statements read at gay pride functions. For the first time, too, pride events were held on the steps of city hall. It was not until his successful campaign for re-election in 1997, however, that he spoke to a pride rally (after having authorized the hanging of gay pride banners on lampposts along the parade route). At the same time, his electoral promises to the community were couched in only the vaguest of terms.

In part, the mayor's lack of concern with the gay and lesbian community reflected that community's own ineffective political mobilization. That began to change with the 1994 state elections. Lesbian and gay participation was encouraged statewide by the Cuomo re-election campaign, which worked closely with the community as a recognized component of the campaign effort, and by the campaign of a lesbian candidate for state attorney general, Karen Burstein. Although both Cuomo and Burstein were defeated in the general election, the visibility of lesbians and gay men in both campaigns was noticed by the county party leadership. In recognition of the role they had played in the campaign, in early 1995, the party chair appointed the first openly gay person to the party's executive committee.

About the time of that appointment, however, the party split over the renomination of the incumbent county executive. The fight within the party forced other politicians to choose sides and also provided openings for newcomers. As a result, a group of younger African Americans not affiliated with the Eve faction and the first Latino candidate ran for city council seats. In this context, an openly identified lesbian, Barbra Kavanaugh, ran as an unendorsed candidate for an at-large city council seat.

Kavanaugh had connections to the city's minority communities and was also well-known among neighborhood organizers. Although she did not have an es-pecially visible record in lesbian and gay activism, she developed a strong cam-paign organization that drew on lesbians, gay men and neighborhood activists, forged relationships with some of the minority candidates running for ward seats, and received the support of politicians associated with both sides of the intraparty conflict. As the campaign proceeded, she gained the quiet support of the county executive and his campaign workers, especially one of his closest associates, who was closeted but known within the lesbian and gay community to be gay.[19]

During the campaign, Kavanaugh received respectful treatment from the media. Her opponents also did not focus attention on her lesbianism. The major local newspaper published a number of flattering photographs and stories about her, including one photograph with her two sons (while carefully excluding pic-tures or mentions of her long-time partner). It was no surprise, then, when the newspaper endorsed her both in the primary and the general election.

In the primary, Kavanaugh coasted to a strong second-place finish in a multi-candidate race and won easily in the general election. Within a short time, she established herself as a visible personality in local politics and an articulate leader on education and housing policy, but she has taken few initiatives directed spe-cifically at benefiting lesbians and gay men. On the other hand, the lesbian and gay community has not pressured her or the regime to move beyond symbolic incorporation.

Syracuse: Culture Wars in a Conservative Bipartisan Regime

Gays and lesbians in Syracuse confront a conservative regime where Republicans are influential in municipal politics and Democratic politicians treat lesbian and gay issues with caution. Although acts of repression have been rare for the past decade, lesbians and gay men have been largely excluded from participation in the local regime, with one notable anomaly discussed below.

Efforts to mobilize the lesbian and gay community have been sporadic since the 1970s and have tended to focus either on AIDS-related issues or gay pride events. Indicative of the exclusionary nature of relations between the regime and the community, in 1985, a controversy arose over the use of a downtown public space where the community had held small pride rallies in the past. The area in question is located near several government buildings and also fronts on the local Catholic cathedral. Municipal authorities asked the Pride Committee to pay $1,000 toward an insurance premium to cover the use of the space for one hour. Although the requirement had existed for many years, it usually had been waived for com-munity groups, including the Pride Committee. When the city demanded the payment, the Pride Committee sued and won. Based on evidence that the requirement had been applied selectively, the court took the city's action to be an infringement of free speech.

In this environment, the Gay and Lesbian Alliance of Syracuse (GLAS) was formed in 1988 primarily as an organization concerned with building social ties within the community. Politically active elements within the group began to chafe at the group's self-imposed constraints, with the result that some members withdrew and joined with others in organizing a political action group under the banner of the AIDS Coalition to Unleash Power (ACT UP).

ACT UP members took the lead in organizing gay pride events in June 1989. They approached the Democratic mayor, Thomas Young, about issuing a proclamation in recognition of the occasion. Young, who had carefully maintained silence on gay and lesbian issues, refused to do so.[20] ACT UP then undertook an action in which they piled cardboard boxes around City Hall to symbolize the "wall of silence" the mayor had maintained. They also supported the candidacy for mayor of one of their members in the city's Democratic primary. Even though he was given little chance to win, the Democratic Party was sufficiently nervous to challenge his nomination petitions and succeeded in getting his name taken off the primary ballot. He then ran on a third-party ticket in the general election where he received only 3.3 percent of the total vote. Young was reelected.

Despite its limited impact, this effort energized organizers of the city's 1990 Gay and Lesbian Pride events to seek the symbolic recognition they had been denied the previous year. This time they approached the city council for a proclamation from that Democrat-controlled body. They were aided in this effort by Charles Anderson, the only African American member, who played what Sharp (1996:750) might characterize as a "responsive" role to these "status quo challengers." The proclamation was brought to the council on June 10 for ratification, but members (both Democrats and Republicans) moved to strike the words "gay," "lesbian," and "pride" from the document. Representatives of the gay and lesbian community refused to accept the proclamation on those terms, setting off an exchange between the council president and lesbians and gay men that resulted in a vote to kill the watered-down resolution entirely.

Angered at this treatment, gays and lesbians created a Fair Practices Committee, which they used as a vehicle for mobilizing the endorsements of an array of local religious, legal, and professional groups. Working through council member Anderson, in August 1990, they brought forward a full-fledged antidiscrimination ordinance designed to prohibit discrimination in employment, housing, and public accommodations. The Cuomo administration assisted this effort by dispatching to Syracuse the head of the Governor's Office of Lesbian and Gay Concerns and another state official, Virginia Apuzzo, who had long been associated with the lesbian and gay rights movement nationally and in New York state. These state officials addressed the city council and presented Governor Cuomo's endorsement of the ordinance.

To the surprise of many observers, the council passed the ordinance 5 to 4 on October 1. Although one Democrat refused to vote for it, one of the four Republicans on the council broke ranks on the issue. There was also some softness on the issue by other moderate Republicans, including the city council president, who indicated that he might have voted in favor of the ordinance had he been called on to break a tie. Passage was made easier by the cover provided by the endorsements of establishment groups and by limited media coverage, which contributed to a limited show of opposition during the legislative process.

Only at a public hearing held by Mayor Young as part of the process of deciding whether to sign the ordinance did representatives of conservative groups turn out. On that occasion, a spokesperson for a right-to-life group threatened that God would no longer love the mayor and he would go to hell if he signed the bill. According to one report, Young responded that "God—He or She—had never said anything about the Fair Practices Law." With respect to the mayor's remarks, a leading lesbian activist later commented, "That really got them upset—the idea that God might be female."

In a statement issued at the time he signed the law, Mayor Young revealed how much his relationship with lesbians and gay men had changed over the preceding eighteen months: "The issue before me, stripped of rhetoric, is quite basic. For two hundred years, what has distinguished our democracy is that we protect freedom, and freedom should not be restrained by government as long as expression of that freedom does not intrude on another's safety or rights."[21]

Despite the self-confidence that passage of the ordinance generated within the gay and lesbian community and the symbolic victory it represented, it was only a small step in the transformation of the regime. In 1993, voters elected a 5 to 4 Republican majority to the city council and a Republican mayor for the first time in twenty-four years. However, Roy Bernardi, the new mayor, had not mentioned gay and lesbian issues during the campaign, and after the election, neither the mayor nor the new council majority moved to rescind the ordinance. Furthermore, within a few months, the defection of a pro-gay Republican to the Democrats changed the council majority back to the Democrats.

Quite independent of the ordinance, elements of the regime continue to be engaged in a series of implicit negotiations over symbolic incorporation of the lesbian and gay community. Even before Bernardi's election, gays and lesbians were included in the city's annual St. Patrick's Day Parade, and they continue to participate without incident. After Bernardi's election, the mayor sought to attract Apple Computer to Syracuse in the wake of a highly publicized rebuff that company received from a suburban county in Texas because of Apple's favorable policies toward lesbian and gay employees. In a letter to the company, Mayor Bernardi pointed to the ordinance as evidence of the positive environment Apple would find in Syracuse.

After Democrats regained control of the city council, they passed gay pride resolutions in 1995 and 1996 with little controversy. In the spring of 1997, however, activists pressed further when they sought a proclamation that included coverage of bisexuals and transgendered persons. The council majority had difficulty accepting these additions. Rather than settle for less inclusive coverage, which they could have gotten, the Pride Committee withdrew the proclamation (*Pink Paper,* 1997:20).

Mayor Bernardi took political advantage of this conflict. After receiving a request from members of the lesbian and gay community, he ordered the city's Department of Public Works to paint a lavender line down the center of a major street where the local lesbian and gay community would hold its annual parade (Casler, 1997).

At the same time, the mayor and other Republican politicians have sought to balance their modest gestures toward the gay and lesbian community with equivalent accommodations to the Christian right. When the New York state chapter of the Christian Coalition met in Syracuse in October 1995, Bernardi welcomed them to the city with remarks that extolled the role they had played in providing "this nation with a refreshing message of community action" (Stonewall Committee, 1996:22).

CONCLUSIONS

Each local regime incorporates into its makeup certain values that shape the responses that it makes to new claimants for participation. Thus, in characteristic fashion, Rochester's pluralist regime moved easily and early to include lesbians and gay men. Indeed, the emergence of the gay and lesbian movement in Rochester coincided with the rising expectations of the Democratic Party in city government. Lesbians and gay men were simply part of the loosely coordinated coalition that has continued to govern the city for the past twenty-five years.

In contrast, Albany's long-established political machine resisted incorporation of lesbians and gay men, much as it resisted sharing power with other groups that challenged its conservative social mores: social liberals, African Americans, women. When the old regime began to disintegrate in the 1980s, however, contenders for succession reached out for allies. More focused on gaining political power than encumbered by moral principles, the contending factions adapted to the new situation by incorporating lesbians and gay men (and other groups) into their electoral organizations and accepting their largely symbolic demands. Indeed, by 1997, the dominant faction of the newly invigorated Democratic Party led by Mayor Jennings had incorporated lesbians and gay men to a point where some critics had come to see them as a pillar of a new machine.

Regime resistance to cultural and political change has been more complicated in Buffalo, where the regime—which consisted for many years of three warring political factions—stalemated on a variety of economic and social issues, only one of which was marginally sympathetic to gays and lesbians. Although one faction quietly began to accommodate itself to gay men and lesbians in the 1980s, it was not until after the 1993 mayoral election that lesbians and gay men were openly welcomed into party work. Gays and lesbians then seized the opportunity provided by conflicts within the dominant party organization to back one of their own for municipal office in 1995. By 1997, Buffalo's political regime had come to be dominated by a party organization and municipal government leadership sensitive to gay and lesbian concerns and prepared, at least, to make low-cost symbolic gestures in the direction of the gay and lesbian community but reluctant to proceed beyond that point.

Finally, the major political parties in Syracuse continue to share certain value biases including unease in dealing with lesbians and gay men. This reflects the generally conservative nature of a regime that one informant described as a network of "good old boys" in which it does not really make much difference whether Democrats or Republicans have the political advantage at any given moment. Although Democrats generally have been less grudging of minor symbolic concessions to lesbians and gay men, they have been hesitant to encourage the incorporation of that population into the inner workings of party and government. Republicans are even less comfortable with such an idea. Nonetheless, the regime seems to be moving cautiously to recognize a more visible gay and lesbian presence if only in ways that are least likely to offend their major constituencies.

Despite variations in the experiences of lesbian and gay residents in the four cities, that population has made important symbolic advances in the past decade. It has done so by taking advantage of the highly partisan politics of New York state to gain access to and influence individuals within state and local Democratic Party circles. However, where Republicans have retained an important measure of power, or where that party has gained strength in recent years (as it has in the governor's office and in some suburban areas), lesbian and gay advances have been held in check. Given the important role of parties in mediating culture wars in New York state, the Republican Party continues to serve as an important vehicle for registering the political concerns of religious fundamentalists and social conservatives who continue to maintain barriers to regime incorporation of gays and lesbians.

NOTES

1. This formulation combines both the "resource mobilization" and "political opportunity" approaches to social movements. In that connection, see McAdam (1982); Morris and Mueller (1992); Tarrow (1994); and Button et al. (1997).

2. The populations of the four cities examined here are predominantly Catholic (though local Catholic bishops vary in their treatment of lesbian and gay issues). The largest segment of urban Protestants consists of African Americans affiliated with doctrinally conservative churches.

3. It is not clear whether Cuomo was personally associated with a campaign poster distributed in parts of New York City during his primary race for Governor in 1982 against

New York City Mayor Ed Koch that urged voters to "Vote for Cuomo, Not the Homo." Yet, according to Shilts (1987:181), gays and lesbians were so offended by Koch's refusal to respond to the initial panic surrounding AIDS that they supported the Cuomo candidacy and his subsequent political leadership despite his occasional lapses.

4. In both of his major works on Atlanta (1976, 1989), Stone accords only passing attention to the cultural or symbolic dimensions of local politics.

5. Sharp (1996) examines six "roles" that government officials play in confronting local "culture wars," but she does not indicate whether there are particular sequences in the responses of local officials.

6. New York's sodomy law was overturned by the state's highest court in 1980 in a case from Buffalo involving gay men and a companion heterosexual case from Syracuse. When Buffalo police subsequently used the existing loitering laws to continue making arrests for allegedly engaging in "deviant" sex, a local activist brought a suit in 1982 that led to a decision by the same court that struck down the loitering law. That decision was appealed to the United States Supreme Court, which avoided dealing with the issue by declaring that no "federal question" existed.

7. On the problematics of substantive incorporation, see Rosenthal (1996b, 1997).

8. The iconography of Rochester was nicely reinforced in 1997 when its African American mayor, William Johnson, greeted Deb Price, a nationally syndicated lesbian columnist, and her lover, Joyce Murdoch, during ceremonies held in conjunction with their service as grand marshals of the city's Gay Pride Parade. Price alluded to the Susan B. Anthony/Frederick Douglass connection in her warm remarks about Rochester (Wilner, 1997:A6).

9. Both Kodak and Xerox have adopted pro-gay employment policies. On another culture-shaping front, the bishop of the Roman Catholic diocese of Rochester broke ranks with the generally conservative prelates of New York state by holding a special mass for lesbians and gay men and their families in March 1997 to welcome them back to the church. Similarly, one of the local Presbyterian churches has played an active role in promoting pro-gay and lesbian attitudes in the national councils of that denomination.

10. This sequence of events appears to approximate Sharp's description of "evasion."

11. Gay and lesbian informants in Rochester did not see this episode as marked by homophobia. Instead, they attributed it to a reluctance on the part of the city government to forgo revenues at a time of major fiscal pressures.

12. There is some uncertainty in New York State about the power of municipal governments to pass antidiscrimination laws. Nonetheless, a number of municipalities (including Albany, Ithaca, and Syracuse) have passed broad-based ordinances, whereas others, including Buffalo and Rochester, have not done so even when lesbians and gay men have had political influence.

13. In the midst of these negotiations, the leadership of the machine issued a symbolically important invitation to ERDC to take part for the first time in the annual Albany County Democratic Party picnic. That participation became a routine matter in the following years.

14. About the same time, ERDC gained credit for helping to pass an antidiscrimination law in Albany County by a vote of 24–13 in the county legislature. The County Executive was Democratic, and Democrats held the majority in the county legislature (Post and D'Aquanni, 1996:1).

15. St. John was defeated for re-election but for reasons, several observers insist, that had more to do with his lack of political skills than his sexual orientation.

16. For a description of that type of community, see Williams and Adrian (1963:27–28).

17. George Arthur, interview by the author, 13 November 1997.

18. It did not become public knowledge until after his death in 1993 that Hoyt's daughter, who lives in California, is a lesbian.

19. During the campaign, a story was leaked to the media that this person was not only gay but had a record of arrests for drunk driving. For the most part, the story was seen as an attempt to embarrass the county executive by his political opponents and not as a direct attack on the individual involved. After the county executive's re-election, this man was appointed to the politically powerful position of commissioner on the County Board of Elections.

20. Citing an article that appeared in the *Syracuse Herald-American,* the newsletter of the gay and lesbian community, *The Pink Paper* (1989:1), reported that Mayor Young was advised against signing the proclamation by his director of communications who was quoted as having said: "A proclamation is a stamp of approval on behalf of the entire city. Generally, we limit it to church groups, veterans and ethnic type affairs. We are reluctant to get involved in proclamations for life style choices, whether it's abortion or gay rights. We don't want to take a stand on it one way or another."

21. One reason informants cite for the mayor's seeming shift in positions was the passage of a referendum in the 1989 election that limited mayors (including the incumbent) to two terms.

Both this and the previous quote come from a story about these events and an interview with one of the leaders of the fight for the ordinance (Jordan, 1991:12).

REFERENCES

Adam, B. D. 1987. *The Rise of a Gay and Lesbian Movement.* Boston: Twayne Publishers.

Button, J. W., B. A. Rienzo, and K. D. Wald. 1997. *Private Lives, Public Conflicts.* Washington, D.C.: Congressional Quarterly Press.

Casler, M. 1997. "Whose Line is it Anyway?" *Pride Inside (Syracuse, N.Y.)* 2(7): 3.

Cohen, C. 1997. "Straight Gay Politics: The Limits of an Ethnic Model of Inclusion." In I. Shapiro and W. Klymicka, eds., *Ethnicity and Group Rights.* New York: New York University Press, pp. 572–616.

Community (Albany, N.Y.). 1988. "Albany County Council Votes Against Lesbian/Gay Civil Rights." 25, #4 (April), p. 1.

Conti, R. 1992. "Activists Pack the Center; Mayor Whalen Says 'Albany Is Ready.'" *Community (Albany, N.Y.),* February, p. 1.

Cruickshank, M. 1992. *The Gay and Lesbian Liberation Movement.* New York: Routledge.

D'Emilio, J. 1983. *Sexual Politics, Sexual Communities.* Chicago: University of Chicago Press.

Easton, D. 1965. *A Systems Analysis of Political Life.* New York: John Wiley.

Erie, S. 1988. *The Rainbow's End.* Berkeley: University of California Press.

Jordan, S. 1991. "Syracuse Passes Ordinance Protecting Gay Freedoms." *Empty Closet (Rochester, N.Y.)* 222 (February), p. 12.

———. 1993. "Landmark Victory! Judge Rules City Discriminated Against Gay Alliance." *Empty Closet (Rochester, N.Y.)* 247 (May), p. 1.

Marotta, T. 1981. *The Politics of Homosexuality.* Boston: Houghton-Mifflin.

McAdam, D. 1982. *Political Process and the Development of Black Insurgency.* Chicago: University of Chicago Press.

Morris, A. D., and C. M. Mueller, eds. 1992. *Frontiers in Social Movement Theory.* New Haven, Conn.: Yale University Press.

Pink Paper, The. (Syracuse, N.Y.). 1989. "Aide Advises Young Against Signing Gay Proclamation." 1, #2 (July).

———. 1997. "1997 Syracuse Pride Proclamation." 9, #1 (June–July).

Post, Libby, and Lissa D'Aquanni. 1996. "Two New Initiatives Extend Rights and Recognition to Lesbian and Gay Community." *Community (Albany, N.Y.)* 24(4), p. 1.

Robinson, F. 1977. *Machine Politics: A Study of Albany's O'Connells.* New Brunswick, N.J.: Transaction Books.

Rosenthal, D. B. 1996a. "Gay and Lesbian Political Mobilization and Regime Responsiveness in Four New York Cities." *Urban Affairs Review* 32 (September): 35–70.

———. 1996b. "Gay and Lesbian Political Incorporation and Agenda Setting in Four New York Cities." Paper presented at the 1996 Annual Meeting of the American Political Science Association, San Francisco, 29 August–1 September.

———. 1997. "Community Building, Bridge Building and Political Opportunities for Lesbians and Gay Men in Four New York Cities." Paper presented at the 1997 Annual Meeting of the American Political Science Association, Washington, D.C., 28–31 August.

Sharp, E. B. 1996. "Culture Wars and City Politics." *Urban Affairs Review* 31 (July): 738–58.

———. 1997. "A Comparative Anatomy of Urban Social Conflict." *Political Research Quarterly* 50 (June): 261–80.

Shilts, R. 1982. *The Mayor of Castro Street.* New York: St. Martin's Press.

———. 1987. *And the Band Played On.* New York: St. Martin's Press.

Stone, C. 1976. *Economic Growth and Neighborhood Discontent.* Chapel Hill: University of North Carolina Press.

———. 1989. *Regime Politics.* Lawrence: University Press of Kansas.

Stonewall Committee (Syracuse, N.Y.). 1996. *Gay Pride 1996.* Syracuse, N.Y.: Stonewall Committee.

Swanstrom, T., and S. Ward. 1987. "Albany's O'Connell Organization." Paper presented at the 1987 Annual Meeting of the American Political Science Association, Chicago, 1–4 September.

Tarrow, S. 1994. *Power in Movement.* Cambridge: Cambridge University Press.

Williams, O. P., and C. R. Adrian. 1963. *Four Cities.* Philadelphia: University of Pennsylvania Press.

Wilner, J. 1997. "Interview: Deb Price and Joyce Murdoch Pay a Visit to Rochester, Their 'Spiritual Home.'" *Empty Closet (Rochester, N.Y.)* 294 (August), pp. A6–A7.

5
The Politics of
Gay Rights Legislation

James W. Button, Kenneth D. Wald,
and Barbara A. Rienzo

Controversies over civil rights laws protective of lesbians and gay men have often been at the heart of culture war issues in local politics.[1] "Gay politics" conjures up images of conflict over gays in the military or the legal recognition of same-sex marriages, but these national debates overshadow the highly contentious nature of local battles over gay rights. Hundreds of American communities have struggled with questions about whether local laws and policies should provide protection against discrimination on the basis of sexual orientation. In some places, such laws have been passed and implemented with little public comment. Elsewhere laws have been passed by local government officials and then overturned in heated public referenda. Many communities have decided against taking legal action, whereas some cities and counties, not content to refrain from action, have passed resolutions outrightly condemning homosexuality as behavior contrary to the standards of the community. Whatever the outcome, the issue of legalized protection against discrimination on the basis of sexual orientation has challenged politics as normal.

This chapter first explains why some communities but not others have adopted gay rights legislation. Our explanations draw on components of social movement theory, yet also test hypotheses concerning the influence of local government structures. Second, and more important, we focus on the different roles that local government officials play in the social controversies surrounding the quest for legal rights protective of lesbians and gays. Although it is assumed that local governments, in an effort to maintain social control, respond to culture war demands in a reactionary and often repressive manner, we shall see that this is not always the case. Indeed, city government roles may actually serve to support gay rights and may even change over the course of such controversy, depending on the local political culture and other factors. At the least, we hope to create greater understanding of one of the most volatile issues in the culture wars confronting American cities.

HOW DID WE STUDY GAY RIGHTS?

Our sources of data are drawn from our national comprehensive study of the politics of gay rights in American communities (Button et al., 1997). These sources are a blend of quantitative and qualitative information. They include a nationwide survey of all U.S. cities and counties with laws or policies prohibiting discrimination on the basis of sexual orientation as of mid-1993. We also surveyed a comparison sample of 125 cities and counties without such legislation selected randomly from a comprehensive list of local jurisdictions in the United States. This chapter will draw most heavily, however, on information from in-depth case studies of five representative, geographically diverse cities that have enacted gay rights laws: Cincinnati, Ohio; Iowa City, Iowa; Philadelphia, Pennsylvania; Raleigh, North Carolina; and Santa Cruz, California. We chose these communities after conducting a cluster analysis of all cities with antidiscrimination laws or policies. This analysis, using a variety of discriminating variables such as social structure, demographic qualities, and political history, divided the cities into four distinct, homogeneous groups. One city representative of each cluster was selected. We decided to study a fifth city that was chosen as quite different from the others. Cincinnati adopted but then repealed its gay rights law and is therefore representative of those locales where opponents of civil rights legislation for lesbians and gay men have been most visible and successful.

In each of the case-study communities, we interviewed a variety of individuals who were considered knowledgeable about the politics of gay rights legislation. These individuals typically included elected city officials, city administrators, gay and lesbian activists, religious and other leaders of opposition groups, members of the business community, and minority group leaders. We also perused local newspapers and available public records. These multiple modes of analysis offered a wide range of sometimes rich sources of information; they also often provided a cross-check on the reliability of any single source. These data yielded evidence of the various roles that local governments played in the controversies surrounding gay rights.

INFLUENCE OF GOVERNMENT STRUCTURE ON ADOPTION OF LEGISLATION: THE NATIONAL DATA

More than one-fifth of Americans now live in communities that provide legal protection to gays, lesbians, and bisexuals. Only eleven states, most in New England, have succeeded in passing such legislation, and the federal government, despite several attempts to add sexual orientation to the 1964 Civil Rights Act, has failed to provide national protection. Thus political battles over gay rights have been waged primarily at the local level. The focus of our initial inquiry is the set of factors, including government institutions, that may have promoted gay rights legislation in a number of cities and counties. To explore this issue, we rely on data from our national survey.

The decision to include sexual orientation in a local antidiscrimination law is typically a significant and contentious one. In attempting to explain the adoption of such legislation, we drew on four major theoretical frameworks. The first approach, urbanism/social diversity, emphasizes sociodemographic factors such as population size, income and race that have commonly predicted public policy outcomes (Skocpol et al., 1993:689). The underlying assumptions of this approach are that public policy depends at base on the social structural qualities of the community and that activist policies are most likely to be found in large and socially complex urban environments. The other three approaches, resource mobilization, political opportunity structure, and communal protest, have been developed from research on social movements. Social movement theory focuses on mass movements that engage and challenge the political system (Mayer, 1991; Morris and Mueller, 1992). The three variants of social movement theory we have used identify different mechanisms that should play a critical role in whether communities add sexual orientation to local civil rights law. Resource mobilization emphasizes the organizational and leadership capabilities available to challenging groups (McCarthy and Zald, 1973). For the problem at hand, explaining the adoption of gay rights ordinances, this perspective calls our attention to measures of the size of the gay community, its prior political outreach, and the strength of gay-related organizations and services. The responsiveness of the political system to new claimants, known as the political opportunity structure, is also considered important (Tarrow, 1991:406). All things being equal, we would expect to find the greatest responsiveness to gay mobilization in communities with strong Democratic voting habits, a progressive state political culture, and a substantial higher education presence. The final framework, communal protest, looks at the opposition to mass movements and includes forces that resist change and innovative policies (Tarrow, 1992:180). Because of the moral dimension that accompanies debates over gay rights, we expected religious composition to play a major role in determining the outcome and included several variables of community religiosity and the presence of morally conservative denominations.

One component of the political opportunity structure approach is the nature of local government. In her study of progress in the women's movement, Anne Costain claimed that an important ingredient was the "openness of government to new interests" (1992:14–15). On the assumption that the nature of institutions "can shape the choices that local leaders make," there is a good deal of research directed at various aspects of local government structures (Sharp, 1997:263). Much work has focused on reform versus nonreform government, with investigations of the impact of separate institutional forms showing the most meaningful and clear-cut results. As Sharp summarizes, "the institutional logic distinguishing city managers from mayors, weak mayors from strong mayors, and at-large from district systems constitutes an important basis for understanding urban phenomena"

(Sharp, 1997:265). Whether structures of local government influence the manner in which public officials respond to culture war conflicts remains to be seen.

Our attempt to explain the adoption of gay rights ordinances or policies used three indicators of local government arrangements: district versus at-large elections, partisan versus nonpartisan elections, and mayor-council versus manager-council systems. District and partisan elections would seem to facilitate gay political power in the same way that they have improved the political representation of racial and ethnic minorities (Welch, 1990). Likewise, it is hypothesized that popularly elected mayors would be more responsive than appointed city managers to the political demands of a mobilized gay constituency and its allies.

A comparison of the local government structures of communities with and without gay rights legislation is shown below.

Government structure	Communities with no ordinance/policy (n = 125)	Communities with ordinance/policy (n = 126)
District (or partly district) elections	51.2%	59.5%
Partisan elections	35.2	42.1
Mayor-council government	59.2	36.5

The nature of local elections meets our expectations; that is, district and partisan arrangements are somewhat more common in cities and counties with gay rights ordinances or policies. As in the case of other unpopular minorities faced with discrimination, gay and lesbian constituencies tend to be neighborhood-based, especially in larger cities where distinctive enclaves are most prevalent (Bailey 1997). In terms of partisan advantages, gays have typically collaborated most closely with the more progressive Democratic Party and, as a result, have gained both votes and other important resources from this affiliation. On the other hand, the results of local executive structures are surprising. City managers, not mayor-council governments, are much more likely to be found in communities with legislation protective of sexual orientation.

Although various forms of local government are associated with the passage of gay rights laws, further statistical analysis indicates that the relationship is spurious. Employing multivariate (logistic regression) analysis with representative indicators of each of our theoretical approaches, we found that no measure of government structure was statistically significant in the final model (Table 5.1; for a further explanation of this model see Wald et al., 1996). In fact, the urbanism/social diversity framework was by far the most powerful predictor. Population size, a key component of the urbanism/social diversity approach, proved to be the most important explanatory factor as locales with legislation averaged 434,214 residents, whereas communities without ordinances averaged only 18,388. As suggested by resource mobilization theory, indicators of the political mobilization of the gay community were also significant factors in the distribution of

Table 5.1. Logistic Regression Results of Gay Rights Ordinance Adoption

Variables	Significant Regression Coefficients
I. Urbanism/social diversity	
Population (in 10,000s)	.453***
Nonfamily households	29.304**
II. Resource mobilization	
Gay-oriented services[a]	71.355*
Gay candidates for public office	1.485**
III. Political opportunity structure	
Congressional support of gay civil rights bill	.941*
IV. Communal protest	
Conservative Protestants	−.091*
Church affiliation	−.070*
Summary statistics: percent correctly predicted overall	95.6

[a]Gay-oriented bars and services that serve as a surrogate variable for gay identity and organizational efforts.
*p < .05; ** p < .01; *** p < .001.

protective ordinances. Finally, in accordance with communal protest theory, we found that the opposition, as measured by the level of church affiliation and the concentration of conservative Protestants, depressed the likelihood of adoption of gay rights.

The political opportunity structure model, however, offered only one modestly significant variable: Communities with ordinances were more likely to be represented by a member of Congress who cosponsored a gay civil rights bill. Thus, differences in government structure associated with passage of gay-friendly legislation are apparently a function of the strong relationship between city size and types of government institutions. According to this analysis, indicators of formal government arrangements have little direct or independent influence on the decision to adopt civil rights legislation protective of gays and lesbians.

ROLES OF LOCAL GOVERNMENTS: ANALYSES OF FIVE CITIES

The data from the national study suggest that local government structure did not, in and of itself, promote passage of legislation. But this general assertion leaves open the question of what roles local officials played in this political process. In explaining and categorizing the various roles that city governments play in responding to demands for antidiscrimination laws and policies, we turned to our intensive study of five representative communities. As part of this analysis, we try to understand the variation in local political roles from one community to another. We also investigate government actions over time from the period of policy initiation to the conclusion of the controversy and beyond. Political roles often change with the course of events and the demands being made, including the period after adoption of gay rights policies. The structure of city governments is also revisited, this time to see whether institutional arrangements shape or mediate the roles that governments play in the culture wars surrounding gay rights. Our discussion of the five locales begins with the cities that were found to be most repressive, and we then analyze those that were most supportive of lesbian and gay demands.[2]

Raleigh

Raleigh is the capital of North Carolina and part of the traditional Baptist South where racism and other forms of discrimination have been embedded in the culture. The state's antisodomy law, a common legal prohibition in the South, has been applied selectively to gays, and incidents of antigay harassment and violence are numerous. Jesse Helms, clearly the most outspoken antigay member of the U.S. Senate, established his political career in Raleigh and resides in the city. Yet Raleigh is considered more progressive than most southern communities. It is an integral part of the Research Triangle (including Durham and Chapel Hill) that has attracted a host of high-tech firms with thousands of employees from outside the South. Raleigh is also a leader in education and the home of North Carolina State University. As a consequence, this North Carolina city is one of the few areas in Dixie where lesbians and gay men have been able to gather and mobilize politically (Button et al., 1997:38–42).

By the mid-1980s, the nearby communities of Chapel Hill and Durham had adopted antidiscrimination policies protective of gays. No such political action had yet occurred, or even been discussed, in Raleigh. In the spring of 1986, however, the Raleigh Director of Parks and Recreation suddenly canceled a park reservation for the annual Gay Freedom Day picnic. The park official reportedly feared that the event would attract hundreds of gays to the public facility. Many gays and their sympathizers were outraged and complained to the city council. City officials soon reversed the decision, allowing the event to proceed as planned.

The park incident proved to be an example of *unintentional instigation.* The initial refusal of park access helped to mobilize gays and convinced them of the need for a city antidiscrimination ordinance. Gay activists appealed to the city's Human Relations and Human Resources Advisory Committee, which in 1987 requested that the city council approve a gay rights resolution. Council members, however, in a classic case of *evasion,* refused to act on the controversial proposal. Instead, city officials asked for more information on treatment of gays in the city. In response, the Human Relations Committee, a quasi-governmental board of nonelected citizens, held a public hearing on gay-related discrimination. In the hearing, a number of lesbians and gay men testified about incidents of being fired from their jobs, harassed by police, and victimized by violence.

No one testified in opposition to gays, and the committee recommended that the city pass a local law prohibiting discrimination on the basis of sexual orientation (Harding, 1988).

Most elected officials continued their evasive tactics, fearing that action on such a recommendation would alienate many citizens and evoke protests from opposition groups. Gays organized further and lobbied on behalf of the bill but also recognized they needed an advocate on the city council to take the lead in promoting the legislation. In the 1987 local elections, gays and their allies, many of whom were concentrated in one district, provided significant support for a candidate, Mary Nooe, who embraced gay rights. Although Raleigh's local government was primarily "reformed" in structure, its council elections were in part by district. Nooe won the district election and soon began to push for city legislation protecting gays. In an example of *entrepreneurial instigation,* Nooe also helped to mobilize liberal groups like NOW, the NAACP, the North Carolina Council of Churches, and various lesbian and gay organizations in support of the ordinance. At a council meeting early in 1988, Mary Nooe made a motion to amend the city's antidiscrimination law to include sexual orientation. With no organized opposition and little debate, the council approved the amendment in a vote of 7–1 (Gaffney, 1988).

The new ordinance, however, was limited in scope, prohibiting discrimination against gays only in city employment, city facilities, and businesses that had city contracts. In this sense, the law was more important symbolically than substantively. Indeed, most city officials, in an evasive mode, provided little support for the law. In the first six years after its enactment, no formal complaints of discrimination were filed, although several gays expressed job-related grievances (Raleigh city official, interview by author, 22 July 1996). An attempt in 1993 to create a more comprehensive ordinance by extending the legislation to the private sector failed to pass in a city council vote. By the 1990s, opposition to gay rights from business owners and fundamentalist churches had crystallized, and these groups dominated committee hearings. Some council members feared that extending the law would create greater tension and divisions within the city. Furthermore, the political process for amending such legislation was more complex and difficult than in the late 1980s. State law now required the city council to first gain approval of the state legislature, because the local bill exceeded the boundaries of state law.

By the mid-1990s, Raleigh city officials had taken a largely *repressive* stance. The city council turned increasingly conservative as Mary Nooe, although successful in winning an at-large seat in the previous election, lost in a citywide race for the mayorship to an antigay Republican. Shortly thereafter, city officials turned down a request for a zoning change to accommodate an AIDS service organization and then closed Raleigh's most popular gay bar, suddenly enforcing more selectively the city's ordinance dealing with adult establishments (Raleigh gay activist, interview by author, 22 July 1996).

In sum, the influence of Raleigh's traditional southern culture and religion was apparent in suppressing the drive for a comprehensive, well-enforced ordinance to protect lesbians and gay men. According to a local gay activist, "It was due to idiosyncratic factors, not to the political strength of the gay community" that a limited anti-discrimination ordinance was adopted (Chapel Hill city official, interview by author, 21 May 1994). In this sense, the law was the result of both unintentional instigation (a city official's refusal to grant access to a public park, thus sparking gays to action) and entrepreneurial instigation (a pro-gay rights official who effectively promoted such a law). Nonetheless, when gays advocated a more extensive law covering the private sector, strong opposition from the religious and business communities emerged, ultimately producing a more conservative city council and mayor. City officials were much less supportive of gay rights, moving to a mode of behavior characterized by evasion and ultimately repression. The mostly reformed structure of the city's local government had little bearing on these outcomes. Only the district election that enabled Mary Nooe, the strong gay rights advocate, to win election initially to the city council was a factor affecting these policy decisions.

Cincinnati

Bounded by the Mason-Dixon line, Cincinnati is a Midwestern city exhibiting both northern and southern cultural influences. Known for its bustling trade, business establishments, and ethnic (mainly German and Irish) neighborhoods, Cincinnati resembles a number of large urban areas of the north. Yet its sizable black population, mainly migrants from the South and largely Baptist, coupled with its conservative, moralistic political traditions, provide the city with a notable southern influence (Button et al., 1997:46–51). Indeed, Cincinnati prides itself on its reputation as a "bastion of traditional family values" and as the "'smut-free' capital of the country" (Rutledge, 1992:340).

This moralistic atmosphere limited the development of an active gay movement. Lesbian and gay political organizations tended to be small and relatively short-lived. In the wake of Anita Bryant's well-publicized campaign against gay rights in Dade County, Florida, however, local gays developed the Coalition for Cincinnati Human Rights Law, which included a variety of progressive groups. In 1977, the Coalition proposed to the city council a civil rights ordinance that included sexual orientation. At the time, Cincinnati had no human rights legislation of any kind, and the proposed bill would have provided protection from discrimination for a number of minority groups.

Opposition to the civil rights legislation, particularly as it related to sexual orientation, surfaced immediately. Business leaders, especially realtors, complained about the prospect of losing their right to rent or sell to whom they pleased. City council members also objected strongly to the proposal. Some opposed gay rights on moral grounds, and others believed that lesbians and gay men faced little discrimination and therefore the law was unnecessary. Several council members also feared the potential controversy surrounding debate over legal protections for homosexuals. In the midst of discussions of the bill, and in a clear indication of a *repressive* response, the city police carried out a massive crackdown on gays in public parks. In a series of police raids, more than sixty men were arrested and charged with public indecency or sexual imposition. Although police harassment of gays in the city was not uncommon, this crackdown was unusually extensive and harsh. Gays protested the raids, in part for what they believed was the blatant political attempt to discredit homosexuals while city officials were considering human rights legislation. Not long after the antigay police actions, the proposed ordinance died in committee for lack of support.

Surprisingly, the police raids had another unanticipated consequence. They stimulated greater unification and organization of the gay community. As a result of this *unintentional instigation,* gays began to carry out voter registration drives, and for the first time, an openly gay man ran for city office (as an unsuccessful write-in candidate). Most important, lesbians and gay men joined together in 1982 to establish what was to become an influential interest group, Stonewall Cincinnati. One of the primary goals of the new organization was to achieve passage of a gay rights ordinance. Stonewall's first major activity, however, was to halt the firing of gay city employees by city officials (Stonewall Cincinnati, 1992).

By the early 1990s, Stonewall Cincinnati was a sizable and relatively powerful interest group. It had mobilized a substantial gay vote that proved influential in the elections of several city council members (all council elections are at-large). With a more liberal council in place, city officials grew more *responsive* to gay demands. In 1991, with virtually no opposition, the city council voted 8–1 to add gays to the city's Equal Employment Opportunity policy, thus prohibiting discrimination based on sexual orientation in municipal jobs and services. A year later, in coalition with other supportive groups, Stonewall proposed a comprehensive human rights law to the city council. Opposition to including sexual orientation in the proposal was substantial, especially among traditional religious black groups and many business leaders. Nevertheless, receptive city officials favored the ordinance, and although the opposition was able to delay action, the council finally voted its approval by a 7–2 margin in late 1992.

The battle over gay rights in Cincinnati, however, was far from over. Adoption of a civil rights law that included sexual orientation enraged and greatly increased the mobilization of opponents. A coalition of pro-family, traditional religious, and conservative groups, along with a number of African Americans, moved to oust city council members who approved the legislation and to create a voter referendum to repeal the law. Well-organized and amply funded, opponents were successful in achieving both goals. In a public referendum in 1993, protection from discrimination for homosexuals was revoked by a 62–38 percent vote margin (Allen, 1995). Gay rights advocates did not relent, however, and resorted to the federal courts to test the constitutionality of the law's repeal. In the meantime, local elections, fueled by well-funded opponents, produced a more conservative city council. When the U.S. District Court ruled to overturn the results of the referendum, the largely new council voted to join the appeal of the court's decision. In 1995, the now antigay city council reconsidered its original decision on gay rights and voted 5–4 to delete "sexual orientation" from the human rights ordinance. This final act emphasized again the primarily repressive role that city officials most often played.

In summary, Cincinnati has a history of political battles over morality issues. With a moralistic, conservative political culture and strong influences from the Christian right, Cincinnati is a northern city with deep southern imprints. Its sizable black population (38 percent) is largely Baptist and conservative on most social issues. As in the case of Raleigh, this predominantly southern and traditional political culture explains the consistently repressive response to gay rights by city officials. This mode of repression has been evident from the police crackdown on gays at the time of the first antidiscrimination initiative in the late 1970s to the 1995 council vote to delete sexual orientation from the human rights law. On the other hand, early police actions served to help mobilize gays politically and ultimately created a more moderate city council. For a brief period in the early 1990s, city officials, lobbied by gays and their allies, were responsive to demands for civil rights protections. However, the ensuing political backlash that repealed gay rights also converted the city council to its traditional repressive mode. Local political structure per se did not unduly influence these actions, although Cincinnati's reformed government, especially its at-large and nonpartisan elections, seemed to constrain lesbians and gays who were geographically concentrated and Democratically aligned. Furthermore, the reformist emphasis on citywide issues and constituencies reinforced the referendum process and the popular repeal of gay rights. This institutional "tyranny of the majority" facilitated Cincinnati's potential for repression of minority rights.

Philadelphia

The "city of brotherly love," Philadelphia, was founded by seekers of religious and political freedom. Symbolized by its Liberty Bell and steeped in colonial history, this large northeastern city attracted immigrants from a variety of countries and is well known for its ethnic and racial diversity. The general atmosphere of tolerance has been reinforced by nonreformed local government with a strong mayor and partisan, mostly district, elections. Such a setting proved to be fertile ground for the early development of a significant gay political movement (Button et al., 1997:32–38).

Gays in Philadelphia first began to organize in the early 1960s. Although relatively small in numbers, these activists protested discrimination against homosexuals at local restaurants. They also helped to sponsor a picket line each July 4 at Independence Hall, claiming that gays were denied basic rights granted all

Americans in the Declaration of Independence. Inspired by the Stonewall rebellion in New York in 1969, the Philadelphia gay movement grew in size and diversity. One mutual goal, however, was the need for a local gay rights ordinance. After several years of lobbying, lesbians and gays convinced the city council in 1974 to begin consideration of such legislation. The city's Commission on Human Relations held public hearings on the proposed measure, then recommended it to the council. Although a variety of gay and lesbian groups and other liberal organizations supported gay rights, several city departments, religious leaders, and the powerful Catholic Archdiocese (an estimated 500,000 Catholics live in the city) firmly opposed it.

In a case of *evasion,* city officials, while sympathetic to gay rights, also realized that the time was not right for moving ahead with the law. Thus, they delayed their response to the antidiscrimination bill, allowing it to languish in committee. In the meantime, the 1975 city elections produced a more conservative council and the re-election of antigay mayor Frank Rizzo, Philadelphia's law-and-order police commissioner of the 1960s. Despite protests by gays to gain council consideration of the measure before the newly elected council members took office, such pleas were denied, and the bill died in committee. In 1977, a similar fate befell a less comprehensive gay rights proposal because of the continuing lack of support from city officials.

With a second defeat, gays in Philadelphia shifted strategies to emphasize electoral politics as the means to create a more supportive lawmaking body. A Lesbian and Gay Task Force was created in 1978, and this major organization played a key role in lobbying, fund-raising, documenting antigay discrimination, and getting out the gay vote. In the 1979 city elections, gays, lesbians, and their allies helped elect a politically moderate mayor to replace Rizzo and a more progressive city council. The new city officials proved to be more *responsive* in meeting gay demands (Philadelphia gay activist, interview by author, 26 July 1994). In 1980, for example, the city issued a policy banning discrimination against homosexuals employed by the municipality.

Two years later, after developing a coalition with other liberal groups including African Americans, gays once again proposed antidiscrimination legislation. A variety of witnesses appeared in public hearings to support the measure, and opposition was late to develop and relatively unorganized. Even the Catholic Archdiocese was ill-prepared and offered only token resistance. The gay rights bill moved quickly out of committee, and the city council voted soon after to approve the legislation by a decisive margin of 13–2. The mayor, who had previously endorsed the bill, surprisingly refused to sign it (but also did not veto it); the measure nonetheless became law after the specified waiting period (Philadelphia Lesbian and Gay Task Force, 1992).

Electoral politics continued to be the primary path to success for Philadelphia's gay and lesbian communities. Wilson Goode, with strong support from gays, became the city's first black mayor in 1983 and won re-election four years later.

Goode appointed several lesbians and gay men to city offices, and created the Commission on Sexual Minorities as an advisory board to the mayor.

Even though gays exerted significant influence in Philadelphia politics, their policy demands in the 1980s met with increasing evasion. City officials repeatedly rejected a resolution recognizing "Lesbian and Gay Pride Week" until finally granting approval by a narrow 9–8 vote in 1989. Many gays perceived this resolution as a significant civil rights issue that gave greater public recognition to homosexuals, but some council members believed the week of celebration to be unnecessary. In a more hostile act, city police beat and mistreated gays who were peacefully protesting when President George Bush visited the city in 1991. An investigation by the city concluded that police homophobia and fear of AIDS were the primary causes of the brutality (Slobodzian and Tulsky, 1992). In response, however, several police found at fault were removed from the force, and city officials established in 1994 a Citizen's Police Advisory Board to monitor police behavior.

In 1993, a major proposal for domestic partner legislation met with stiff resistance from a less progressive city council. The Catholic Archdiocese and other opponents (including many blacks) were well organized in opposition to this issue, arguing that granting gays the same city benefits as married heterosexual couples was immoral and a threat to the traditional family. Given the strength of the opposition, city officials, including the pro-gay mayor, decided to table further discussion of this controversial proposal. Finally, the Commission on Human Relations, the enforcement agency for gay rights and other civil rights provisions, suffered significant budget and staff cuts in the 1990s, which resulted in lower numbers of formal complaints of discrimination (Philadelphia city official, interview by author, 24 July 1994).

Thus, in Philadelphia, the responses of city officials to gay demands have varied a good deal. Although gays and lesbians began to organize politically early on, proposing an antidiscrimination law by the mid-1970s, city government initially evaded action on the proposal. The traditional political culture of the city, reflected in the large white ethnic and Catholic populations, dominated local politics. Gays, nevertheless, mobilized electorally and, along with liberal allies, were able to create a more responsive city council and mayor. By the early 1980s, city officials overwhelmingly approved a gay rights measure and, later in the decade, adopted other policies beneficial to lesbians and gay men. More traditional forces soon reasserted themselves, however. The Catholic Archdiocese along with a number of African Americans were able to block domestic partner benefits legislation, the major gay demand of the 1990s. In terms of government structure, Philadelphia's nonreformed system, especially partisan and district elections, enabled gays and lesbians to elect progressive officeholders. Yet, the same structure also allowed neighborhood-based white ethnics to recapture control of city hall and to evade gay demands once again.

Santa Cruz

Santa Cruz is a burgeoning but still charming seaside resort community less than one hundred miles south of San Francisco. The visibility of lesbians and gays, a nearby University of California campus, and its relative proximity to San Francisco make it a "forward-thinking and progressive" city (Honig, 1991). In 1975 when Santa Cruz County officials passed the first countywide gay rights measure in the United States, it generated little surprise locally (Button et al., 1997:42–46).

Gays and lesbians began to mobilize politically in the later 1970s. They were galvanized by the publicity emanating from Dade County (which includes Miami), Florida's repeal of its antidiscrimination ordinance and by the threat posed by California's Briggs Initiative. State Senator John Briggs had engineered a statewide referendum on a proposal that would force schools to fire teachers who were gay or who promoted homosexuality. This controversial initiative was defeated in the 1978 state elections. Recognizing the importance of the electoral process, gays and other liberals joined together to vote progressive candidates into local office. By the early 1980s, they had developed their own local political action committee (PAC) and helped elect a decidedly more liberal city council, including an openly gay candidate, John Laird, as mayor (Santa Cruz city official, interview by author, 25 June 1994).

Mayor Laird and the progressive council soon instituted policies to meet the demands of gay constituents. In the role best characterized as *hyperactive responsiveness,* the city council passed policies to prohibit antigay discrimination in municipal employment and to include sexual orientation in the city's sexual harassment program. The council also enacted a law declaring AIDS nondiscrimination and a resolution to increase AIDS funding. In addition, the mayor played a key role in establishing a Human Rights Commission in 1986 to help document acts of discrimination against gays and lesbians. Santa Cruz had a history of antigay harassment and even violence, although many of these incidents were attributed to outsiders and tourists. Finally, city officials established domestic partner benefits for gays in 1987, a policy accomplishment well in advance of most other communities even in California (Musitelli, 1993). All of these actions were carried out with unusual haste and depicted aggressive support for gays and lesbians.

Santa Cruz nonetheless still had no gay rights legislation, perhaps because the above policies served to protect gay and lesbian interests adequately. In 1991, California Governor Pete Wilson, who had promised to sign a statewide employment antidiscrimination law inclusive of sexual orientation, surprisingly vetoed such legislation. The Governor's veto triggered angry protests and riots around the state by gays who felt betrayed. In response to the veto, lesbians and gay men in Santa Cruz mobilized specifically to gain passage of a local antidiscrimination measure. Thus, the Governor's action proved to be a form of *unintentional insti-*

gation, providing the spark that was necessary to motivate gays to push for gay rights legislation.

Lesbian and gay activists worked to secure broad-based support, developed coalitions, and lobbied the city council for a local ordinance. The Human Rights Commission formally recommended antidiscrimination legislation to the council, presenting ample evidence of antigay harassment and ill-treatment. The inclusion of sexual orientation in the legislation received support from most sectors of the community, including many business leaders. However, "physical appearance" was also a proposed category for protection from discrimination, and this generated extensive controversy and discussion about which specific characteristics were to be covered. The council appointed a task force to rewrite the proposed ordinance to clarify this issue. The revised measure faced opposition from some fundamentalist church groups that regarded homosexuality as immoral activity and unworthy of legal protection. City officials, however, were supportive of the revised ordinance and, in a *responsive* mode, the council approved it by a 5–2 vote in 1992. Coverage of sexual orientation had support from all council members, although two councilmen objected to the physical appearance component of the bill (Starr and Brookie, 1992).

Thus, Santa Cruz, known as a lesbian mecca, was influenced greatly by the gay movement in San Francisco. Lesbians and gay men were organized politically by the late 1970s and helped to forge a progressive city government, including the election of a gay mayor. In a role characterized as hyperactive responsiveness, city officials began to take aggressive action in support of lesbian and gay demands. Mayor Laird mobilized gay and other community support on behalf of these issues; at other times, he personally promoted policies to benefit homosexuals. With a pure reformed local government, Santa Cruz offered little countervailing representation and relative homogeneity. As a result, most city officials were co-opted by progressive forces led by lesbians and gay men. In this setting, the adoption of gay rights legislation in the early 1990s was the capstone to more than a decade of local government initiatives guaranteeing protection and assistance to gays.

Iowa City

The quintessential college town, Iowa City is dominated by the University of Iowa with its twenty-seven thousand students. As a result, the city's populace is relatively young, well-educated, and liberal. In a state controlled by Republicans, Iowa City is one of the few places where Democratic candidates can consistently claim victory (Button et al., 1997:28–32). For lesbian and gay men, the city is considered a safe haven and enjoys the reputation of being a "gay center of the Midwest" (Miller, 1988).

Homophobia and discrimination against gays, however, have not been uncommon in the community. Yet the prevailing atmosphere of tolerance, especially within the university, enabled gays and lesbians to begin to organize relatively early. Motivated by the Stonewall riot, gays and other student activists established the Gay Liberation Front in the early 1970s. Centered at the university, this organization promoted issues of concern to gays. One of the first and foremost issues was the need for local antidiscrimination legislation that would help to protect homosexuals (Iowa City lesbian activist, interview by author, 9 June 1994).

By the mid-1970s, gay students and others had successfully lobbied the city's Human Relations Commission to begin discussions of gay rights legislation. After two years of deliberation, the Commission recommended such legislation to the city council. Iowa City's reformed local government was generally responsive to the proposal. In a public hearing, a number of persons including several ministers testified in support of legal protection for gays. Despite a lack of organized opposition, several council members and others in the community voiced concern over what was perceived as a controversial issue. One council member expressed fear that such legislation might force employers to hire gays and lesbians. A few opponents, especially several clergymen, maintained that gay rights legislation would have the effect of advocating homosexuality and encouraging promiscuous sex.

Although most city officials favored the proposed legislation, they were also sensitive to the concerns of landlords and rental property owners whose objections were voiced most strongly. These influential business interests argued that gay rights would result in costly liability suits and force them to condone immoral sexual activity. With local elections approaching, council members decided to delete housing from the antidiscrimination bill. Having dropped the most controversial provision, the council, in a style best characterized as *responsive,* voted 4–3 to adopt the gay rights law in the spring of 1977. Iowa City thus joined a handful of other university communities and several large cities as the first locales to formally pass legislation protecting lesbians and gay men.

A few years later, city officials added housing to the coverage of the original gay rights ordinance. The extension to housing was relatively free of controversy because the original legislation had proven to be workable, with relatively few formal complaints. By this time, the university had included sexual orientation in its own nondiscrimination policy in response to an antigay incident on campus. Lesbian and gay students were increasingly well-organized and, in addition to promoting university policies, programs, and classes to meet the needs of gays, they continued to be active in city politics.

By the early 1990s, gays had become an influential part of the liberal coalition that dominated city hall, and the gay and lesbian vote was perceived as crucial to the success of progressive candidates for local office. In what might be described as a high level of responsiveness to gay demands, city officials in 1994 gave consensus approval to domestic partner health benefits for municipal employees. Just a year later, the city council voted unanimously to amend the local human rights law to include transgendered persons, and added a half-time staff person to help investigate issues of discrimination (Iowa City public official, tele-phone interview by author, 10 September 1996). A few city officials even appeared in the annual Gay Pride Parade and at other gay events, and several openly les-bian and gay candidates have felt free to compete (though unsuccessfully) for public office.

In sum, because of the influence of a liberal university culture, Iowa City has been in the vanguard of the movement for gay rights. Progressive and gay stu-dents of the University of Iowa, moved by the politics of protest of the 1960s, organized early on to fashion political issues both at the university and in the community. City officials proved to be hesitant, but generally responsive, to the initial demands for gay rights legislation. While removing the most controversial provision (housing) in the first proposed ordinance in the mid-1970s, the city council proceeded to approve the measure, and then in incremental form, added housing a few years later. Politically active gays and other university students, faculty, and staff continued to exert a significant influence on local government. By the 1990s, Iowa City's reformed government had been virtually co-opted by these political forces, and acting in a highly responsive mode, approved a host of policies benefiting the gay community. As summarized by one city official, "The university makes the city more diverse and creates an atmosphere of tolerance and understanding that would not normally be here" (Iowa City city official, in-terview by author, 7 June 1994).

CONCLUSION

The culture wars waged locally over gay and lesbian rights have challenged some of the assumptions of institutionalists. In our aggregate analysis of the adoption of antidiscrimination legislation, we have found that the structure of local gov-ernments had no direct causal influence. Yet the nature of local elections did, in some cities, affect gay electoral power, which in turn influenced the modes of local government actions. For example, district elections in Raleigh and Philadelphia enabled geographically concentrated gays to translate their numbers into politi-cal power. On the other hand, Cincinnati's at-large council elections served to minimize gay balloting power and to benefit the opposition. In Santa Cruz and Iowa City, where gay and lesbian political power was most pervasive, the nature of the local election systems mattered little. Nonetheless, reformed structures in general in these cities helped to reduce the influence of opposition (now minor-ity) forces, thereby enhancing the ability of gays to control the political agenda and even co-opt local officials.

In terms of the roles that local officials assume in the controversies surrounding gay demands, our findings indicated that such roles may vary a great deal over time and from one city to another (see Table 5.2). Political culture in particular affects the ways in which local governments respond to issues of lesbian and gay

Table 5.2. Local Government Responses in Conflicts over Gay Rights

	Responses over Time
Raleigh, N.C.	Unintentional instigation → evasion → entrepreneurial instigation → evasion → repression
Cincinnati, Ohio	Repression → unintentional instigation → responsiveness → repression
Philadelphia, Pa.	Evasion → responsiveness → evasion
Santa Cruz, Calif.	Hyperactive responsiveness → unintentional instigation → responsiveness
Iowa City, Iowa	Responsiveness → responsiveness (high level)

Note: Government role during time period in which gay rights legislation was adopted was "responsiveness" in all cities but Raleigh, where it was "entrepreneurial instigation."

rights. Cities with predominantly conservative cultures, like Raleigh and Cincinnati (and to a lesser degree Philadelphia), responded primarily in evasive and repressive modes. In these cities, traditional religious and other opposition groups proved relatively well-organized and dominated local government; in contrast, attempts by gays to mobilize politically were often thwarted. Furthermore, the adoption of legislation protective of homosexuals in Raleigh and Cincinnati required either unintentional or entrepreneurial instigation for challengers to overcome city government resistance. In cities dominated by a more liberal political culture, as in Santa Cruz and Iowa City, gays organized relatively easily and early while political opposition was minimal. In this environment, city officials proved consistently responsive, at times even hyperactive or highly responsive in their reactions, to gay demands.[3] As a result, city governments in these two settings adopted a number of policies or programs, such as domestic partner benefits, that went well beyond basic demands for civil rights laws.

More generally, the passage of gay rights legislation was affected by several social movement forces that went beyond the specific actions of public officials. According to the analysis of our theoretical models, laws or policies protective of gays and lesbians depend to some extent on community size and social diversity, a favorable political environment, the organizational and political resources of the gay community, and the influence of traditional religious and other opposition groups. Unlike political culture, many of these forces are prone to change depending on local circumstances and political actors. Yet a full understanding of the struggle over gay rights requires attention to its character as a social movement as well as its more clearly political dimensions.

NOTES

1. We use the terms *gay* or *lesbians and gay men* (or vice versa) inclusively to refer to male homosexuals, female homosexuals, and bisexuals without intending disrespect to any particular group.

2. Detailed information about these five case-study communities, and about the lesbian and gay political movements in each, can be found in Button et al. (1997), especially chapter two. A complete listing of references for each city is also found in the book.

3. In each of the cities except Cincinnati, the local human rights (or relations) board, the quasi-governmental body of citizens (or professional administrators in large cities) appointed by the mayor or council, played an important role in promoting gay rights. These independent boards, typically created during the black civil rights era of the 1950s and 1960s to monitor human rights issues, gathered evidence of antigay discrimination, held public hearings on proposed ordinances, and often lobbied city officials.

REFERENCES

Allen, C. 1995. "Strange Bedfellows: Cincinnati's Anti-Gay Rights Initiative 'Issue 3' as a Test for a Christian Right and African-American Political Alliance?" Paper delivered at the Annual Meeting of the American Political Science Association, Chicago, 31 August–3 September.

Bailey, R. W. 1998. *Gay Politics, Urban Politics: Identity and Economics in the Urban Setting.* New York: Columbia University Press.

Button, J. W., B. A. Rienzo, and K. D. Wald. 1997. *Private Lives, Public Conflicts: Battles Over Gay Rights in American Communities.* Washington, D.C.: Congressional Quarterly Press.

Costain, A. H. 1992. *Inviting Women's Rebellion: A Political Process Interpretation of the Women's Movement.* Baltimore: Johns Hopkins University Press.

Gaffney, P. 1988. "City Passes Law Protecting Gays." *Raleigh (N.C.) News and Observer,* 6 January, n.p.

Harding, R. 1988. "Gays Win Protection in Raleigh, N.C." *Advocate,* 1 March, p. 11.

Honig, T. 1991. "Challenges to Traditional Values Constantly Test a Community." *Santa Cruz (Calif.) Sentinel,* 4 August, n.p.

Mayer, M. 1991. "Social Movement Research and Social Movement Practice: The U.S. Pattern." In D. Rucht, ed., *Research on Social Movements.* Frankfurt: Campus Verlag, pp. 47–120.

McCarthy, J. D., and M. Zald. 1973. *The Trend of Social Movements in America: Professionalism and Resource Mobilization.* Morristown, N.J.: General Learning Press.

Miller, M. 1988. "Iowa City 'Cool Place' for Gays, Lesbians." *Iowa City Press-Citizen,* 25 June, p. 1B.

Morris, A. D., and C. M. Mueller, eds. 1992. *Frontiers in Social Movement Theory.* New Haven, Conn.: Yale University Press.

Musitelli, R. 1993. "Laird Hopes to Make History." *Santa Cruz (Calif.) Sentinel,* 25 August, p. A1+.

Philadelphia Lesbian and Gay Task Force. 1992. "The Celebration of a Decade, 1982–1992." Report. Philadelphia: Philadelphia Lesbian and Gay Task Force.

Rutledge, L. 1992. *The Gay Decades.* New York: Plume.

Sharp, E. B. 1997. "A Comparative Anatomy of Urban Social Conflict." *Political Research Quarterly* 50 (June): 261–80.

Skocpol, T., M. Abend-Wien, C. Howard, and S. G. Lehmann. 1993. "Women's Associations and the Enactment of Mothers' Pensions in the United States." *American Political Science Review* 87: 686–701.

Slobodzian, J. A., and F. N. Tulsky. 1992. "AIDS Fears and Homophobia Led City Police
to Abuse Protesters." *Philadelphia Inquirer,* 19 March, p. A1.

Starr, B., and S. Brookie. 1992. "Queers Victorious: Anti-Bias Bill Passes, 5–2." *Lavender Reader,* Summer: 19.

Stonewall Cincinnati. 1992. *Stonewall Cincinnati: Ten Years of Challenge, Change, and
Championing Our Rights.* Report. Cincinnati, Ohio: Stonewall Cincinnati.

Tarrow, S. 1991. "Comparing Social Movement Participation in Western Europe and the
United States: Problems, Uses, and a Proposal for Synthesis." In D. Rucht, ed., *Research on Social Movements.* Frankfurt: Campus Verlag, pp. 392–420.

———. 1992. "Mentalities, Political Cultures and Collective Action Frames: Constructing Meanings through Action." In A. D. Morris and C. M. Mueller, eds., *Frontiers in
Social Movement Theory.* New Haven, Conn.: Yale University Press, pp. 174–202.

Wald, K. D., J. W. Button and B. A. Rienzo. 1996. "The Politics of Gay Rights in American Communities: Explaining Anti-Discrimination Ordinances and Policies." *American Journal of Political Science* 40: 1152–78.

Welch, S. 1990. "The Impact of At-Large Elections on the Representation of Blacks and
Hispanics." *Journal of Politics* 52: 1050–76.

6
Conflicts over Sexual Orientation Issues in the Schools

Barbara A. Rienzo, James W. Button, and Kenneth D. Wald

As purveyors of social norms and values of the dominant culture, public schools tend to deny the existence of homosexuality and to reinforce society's heterosexism and antihomosexual bias. Educators and health professionals cite such prejudicial practices as omission of homosexuality in formal curricula, tolerance of antigay jokes and harassment, and the sponsoring of social events that only affirm heterosexual couples as evidence of how schools create a hostile and harmful environment for gay students.[1] They contend that institutionalized change is not only necessary for gay and lesbian students, but would be beneficial for all youth, their parents, school staff, and, ultimately, society in general (Telljohann and Price, 1993; Unks, 1993–94).

As the largest and perhaps most important institution of local government, schools seem a likely setting for a culture war over the quest to change policy and programs to those more inclusive of gay and lesbian interests. As legal and education scholar Karen Harbeck has observed, the controversy over combining homosexuality and education evokes "one of the most publicly volatile and personally threatening debates in our national history (because of the threat to) the traditional cultural ideology set forth in the schools" (Harbeck, 1992). In order to study these culture wars, we first investigated differences in policy and program offerings related to sexual orientation in school districts located in jurisdictions with local antidiscrimination legislation (see chap. 5) to a control group of districts not embedded in gay-friendly political environments. Second, we conducted case studies of representative school districts to explore the ways in which school officials responded to demands for programs addressing such issues.

* * *

SURVEY OF SCHOOLS

This exploration of public schools was conducted within our larger study of U.S. cities and counties with and without legislative protection on the basis of sexual orientation. The methodology was virtually identical to that described in chapter five. Thus, we surveyed school district officials—usually health education/services coordinators or curriculum coordinators—in the 126 communities with such legislation as well as in the 125 without. In cities and counties with more than one school district, we randomly selected up to five districts. We received responses from school districts within 81 percent of communities with gay rights legislation and from districts within 94 percent of locales without such legislation (Rienzo et al., 1996).

Not surprisingly, the majority of U.S. schools do not offer the policies and programs addressing sexual orientation that are supported by health professionals and advocates. However, our survey documented that school districts in communities with gay rights legislation provided significantly more programs and policies inclusive of sexual orientation than did those without such legislation. For example, instruction about sexual orientation was reported by half of the districts within ordinance communities, whereas only about one-third of districts without legislation offered such education. Similarly, policies that prohibit antigay language and behavior were found within almost a quarter of districts in communities with legislation versus 14 percent in those without. The same pattern emerged for other recommended programs, such as the provision of support groups, counseling, and in-service training for staff.

This study pointed to the significance of political factors as most crucial to successful efforts for such changes in schools. Variables associated with urbanism/social diversity theory—such as population size, level of education, and percentage of nonfamily households—contributed strongly to the institution of programs related to sexual orientation in schools. In addition, the political variables associated with resource mobilization theory, including number of gay public officials, active gay rights supporters in school board elections, and the extensiveness of the district's state gay rights law, proved significant to district efforts on behalf of sexual orientation (Rienzo et al., 1996). These findings suggested that certain political variables in the larger community influenced school outcomes. Unfortunately, we did not include questions related to the governmental structural characteristics of the school districts in this national survey, nor are such data published elsewhere. Thus, we are not able to explain how political characteristics of the school boards and school superintendent's offices may have influenced these findings.

The next phase of our research, intensive case studies of five communities, documented the underlying processes involved in such changes. Studying these individual school district efforts closely allowed us to understand more thoroughly the process underlying the events surrounding requests for modifications in school practices. Thus, we could better explain the different reactions of school officials to the range of policy and programs supportive of lesbian and gay youths requested by proponents for change in these communities.

CASE STUDIES OF SCHOOL DISTRICTS

We interviewed persons considered knowledgeable about their school district's experience with sexual orientation issues within five representative cities (Cincinnati, Ohio; Iowa City, Iowa; Philadelphia, Pa.; Raleigh, N.C.; and Santa Cruz, Calif.). Each of these communities was representative of a cluster of sites within the United States that passed gay rights ordinances (see chap. 5). Iowa City is a university community, among the first cluster of cities to pass such legislation. Philadelphia is representative of larger, urban cities, whereas Santa Cruz exemplifies the coastal and suburban communities with gay rights ordinances. Raleigh was chosen as a prototypical southern or border South city with legal protection for gays. Finally, Cincinnati is a city that passed and then rescinded its ordinance, a site where the forces resisting such efforts were manifest. We interviewed school board members, school administrators, teachers, counselors, parents, community agency representatives, elected officials, and representatives of organizations opposed to school efforts to address sexual orientation in each locale. We also consulted public documents and newspapers to augment these interview data. Each of the communities had faced, to some degree, pressure to institute changes addressing sexual orientation in their schools, and this pressure had resulted in a range of responses and outcomes (Button et al., 1997).[2] For each community, the response patterns of school district officials to sexual orientation issues will be described and analyzed. These reactions are ordered from school districts found to be most resistant to those most responsive.

Resistant Reactions to Gay Rights Initiatives

REPRESSION. Not surprisingly, Raleigh, exhibiting most characteristics of the prototypical South, offered *no* policies and programs inclusive of sexual orientation. In fact, as a long-term school board member from Raleigh explained it, "Sexual orientation has never been discussed by the school board in all the years I have been on it—by proponents or opponents. No letters, no phone calls. Neither has the issue been brought up at the portion of school board meetings devoted to public (input). . . . The issue has never been brought to the school board" (interview by author, 20 May 1994).

However, gay and lesbian issues had been raised in a committee concerned with school health issues, the School Health Advisory Council (SHAC). Appointed by the school board, SHAC is composed of a balance of school personnel and individuals reflecting the community more generally. In 1994, school staff brought the issue of sexual orientation to SHAC because classroom teachers struggled with whether and how the topic should be taught. At the time, some SHAC members perceived that this issue would not become part of its agenda, reasoning that the timing was not right, even though SHAC probably would decide in the future that this was a topic that should be addressed. Subsequently, SHAC did, in fact, table the concerns raised about sexual orientation issues (Button et al., 1997:148–52). As a SHAC member explained, "Raleigh is in the Bible-belt and the South, (and the community is) opposed to sex education in general. Although the city is liberal to some degree and doesn't support (Senator Jesse) Helms, right-wing fundamentalists are powerful here—they squelch things before they even come up" (interview by author, 25 May 1994).

This type of repressive response has also been termed the "non-decisionmaking hypothesis" by scholars of urban politics (Bachrach and Baratz, 1970:43–46). School leaders use their power to determine the agenda and keep certain issues off the table. Several other examples of this repressive reaction were revealed. For instance, a presentation about sexual orientation issues pertinent to youth was delivered to school counselors in the latter 1980s. However, subsequent initiatives to provide similar training for school personnel were discouraged by school administrators. Likewise, OUTRIGHT, nearby Durham's community agency for gay and lesbian youth, has attempted on several occasions to place advertisements about their services in Raleigh high school newspapers. These ads have been consistently rejected by school administrators (Raleigh school official, telephone interview by author, May 1994).

The repressive response is further illustrated in the reaction of Raleigh administrators and school board members to an incident that occurred in 1994. As in many communities, students are increasingly mobilized in reaction to gay/lesbian issues (Button et al., 1997:163–64). Six Enloe High School students in Raleigh, who became known as the "Enloe 6," produced a pamphlet response to a poster with homophobic content displayed in school by other students. The school principal's reaction was to suspend both sets of students. Hundreds of students signed petitions in support of the Enloe 6. The six students protested their punishment to the school board, which changed the suspension to detention (Silberman, 1994). Although the homosexual nature of the incident was discussed in private, the school board's public response—and the sole issue reported by the media—was centered on free speech. "No one ever dealt with the underlying issue of tolerance," according to one high-level school official (telephone interview by author, May 1994).

Repression is typically in response to a "perceived threat (that) occurs when authorities fear loss of control because of the disruption . . . potential represented by status quo challengers"(Sharp, 1997:275). For school officials, issues that they perceive cause turmoil elicit this fear. When asked to estimate the level of controversy sexual orientation issues would induce, Raleigh interviewees averaged 9 on a scale of 1 (low) to 10 (high). According to a Raleigh school official, "Controversy causes administration to go into denial—to pretend sexual orientation doesn't exist—and hope that nothing forces us to handle the issue. . . . I believe there are teachers who will talk with students one-on-one, but they don't feel like they can say anything about sexual orientation aloud in the classroom—they are out on a limb" (telephone interview by author, May 1994).

Teachers, administrators, and elected school board members fear that their jobs would be threatened if they appeared to support homosexuality. Most Raleigh school district administrators who were asked to participate in this study would not consent to be interviewed. This was the only study city in which school administrators considered knowledgeable about sexual orientation issues refused to participate. As was the case in every school district we studied, many participants referred to the well-publicized ousting of New York City's School Chancellor Joseph Fernandez over this issue in 1992. Although New York's "Children of the Rainbow" multicultural education curriculum, which the Chancellor supported, actually contained only a very minor segment devoted to sexual orientation issues (and that was confined to the teachers' guide), it aroused vehement public protest and national media coverage (Myers, 1992).

The structure of school government alone does not sufficiently explain these responses. Raleigh's school district superintendent, like most, is appointed by its elected school board. The nonpartisan school board elections are by district. Although district elections tend to promote minority representation on the board, this seemed to have little influence on school officials' reactions in this case because no advocates for gay issues had been elected to the school board.

Raleigh's political culture, on the other hand, does seem to predict school officials' repressive response to demands for nontraditional school programs. As stated earlier, the politically conservative nature of the South is apparent in Raleigh. The city's antidiscrimination ordinance is very limited in scope and poorly enforced. The school board response to the "Enloe 6" incident—*repression*—was described as a reaction to the "tenor of the community" by a local public official (interview by author, 23 May 1994). Conservatives at the state level, moreover, have increased pressures on North Carolina schools to maintain traditional norms. In 1995, the state legislature passed the "Teaching Abstinence until Marriage Bill," which, among other things, mandates that schools discuss marriage as a heterosexual union only and that they teach that homosexuality is illegal under North Carolina's sodomy law. No current school board members publicly support programs that address sexual orientation (Button et al., 1997: 38–42, 212). Not surprisingly, given this political climate, there have been no efforts to establish school-based programs to meet the needs of gay and lesbian students.

RESPONSIVE, THEN REPRESSIVE. A second type of reaction by school officials to appeals to address sexual orientation issues was a responsiveness when first approached, but a subsequent stance marked by repression. This twofold outcome was evident in two communities, Cincinnati and Philadelphia.

In Cincinnati, a proposal to add sexual orientation to its antidiscrimination statement for employees was brought to the school board by one of its members in 1991. The proposal was presented at a time the board was examining other civil rights and affirmative action policies, such as whether to terminate the district's investments in South Africa. The antidiscrimination proposal passed relatively easily and without much discussion. The lack of expressed opposition by any board members was attributed to a reluctance to bring public attention to the possibility that "gay teachers existed" in Cincinnati's schools (school official, interview by author, November 1994). Thus, this passage qualifies as a *responsive* school board reaction in that it was brought to the board in the usual route and passed after some—albeit subdued—discussion.

Another example of responsiveness in Cincinnati's school district was the establishment of a network of gay/lesbian teachers, originally called GLUE (Gays and Lesbians United in Education). This network has quietly but consistently worked to foster gay-friendly change in the schools. For instance, GLUE (now officially GLSTN—Gay-Lesbian-Straight Teacher Network, a chapter of that national organization) regularly questions school board candidates during their campaigns to determine their stance on gay/lesbian issues. Some members have marched behind their organization's banner in Cincinnati's annual Gay Pride Parade. In the early 1990s, GLUE members participated in a meeting of school counselors to discuss youth sexual orientation issues and worked to obtain the teachers' union support for gay-friendly policies such as domestic partner benefits. The union did secure an extension in the district's bereavement leave policy to include "permanent members of the household" in addition to immediate family members. Passage of this benefit, however, was purposely "buried in other language" so as to not draw attention to gays, and was passed quietly by the school board. Although the union maintained support for domestic partner benefits for gays, their ability to negotiate successfully for this issue was considered very unlikely after the citywide referendum that repudiated gay rights in 1993 (Button et al., 1997:139, 151; interviews by author, Cincinnati school teacher, school official, November 1994).

Thus, certain forces in Cincinnati have encouraged responsive reactions by school officials to demands for change on behalf of gay/lesbian teachers and students. Some school board candidates have even sought the endorsement of the city's major gay-lesbian organization, Stonewall Cincinnati. However, two prominent events squelched support for gay rights in schools. The first incident was the aforementioned furor that occurred in New York City over the inclusion of sexual orientation within its proposed multicultural education program. As one Cincinnati school board member reflected, "sexual orientation is not an issue raised in the schools here . . . like in New York. Whatever level of controversy happens in the community, multiply it in the schools—even close-by incidents raise all kinds of problems" (interview by author, November 1994). Secondly, the successful referendum in 1993 to revoke the sexual orientation segment from the city's antidiscrimination ordinance was reported to have a "chilling effect" on the school district's approach to all issues that involved sexual content. In fact, officials have not had to respond to demands—the issues have not been raised. According to a school board member, "the subject has never arisen in the context of the schools since 1992" (interview by author, November 1994). Consequently, policies and programs that address sexual orientation on behalf of students have not been implemented in Cincinnati's schools (Button et al., 1997:148–52).

The school district government structure for Cincinnati includes a superintendent appointed by its school board whose seven nonpartisan members are elected by district. District elections probably fostered the election of a school board member willing to bring the antidiscrimination policy on behalf of gay and lesbian employees to the school board. However, its passage did not mobilize the community to support gay rights issues; in fact, the policy change was, and remains, unpublicized. During the 1993 campaign to rescind the gay rights portion of the city's human rights ordinance, school personnel and gay rights advocates were relieved that the school antidiscrimination policy never emerged in public discussion (gay activist, interview by author, 4 November 1994).

The school board's repressive response to gay rights when the issue became public seems to reflect the community's very conservative political culture more than its governmental structure. The school board member who had sponsored the gay rights antidiscrimination policy subsequently lost a bid for a city council seat in the 1993 elections. That loss was attributed to an "unfair" attack by the right wing on her support of sex education (Wilkinson 1995; school teacher, school administrator, interviews by author, 2 November 1994). Another school board member described threats from opponents who said they would withdraw their children from the schools and "beat us at the ballot box." It was believed that conservatives would attempt to defeat those school board members who appeared to support sexual orientation issues in the following school board election (school board member, interview by author, November 1994; Wilkinson, 1994).

A school official summarized the power of the conservative forces controlling Cincinnati subsequent to the 1993 elections as follows: "In November 1993, the same people backing the repeal of the ordinance were against a school tax levy—both went down to defeat. That election campaign and its results served to reinforce the perceived power of those conservatives—more power than they should have, given their numbers" (interview by author, November 1994).

These conservative forces in the electorate were credited with evoking such fear in school officials that it resulted in their suppressing a host of initiatives—including and going beyond those involving sexual orientation—in the schools. For example, although supportive prior to the election, the teachers' union considered the prospect of negotiating for domestic partner benefits on behalf of people with "non-traditional lifestyles" untenable "because people will kill school levies" in response. In addition, the school district was perceived to have become "more cautious" in all potentially controversial areas, such as sex education (teachers union official, interview by author, November 1994). GLSTN members who presented information on sexual orientation issues in a meeting with school counselors were told that Cincinnati did not have gay or lesbian students. Administrators and teachers described their fears of losing their jobs should they be perceived as gay or lesbian or as an advocate on behalf of gay/lesbian issues. Furthermore, school personnel who wanted to acknowledge their homosexual orientation were afraid of "outing" their partners in such a conservative city. "Cincinnati is not welcoming (to gays and lesbians), and the school policy has never been tested. We're not sure how effective it is," stated one school official (interview by author, November 1994). As a result, the vast majority of gay teachers (and other staff) are not open about their sexual identity despite the legal protection afforded them by their district's antidiscrimination policy (Button et al., 1997:148–52).

Philadelphia provides a similar twofold response on the part of its school district's decision makers to gay rights initiatives, with very similar results. Its school board was approached in the early 1990s by a local organization, the city's Lesbian and Gay Task Force, to consider inclusion of sexual orientation policies and programming in the schools. The board's reaction was, at first, responsive in nature. The proposals—first for a policy on sex/gender equity in which sexual orientation was explicitly included, next for a multicultural education policy that included sexual orientation—were handled in the same manner as all initiatives. Both went to school-community representative committees for consideration, and the policies came back from those committees as proposals to the board. The school board passed both. Implementation of these policies, however, has been a different story, one that illustrates the subsequent repressive stance by school officials.

The more potentially transforming of the two policies, the Multiethnic-Multiracial-Gender Equity Policy (Policy 102), serves as a good illustration of this twofold response. This policy was intended to promote "an educational process designed to foster knowledge about and respect for those of all races, ethnic groups, social classes, genders, religions, disabilities, and sexual orientations." Its purpose was to "ensure equity and justice for all members of the school community, and society as a whole, and to give those members the skills and knowledge they need to understand and overcome individual biases and institutional barriers to full equality" (School District of Philadelphia Board of Education, 1994:1). The city's Task Force had argued forcefully for this policy's adoption by presenting data from its comprehensive survey of antigay discrimination and violence, including information concerning school experiences. Between one-quarter and one-third of women, and almost three of five men, reported experiencing harassment in school, mostly by peers. About 15 percent of gay men claimed that they had been abused by teachers or school officials. Comparisons with previous studies of Philadelphia indicated these problems were increasing. The Task Force presented other local data showing that teenage and young adult males accounted for the majority of perpetrators of antigay and antilesbian violence. Thus, they were able to contend convincingly to the school board that Philadelphia's schools were inadequately protecting young gays and lesbians, not providing accurate, comprehensive education about sexual orientation, and neglecting to condemn violence (Gross and Aurand, 1992). Policy 102 was adopted by the board of education in January 1994.

After passage of the policy, the Task Force continued to press the school board to carry out the policy's educational mission, including its stipulations with respect to sexual orientation. Supporters, including gay and lesbian youth, provided testimony at the board's public hearings regarding the policy's implementation. In 1994, however, the board of education appointed a new superintendent who presented a school reform plan that did not incorporate sexual orientation issues or other specific components from Policy 102. Seventy members of the policy planning committee signed a petition asking that the superintendent change his initiative to include the policy recommendations. In a *repressive* response, the superintendent did not make these requested changes or appoint any policy planning members to his committees to design school reform. In essence, he has "virtually disbanded" the policy planning committee (Gross and Aurand, 1996:24–25; Philadelphia Lesbian and Gay Task Force, 1995:1–4; Philadelphia gay activist, telephone interview by author, 28 May 1996).

The Philadelphia Lesbian and Gay Task Force, which had initiated the city's antidiscrimination ordinance, also spearheaded the effort to support the inclusion of sexual orientation in school programs. Passage of two school policies that included sexual orientation was due to the significant effort by the task force to develop a broad-based coalition of individuals and organizations supportive of gay rights. Individuals representing a range of community organizations testified in support at the school board public hearings. On the other hand, as in other cities we studied, Philadelphia's school board members expressed reluctance to support initiatives, such as Policy 102, that provoked serious controversy. Virtually all the contentious discussion at the public hearings on that policy and its implementation focused on the inclusion of sexual orientation. Moreover, the two board members who were supportive of sexual orientation and Policy 102 ended their terms shortly after its passage and no longer serve on the board of education. One of these members was not appointed president "on his turn" (a position that typically was given in succession) and was not reappointed by the city council to the board. Although some board members are perceived as supportive, none are considered as powerful as those who served previously, and none are advocating for gay rights initiatives. Finally, the school superintendent hired by the school board has demonstrated no support for gay rights initiatives and, in fact, has repressed such demands from gay rights advocates (Button et al., 1997:148–52, 163–64, 168; Philadelphia gay activist, telephone interview by author, 28 May 1996).

Certainly it may be argued that the outcome in Philadelphia incorporates more substantive changes than those found in Cincinnati, although school officials' reactions were somewhat similar. At the time they were responsive, Philadelphia's board of education was much more public in its handling of the issues. The outcome—passage of two policies that include sexual orientation explicitly—was conceived as advantageous in affecting further desired changes. Establishing a policy is often deemed to be a required initial step toward implementing institutionalized change. Nevertheless, the students and staff in Philadelphia's schools do not currently have official sanction to implement the vast majority of sexual orientation programs that were officially adopted as part of those policies.

As is commonly the case, Philadelphia's school superintendent is appointed. Its board of education, however, is also appointed—by the city council. Council members are elected in partisan races by district. This results in a very nonreformed system, one that is more subject to political influence. District and partisan local elections enabled gays to influence council membership and therefore the appointments to the school board. But such an election system also served to enhance the political power of the many white ethnics, African Americans, and Hispanics, who dominated the city demographically. Other than African Americans, these groups were typically opposed to gay initiatives (Button et al., 1997:32–38). Yet the reactions of school officials to lesbian and gay demands are best explained by the political culture of Philadelphia. Founded by those seeking political and religious freedom, the city has enjoyed a reputation for tolerance and encouraging diversity. At the same time, large numbers of ethnic whites and suburban Republicans have provided the community with a more conservative culture of "blue laws, mediocity and industry" (Tucker, 1982). This clash of cultures probably provides the best understanding of the shift in the reactions of school officials to gay initiatives.

Supportive Reactions to Sexual Orientation Issues

ENTREPRENEURIAL INSTIGATION AND RESPONSIVENESS. Iowa City provides a look at how a school district responds in an way that instigates change. The district was first asked to address sexual orientation issues in the early 1990s by one of its long-term high school teachers. This teacher credited his motivation to two almost-concurrent events, one national and one local: the 1992 Republican national convention in which gays were publicly derided, and an incident in his school in which the principal made an antigay remark in a meeting with parents. In the process, the teacher decided to "out" himself to his coworkers, the first among school personnel to do so in the district (Button et al., 1997:162).

The method this teacher employed to bring sexual orientation issues to school officials reflects the relatively tolerant nature of the district and the city. Initially, the teacher called a meeting (off-campus, with assured anonymity) of gay and lesbian teachers and students. Together they discussed the program changes they wished to see in their schools and drew up a list of concerns. This list was taken by the teacher to the coordinator of the school district's Equity Committee. Iowa state law mandates that each school district maintain an equity committee to manage multicultural concerns, such as providing in-service education and suggesting and monitoring policy. However, this school district's equity committee co-ordinator, unlike those in the vast majority in the state, agreed to include sexual orientation in the domain of the committee's responsibilities. Thus, the teacher and the group had an official place to take their concerns, a committee with the responsibility to correct unfair, prejudicial practices. As such, the equity commit-tee could—and chose to—undertake policy initiatives that addressed the identi-fied concerns of gays and frame them in rights-oriented terms. Moreover, because of its title and designated purpose, this committee *had to* frame these concerns in terms of "rights" and justice in order to justify its intervention. Such actions qualify the official reaction as *entrepreneurial instigation* (Sharp, 1996:752). Within the first year, the school district's equity statement (which is included on all docu-ments produced by the district) and its antiharassment policy were changed to include sexual orientation explicitly. In addition, the equity committee coordina-tor developed and delivered in-service training for teachers and administrators on sexual orientation (Button et al., 1997:152–67).

Other changes that have taken place within the district since may be classi-fied as *responsive*. As one school official stated, the gay rights movement does not elicit a "big outcry like the civil rights movement. Whispering changes that are gradual result in a positive impact" (interview by author, 1996). Thus, changes have evolved in an organized manner, developed through using the school system's standard strategies in a step-by-step process. For example, one high school prin-cipal supported the formation of SAID, Students Against Intolerance and Dis-crimination, initiated by students in response to an antigay incident. This school organization, as is the case for all official school clubs, was assigned a paid fac-ulty sponsor. SAID subsequently enlarged its scope to include discrimination issues of all kinds. The equity committee coordinator has conducted training workshops about sexual orientation issues for faculty and administrators during each ensuing academic year. Finally, the same teacher who brought the list of concerns to the equity committee also effectively lobbied for domestic partner benefits. In 1994, the teacher union representative negotiated successfully with the board to add domestic partner benefits for same-sex partners. Domestic part-ner benefits, rarely provided by school districts or other public agencies, are among the most coveted desires of many gays and lesbians (Button et al., 1997:152–67).

These policy and program changes, which have come about relatively gradu-ally, are generally viewed as acceptable by the community. As a school official stated, "We did receive some criticism for (these) initiatives, which we ignored and they went away" (telephone interview by author, 21 May 1996). Although instruction about sexual orientation is not yet included in the school district cur-riculum guidelines (for inclusion in health or in other subjects), the equity com-mittee continues to develop methods to address the identified concerns from the original list. These needs include supplying materials for the media centers and training counselors to handle sexual orientation issues with students and their parents.

Iowa City's school government consists of a seven-member, nonpartisan school board that is elected at-large and appoints the school district superintendent. The school officials' level of support and acquiescence to requests for change would not be best explained by a reformed government structure, although such a structure does help to reduce countervailing representation. This responsiveness to change—even school officials' initial instigation—is more understandable when the political culture of the community is considered.

Iowa City is representative of "university communities" nationally, and therefore exhibits a more progressive political atmosphere than the norm. The University of Iowa can readily be seen as a major influence on the nature of both the city and school district's reactions to gay rights initiatives. University-sponsored workshops on sexual orientation issues served to educate its citizens both directly through participants' attendance and indirectly through media coverage of such events. The university's inclusion of sexual orientation in its antidiscrimination policy and in its domestic partner benefits plan served as models for school district officials to develop almost identical documents for school personnel.

Iowa City has earned the reputation of being strongly committed to equality, an atmosphere in which gays and lesbians live comfortably and, in large part, openly. Gay and lesbian parents and teachers are increasingly revealing their sexual identity to school district personnel, an action that further presses the schools to address these issues. Both the school board and the superintendent were perceived as very supportive of equity and conceived of gay rights as inherently issues of justice and fairness. Thus, even the highly publicized defeat of an openly gay school board incumbent in nearby Des Moines in 1995 did not seem to affect the continuing efforts in this community to provide services and policies that address sexual orientation issues in the schools. As one school official asserted, "That election (Des Moines) reflects the same efforts going on all over the country with opponents' efforts. It did not have any effect on this school district" (telephone interview by author, 21 May 1996).

RESPONSIVENESS AND ENTREPRENEURIAL INSTIGATION. School officials in Santa Cruz reacted in a *responsive* way from the outset to suggestions for school programs that addressed sexual orientation issues. Initial groundwork for change was attributed to a high school health teacher who, in the early 1990s, accepted the offer of a local gay and lesbian network, Triangle Speakers, to make presentations to her classes. Next, the teacher made a request to the appropriate middle-level administrator to incorporate official instruction about sexual orientation into the district's health curriculum. The school administration responded by referring the issue to a standing committee, the Substance Abuse/Student Assistance Advisory Committee. This was a logical placement because risks for substance abuse (as well as other mental and emotional health problems) among gay and lesbian students were documented to be greater than among their peers, according to a federal government report published in 1989 (Gibson, 1989:110–42).

A task force, cochaired by the health teacher, was established to address the needs of gay/lesbian students and their families. Thus, this initiative was treated by school officials in a responsive way in that they utilized appropriate committees and a structured process. Then, in the mode of *entrepreneurial instigation,* the task force coordinated a host of additional efforts to identify and address sexual orientation issues, albeit proceeding in a deliberate, careful manner. Several changes were instituted through the sponsorship of this task force, and when some objections were raised to the school board, the systematic process used by this committee was credited with saving the initiatives from compromise or elimination.

The task force began the process of instituting change by educating school administrators in a workshop designed to present information on sexual orientation. This educational effort was considered a key factor in building awareness and gaining administrative support. The task force believed strongly that securing the support of central administration was critical to its ability to proceed further in this endeavor. This perspective was confirmed when the program came under attack in the larger community. In 1990, "a few ultra-conservative parents" went to the county school board with their concern that Triangle Speakers were corrupting and recruiting their children. The editor of a locally published conservative newspaper (*The Forum*) adopted the issue and organized a "very loud, ugly" protest directed at the district's school board members in public hearings. These vociferous school board hearings motivated lesbian and gay activists and their allies to increase their involvement in supporting school district policies and programs. In fact, a group of supporters formally organized to counter the protesters and to support comprehensive sexuality education (including sexual orientation) in the schools. Triangle Speakers were increasingly motivated to participate in school programs. The Speakers were key participants in the training programs for school personnel sponsored by the task force and fought to continue their presentations for high school classes by appearing at public hearings and by speaking out through the media (Button et al., 1997:165). The Santa Cruz school board did not recant in its support of the program. Reflecting the entrepreneurial instigation response, one board member stated, "we've continued to push forward. School board members need to initiate these policies. It's important to speak out publicly on this (issue)" (interview by author, 28 June 1994).

Subsequently, Santa Cruz schools have established numerous initiatives addressing sexual orientation, several modeled after Los Angeles' nationally renowned model program, Project 10, as well as the innovative programs established in the San Francisco school district. The school board has enacted antigay harassment and equity statement policies that include sexual orientation. Training for staff (counselors, psychologists, elementary and junior high teachers) and for school teams (composed of teachers, parents, staff, and counselors) about sexual orientation issues has been conducted by the task force for all secondary schools. More so than in other cities we studied, school administrators discussed the need to educate their staff to respond sensitively to the increasing numbers of gay and lesbian parents that attended typical school meetings. District curriculum guidelines include two-day units on sexual orientation within health classes. Instruction also takes place within English and history classes, and posters on gay rights and famous gay and lesbian individuals are prominently displayed in the high schools. In July 1995, domestic partner benefits for school personnel were passed by the school board. Although antigay harassment still occurs occasionally in school, such incidents are typically reported and punished (Button et al., 1997: 166–67).

Santa Cruz's school superintendent is appointed by its nonpartisan, seven-member school board, which is elected both by district and at-large, thus making school government mostly reformed. Such a political structure may enhance the homogeneity of the school board and reduce the representation of the opposition. But reformed government is not the best predictor of the substantial inroads that have been made to incorporate these innovative, institutionalized changes. Again, this responsive reaction seems more related to factors that reflect the progressive political culture of this city.

Santa Cruz, a distant suburb of San Francisco, passed an antidiscrimination ordinance with exceptionally broad coverage. Lesbians and gay men in Santa Cruz live quite openly without much public harassment or related problems. The local newspaper editorialized on behalf of Triangle Speakers and is generally considered supportive of gay and lesbian issues. Although there has not been an openly gay candidate for the school board, several gays have been elected to the city council. There are some openly gay school administrators, teachers, and students, with increasing numbers publicly acknowledging their sexual orientation. The superintendent, in particular, is credited with creating an atmosphere in which much has been accomplished in changing the nature of the institution to include sexual orientation policy and programming. In the words of one senior school administrator, "I must commend our administration. We couldn't do it without their support—and they have been supportive from the beginning. Even a change in administration did not change this support. They are caring, fair-minded, all straight except one. They care for kids and we have, from the beginning, approached this as a kids issue—for their learning, safety, and self-esteem" (interview by author, 1994).

CONCLUSION

School districts nationally are not typically addressing sexual orientation issues through policies and programs. Our in-depth studies of five representative school districts enabled us to analyze the process by which school officials deal with advocates' demands for such programs. As summarized in Table 6.1, initially officials in four of the five districts acted in a responsive manner. This support was not always sustained, however, and such endeavors often confronted repres-

Table 6.1. Responses of School Officials to Gay Initiatives

	Responses over Time
Raleigh, N.C.	Repressive (1994+)
Cincinnati, Ohio	Responsive (early 1990s) → repressive (1992+)
Philadelphia, Pa.	Responsive (1985–1994) → repressive (1994+)
Iowa City, Iowa	Entrepreneurial instigation (1992) → responsive (1993+)
Santa Cruz, Calif.	Responsive (1990) → entrepreneurial instigation (1990+)

sive and evasive reactions to program change. Nonetheless, two school districts (Santa Cruz and Iowa City) demonstrated an official reaction that was responsive, even instigating, and significant innovative programs were instituted.

The ultimate outcome of sexual orientation initiatives in these school districts was best explained by analyzing political culture rather than governmental structure. Cities with school districts that incorporated programs and policies inclusive of sexual orientation had a political culture that was considered liberal or progressive. Gay and lesbian citizens could openly disclose their sexual identity to many parts of these communities, including school personnel. Some openly gay candidates were elected to public office (though none as yet to the school boards in these districts). Each of these cities increasingly employed openly gay and lesbian school teachers and administrators.

The reformed structure for electing school government found in Raleigh, Santa Cruz, and Iowa City probably made it more difficult for opponents of the predominant political culture to gain representation. School district decision makers in Iowa City and Santa Cruz supported gay-friendly initiatives based on principles of justice and equity because they functioned in a larger environment that promoted these values. In Raleigh, school district officials were those who represented their community's conservative values, and those values were reflected in officials' repressive reactions to proposals for change. Those who would promote sexual orientation issues—who would oppose Raleigh's dominant political culture—were neither elected nor appointed to office. Thus, the reformed government structure in these cities seemed to act as a moderating influence on change in the schools in that it enhanced the ability of those representing the dominant political culture to maintain their power. On the other hand, both Philadelphia and Cincinnati operated under nonreformed school district structures that made their systems more open to political actors on both sides of the issue. As a result, proponents for sexual orientation initiatives in these school districts were able to influence the system through elections to accommodate some responsiveness to change. However, opponents to such initiatives also were successful in using the system to repress change and maintain the status quo. Thus government structure had a modest impact on the overall reactions of school officials.

School districts that were responsive to gay demands had a political opportunity structure supportive of gay rights in the larger community. This entailed mobilization on the part of gays and their allies that laid the groundwork in advance for school-based programs. Electing supportive public officials, passing a gay rights ordinance, and undertaking other endeavors that increased public visibility and education about gay issues seemed to pave the way for subsequent changes in those institutions, such as schools, that are strongly resistant to controversial initiatives. Thus, although gay rights campaigns emerged in these cities in the 1970s and 1980s, similar proposals were not brought to the school boards in these communities until the 1990s.

As stated in the beginning of this chapter, schools are the purveyors of social norms of the dominant culture. We would argue that school officials look locally for the norms under which they operate and that political culture rather than political structure is the predominant influence on school governments embroiled in this culture war issue.

NOTES

1. We use the terms *gay* and *lesbians and gay men* (or vice versa) inclusively to refer to male homosexuals, female homosexuals, and bisexuals without intending disrespect to any particular group.

2. Detailed information about these five school districts and their communities can be found in our recent book (Button et al., 1997), especially chapters two and five. A complete listing of references for each school district is also found in the book.

REFERENCES

Bachrach, P., and M. S. Baratz. 1970. *Power and Poverty: Theory and Practice*. New York: Oxford University Press.

Button, J. W., B. A. Rienzo, and K. D. Wald. 1997. *Private Lives, Public Conflicts: Battles Over Gay Rights in American Communities*. Washington, D.C.: Congressional Quarterly Press.

Gibson, P. 1989. "Gay and Lesbian Youth Suicide." In *Report of the Secretary's Task Force on Youth Suicide, Volume 3: Prevention and Intervention in Youth Suicide*. Washington, D.C.: U.S. Department of Health and Human Services, pp. 110–42.

Gross, L., and S. K. Aurand. 1992. *Discrimination and Violence against Lesbian Women and Gay Men in Philadelphia and the Commonwealth of Pennsylvania: A Study by the Philadelphia Lesbian and Gay Task Force*. Philadelphia: Philadelphia Lesbian and Gay Task Force.

———. 1996. *Discrimination and Violence against Lesbian Women and Gay Men in Philadelphia and the Commonwealth of Pennsylvania: A Study by the Philadelphia Lesbian and Gay Task Force*. Philadelphia: Philadelphia Lesbian and Gay Task Force.

Harbeck, K. M., ed. 1992. "Introduction." In K. M. Harbeck, ed., *Coming Out of the Classroom Closet: Gay and Lesbian Students, Teachers and Curricula*. New York: Harrington Park Press, p. 2.

Myers, S. L. 1992. "Values in Conflict: Schools Diversify the Golden Rule." *New York Times,* 6 October, pp. B1,12.

Philadelphia Lesbian and Gay Task Force. 1995. *Addessa Testimony to the Board of Education.* Philadelphia: Philadelphia Lesbian and Gay Task Force. Report.

Rienzo, B. A., J. Button, and K. D. Wald. 1996. "The Politics of School-Based Programs That Address Sexual Orientation." *Journal of School Health* 66:33–40.

School District of Philadelphia Board of Education. 1994. *Policy 102: Multicultural-Multiracial-Gender Education.* Report.

Sharp, E. B. 1996. "Culture Wars and City Politics: Local Government's Role in Social Conflict." *Urban Affairs Review* 31:738–58.

———. 1997. "A Comparative Anatomy of Urban Social Conflict." *Political Research Quarterly* 50 (June): 261–80.

Silberman, T. 1994. "Enloe Principal Upholds Students' Suspensions." *News and Observer (Raleigh, N.C.),* 10 March, p. B8.

Telljohann, S. K., and J. H. Price. 1993. "A Qualitative Examination of Adolescent Homosexuals' Life Experiences: Ramifications for Secondary School Personnel." *Journal of Homosexuality* 26:41–56.

Tucker, S. 1982. "Philadelphia: Home of Great Spirits." *Advocate (Philadelphia),* 2 September, p. 26.

Unks, G. 1993–94. "Thinking About the Homosexual Adolescent." *High School Journal* 77:1–6.

Wilkinson, H. 1994. "Anti-Gay Rights Group Targets 5 on Council." *Cincinnati Enquirer,* 8 September, n.p.

———. 1995. "95 Campaign: Republicans Revving Up TV Assault: 2 Council Candidates Focus of Negative Ads." *Cincinnati Enquirer,* 24 October, p. B2.

7
San Francisco and Domestic Partners: New Fields of Battle in the Culture War

Richard DeLeon

In a recent article, *Business Week* writer Linda Himelstein noted that "these days municipalities are pushing their clout way past potholes and police. Local governments are foisting their social vision on industry by passing bold laws that give them a say in everything from human-rights issues to compensation" (Himelstein, 1997:98). The centerpiece of her story was San Francisco and its new domestic partners law that required private companies doing business with the city to offer domestic partners of employees the same benefits as legally married spouses. San Francisco's enforcement of that law has placed the city on a collision course with United Airlines and other multinational corporations that have challenged the authority of local governments to throw their weight around and meddle with business prerogatives. There would be no story here, of course, if gay and lesbian couples had access to the same privileges of officially sanctioned marriage enjoyed by heterosexual couples under state laws. But same-sex marriages remain a distant prospect and are currently one of the most intensely contested issues in the nation's still unfolding culture war. By passing its domestic partners law, San Francisco fired a new shot from the left in that war and exposed the linkages between capital and culture in ways that could not have been anticipated. This chapter examines the political origins of San Francisco's landmark legislation, its impacts on the private sector, and its potential use as a weapon in the cause of social justice.

Culture war is characterized by "intense social conflict centered on fundamental issues of morality and social justice" (Sharp, 1997:261; cf. Hunter, 1991:42). In San Francisco, as reflected in the way the city's diverse people live and work together and resolve their disputes, the local culture war is essentially over, and the progressives have won. Small-scale battles and skirmishes still flare up from time to time, especially around issues—like prostitution, homelessness, or the quality of life—that are linked to the defense of neighborhood space. And there are enclaves of residents who remain intolerant of gays and lesbians, abortion rights activists, newly arrived immigrants, HIV carriers, welfare recipients, and other groups. But overall, after decades of sporadically violent struggle, San Franciscans have achieved a communal peace of mind on fundamental issues of morality and justice. The taproot of that moral consensus is an ethos of mutual tolerance and civility combined with a love of place and an appreciation of social, ethnic, and cultural diversity. A term for this is "rooted cosmopolitanism" (Cohen, 1992; also Hollinger, 1995:83–87). As a short description of political culture, it fits San Francisco well. It also helps to explain San Francisco's reputation as the "Sanctuary City," as the "Left Coast City," and as the nation's capital of progressivism (DeLeon, 1992, 1997). San Franciscans do fight and bicker a lot, but at the deeper level of political culture, they are not at war with themselves.

But they are at war with others. San Francisco's local government leaders have become deeply engaged in waging cultural war outside the city limits. Indeed, San Francisco's various official interventions on multiple fronts in that war illustrate Sidney Tarrow's point that the state serves "not only as the *target* of collective claims, but increasingly as a *fulcrum* of claims against others" (Tarrow, 1994:6). In some cases, such as California's recent battle over the medicinal use of marijuana, those claims in San Francisco have taken the form of asserting local government autonomy vis-à-vis state and federal regulatory authority. In other cases, such as the recent prohibition on contracts with firms doing business with Burma, those claims have leveraged city hall's economic clout into an instrument of local foreign policy (cf. *San Francisco Examiner,* 1997b). And in the continuing conflicts over gay rights at all levels of government (Button et al., 1997), San Francisco itself has become less a local scene of battle and more a staging area for doing battle in the national culture war.

ENTREPRENEURIAL INSTIGATION IN THE CULTURE WAR

In work on social movements, "comparatively little attention has been paid to the question of government officials' responses to social movements or their role in the development of those movements" (Sharp, 1997:265). One such role highlighted in Sharp's study was that of the "entrepreneurial instigation" of culture wars by local officials who capitalize on their "awareness of disequilibrium or alertness to latent discontents" in the communities they represent (Sharp, 1997:266; also see Schneider and Teske, 1992:738).

This chapter provides a case study of how gay rights activists and government officials in San Francisco used the power and apparatus of the local state to instigate the adoption of domestic partners programs by thousands of private firms and other contractors that do business with the city. Having reached the limits of what was possible within the confines of the local public sector, these entrepreneurial instigators succeeded in passing a new domestic partners ordinance that

triggered a chain reaction of social reform in the private sector that is now causing national and even international reverberations. In doing so, they tapped their
awareness of discontent among gay and lesbian business employees across the
country; applied their knowledge of the disequilibria and vulnerabilities of
powerholders in the private sector (Tarrow, 1994:86); exploited their access to
local political opportunity structures and movement social networks (Tarrow,
1994:85–90); and framed the public interpretation of consequent actions and reactions in ideological terms that served the movement's goals. This admittedly is
only a single case study, but it is a substantively important case in policy terms. It
is one that offers useful political lessons and valuable insights into the structured
fields of power that typically constrain local government action but that also can
mediate entrepreneurial instigation, amplify its effects, escalate social conflicts,
and potentially transform the broader context of the culture war itself.

The political campaign for domestic partners in San Francisco developed
through two distinct phases, the second a major escalation of the first. The special
meaning of *escalation,* as the term is used here, "is the step-by-step passage from
context-preserving to context-transforming conflicts. The quarrels about practical adjustments, collective identities, and moral ideals that take the framework
for granted pass into struggles that bring the framework into question" (Unger,
1987:275). The first phase of the domestic partners campaign, although it provided an anticipatory experiment in social reform that drew national attention, was
confined to the public sector and stayed within the city limits. It was a *context-
preserving* struggle because it did not challenge the structures of federalism and
capitalism in which it took place. The second phase, and the main focus of this
chapter, was a *context-transforming* escalation of conflict that crossed the border into the private sector and asserted local autonomy against state and federal
authority.

PHASE I: SEIZING THE LOCAL TERRAIN

The first phase of San Francisco's development of domestic partners policies began
in 1982 and, after a long struggle, ended in 1996. (For an excellent study, see Bailey
1998; also see DeLeon, 1992.) In 1982, the San Francisco Board of Supervisors
passed a domestic partners ordinance drafted by gay Supervisor Harry Britt. It
established a domestic registry and offered full bereavement, visitation, and health
benefits to partners of public employees of the City and County of San Francisco.
Mayor Dianne Feinstein vetoed the bill, however, bowing to pressure from the
city's religious and fiscal conservatives. Her veto angered many gays and lesbians and added fuel to a successful petition campaign calling for a recall election
in 1983. Mayor Feinstein routed her opponents in that election, winning 82 percent of the vote. Stung by defeat and lacking mayoral support, advocates of domestic partners legislation decided to retreat until 1987, when a broad-based

grassroots coalition elected liberal state assemblyman Art Agnos as mayor. Agnos had championed gay rights in the assembly and authored a major bill banning discrimination based on sexual orientation. Campaigning for mayor, he pledged support for domestic partners legislation and attracted many votes from the gay and lesbian community.

In 1989, with Mayor Agnos's support, Supervisor Britt introduced a new version of the domestic partnership ordinance that would allow unmarried, cohabiting couples (gay or straight) to register their relationship with the city clerk for a $35 fee. Although lacking the health insurance benefits included in the 1982 proposal, this legislation did give city and county public employees bereavement and hospital visitation rights equivalent to those of married couples under California law. The Board of Supervisors passed the new ordinance, and Mayor Agnos signed it. Before it took effect, however, conservative groups led by the Roman Catholic Archdiocese organized a successful petition campaign to require voter approval of an initiative referendum (Proposition S) at the general municipal election to be held later that year.

The prospects of victory for domestic partners looked good at the time. As a group, the city's gays and lesbians were highly mobilized, politically sophisticated, and constituted 15 to 20 percent of the entire electorate. Although divided on many issues, they were united in their support of domestic partners. The growing AIDS and HIV epidemic in San Francisco had aroused public sympathy for people with AIDS and compassion for their loved ones. One poll found, for example, that over 93 percent of all San Franciscans supported hospital visitation rights for life partners and extended bereavement leaves for gay and lesbian city employees who lost their partners. Nearly all elected officials endorsed Proposition S, as did most of the city's major newspaper editors, many corporate business leaders, and even some religious leaders who had opposed domestic partners in 1982. Many older residents, homeowners, and fiscal conservatives continued to be concerned about the long-run costs, however, and conservative Catholic, Protestant, and Jewish leaders mobilized opposition to Proposition S based on its perceived threat to traditional family values and conceptions of marriage. Partly in response to these religious objections, many of the city's African Americans opposed Proposition S or were undecided. Many Asians also were inclined to vote against it on cultural or financial grounds. Despite this opposition, however, the balance of electoral forces clearly favored passage of domestic partners into law.

Then came the Loma Prieta earthquake on October 17, three weeks before the election. Political campaigning virtually ceased as leaders and citizens coped with the destruction. By election day, it became clear that Proposition S was in trouble. In a low-turnout election, the referendum lost by one percentage point and a few thousand votes. Domestic partners legislation was back to square one.

In 1990, the push for domestic partners started up again. Supervisor Britt introduced yet another domestic partners proposal as a board-sponsored ballot initiative, Proposition K, for voter approval in the November 1990 general election. This measure would create a domestic partners registry for city employees and grant only limited benefits that excluded health insurance. Health-care benefits for domestic partners of city employees were quietly folded into the city's personnel policies by mayoral executive orders and administrative regulations (Bailey, 1998). Adding further incentive to gays and lesbians to turn out and vote, lesbian activists Carole Migden and Roberta Achtenberg ran as candidates for the Board of Supervisors, openly gay Tom Ammiano ran for a seat on the Board of Education, and lesbian Donna Hitchens ran for a judgeship on the Superior Court. Proposition K won handily, partly as a result of greater support from taxpayer groups, older homeowners, and African Americans. And Migden, Achtenberg, Ammiano, and Hitchens all won their races in what reporters described as a "Lavender Sweep." Combined with administrative policy reforms, the passage of Proposition K established domestic partner benefits for San Francisco city workers. One last attempt by religious conservatives to repeal it by referendum in 1991 failed miserably, winning only 40 percent of the vote.

PHASE II: CROSSING BORDERS AT THE LEVEL OF REGIME

In the 1994 elections, Tom Ammiano won election to the Board of Supervisors and the city's voters decisively countered the Republican Party's national onslaught in every local race; and in the 1995 mayoral election, former assembly speaker Willie Brown defeated incumbent Frank Jordan and challenger Roberta Achtenberg to become the city's first African American mayor. By early 1996, San Francisco's domestic partners policies had become widely accepted, routine, and beyond debate. Meanwhile, the city's gay and lesbian community had achieved a pinnacle of political incorporation and governing power.

In Robert Bailey's terms, the gay and lesbian presence in San Francisco had become "embedded" at three different levels (political organization, government authority, and public ideology) in the city's structures of power and authority. The fourth layer of embedding at the level of the urban regime (cf., Stone, 1989:6) was within reach. "To be embedded at the regime level," Bailey writes, "means sufficient political organization, sufficient presence in the administrative bureaucracy, and the addition of its issues to the political agenda and its language to the regime's discourse. Finally, it requires admission to the points of overlap between private power and public instrumentalities" (Bailey, 1998:332; see also Zukin and DiMaggio, 1990:14–23).

With gay rights champion Willie Brown in the mayor's office and with one gay male (Tom Ammiano) and two lesbians (Carole Migden and Susan Leal) on the Board of Supervisors, the political stage was set for a second wave of innovation that would extend the reach of San Francisco's domestic partners policies beyond the public sector and outside the city limits into new and treacherous territory.

As a prelude, in January 1996, the Board of Supervisors unanimously passed an ordinance drafted by Supervisor Migden that would allow the county clerk's office to perform same-sex wedding ceremonies for couples registered as domestic partners. In March, Mayor Brown and Supervisor Migden presided at city hall in the wedding of 150 gay and lesbian couples. Although not officially recognized under state law, these marriage ceremonies were traditional in every other way. San Francisco thus became the first U.S. city to initiate vows between domestic partners with a mass public ceremony (Lynch, 1996).

In May 1996, Geoff Kors, Carol Stuart, and Jeff Sheehy of the Harvey Milk Lesbian/Gay/Bisexual Democratic Club drafted legislation for the Board of Supervisors that would require private firms and nonprofits doing business with the city to provide their employees with equal benefits protection for registered domestic partners. Supervisors Ammiano and Leslie Katz cosponsored the draft legislation and mobilized support for it over the summer and into the fall of 1996. The Board unanimously approved the bill, and Mayor Willie Brown signed it into law on November 8, 1996.

This domestic partners initiative fell far short of the sponsors' ultimate goal of fully sanctioned same-sex marriages under state and national law, but it would certainly move things in that direction, especially if the border crossing into the private sector were to spread reform via chain reaction to other cities and states. An estimated sixteen thousand companies did business with the city, and many of these were large national or multinational corporations. Because the draft legislation required a city contractor to provide domestic partners benefits to *all* of its employees, regardless of their location, the potential scope of impact stretched far beyond the city limits. Scattered throughout regional and national business networks—in companies like Bank of America, Chevron, and United Airlines—were well-established gay and lesbian employee groups that had been lobbying corporate managers for years to provide domestic partners benefits. These enclaves of gay rights advocates within the corporate structure were connected by their own social networks to one another and to the broader reform movement. Most were tuned to San Francisco's political frequency and were prepared to resonate with any reform initiative targeting the private sector. The injection of even a small voltage of political power into the local grid of firms doing business with the city might well cascade through these various networks to achieve a major amplification of reform.

BUSINESS NOT AS USUAL IN SAN FRANCISCO POLITICS

Leaders of San Francisco's downtown corporate business community were gentle in their criticism of the proposed ordinance, and some even took positions openly endorsing it. The Chamber of Commerce, for example, took no official position on the proposal beyond expressing concerns about its impacts on business costs and competitive advantage. Kira Keane, executive director of the Committee on Jobs, the city's leading downtown business lobbying organization, stated that there was no discernible opposition to the legislation. "Large companies paved the way for it," she said. "We think it's the right thing to do" (Lewis, 1996a).

It is true that large firms had paved the way. Earlier in the decade, large Bay Area firms such as Levi Strauss & Co., Apple Computer, Inc., Genentech Corp., and Silicon Graphics, Inc. had extended health and other benefits to the domestic partners of their gay and lesbian employees. In more recent years, other large firms, including IBM, American Express Co., and Walt Disney Co. followed suit, in some cases incurring the wrath and boycotts of outraged religious conservatives (*San Francisco Examiner*, 1996). These firms, many of them located in the highly competitive high-tech industry, were compelled to offer domestic partners benefits as necessary incentives for recruiting top talent in their fields. Internal pressure from gay and lesbian employee groups put steam behind that decision, and the relatively small financial costs involved proved to be no obstacle (Raine, 1997). The advantage of bigness was a key factor explaining why large companies rather than small ones had taken the lead in offering domestic partners benefits. Large firms had sufficient leverage with their big accounts to force recalcitrant insurance companies to provide affordable domestic partners coverage to their employees. Small firms lacked such bargaining power and were unable to find providers willing to sell coverage at affordable rates.

In summary, even before Ammiano and his associates introduced their bill, momentum was building among large firms in some industries to adopt domestic partners voluntarily and for solid economic reasons. The conditions were ripe for instigating a major escalation of social reform throughout the entire private sector.

LEAVING CLINTON BEHIND: POLITICAL TIMING AND THE 1996 PRESIDENTIAL ELECTION

The political climate surrounding San Francisco's domestic partners initiative also bolstered local support and dampened opposition. The 1996 presidential election campaign was heating up, and the city's progressives were on red alert defending immigrants, welfare recipients, and racial minorities against attacks from state and federal politicians. Gay and lesbian leaders were outraged by President Bill Clinton's election-year pandering to the cultural right and especially incensed by his decision to speak at a fund-raising event in San Francisco in early June. Clinton had publicly condemned same-sex marriages and announced his intention to sign the Congressional Defense of Marriage Act, which defined marriage exclusively as the union between a man and a women. Many local observers viewed Clinton's campaign stop in San Francisco as a transparent attempt to provoke confrontation with angry gay and lesbian activists and to pose for the media as a defender of family values in the land of Sodom. Even the staid *Chronicle* editors drolly remarked that Clinton's visit "would play well among Middle American voters, many of whom regard San Francisco—incorrectly, to be sure—as a strange liberal outpost on the Far-Left Coast inhabited by an equally weird population" (*San Francisco Chronicle,* 1996).

Despite Mayor Brown's warning to stay away, Clinton came and spoke but attracted only quiet and civil protest. The city's political elite, including Mayor Brown, Assemblywoman Carol Migden, and Supervisors Ammiano, Katz, and Leal, snubbed Clinton while he was in town and made it clear that San Francisco would fight its own cultural battles without him (Brazil, 1996). These political theatrics set the stage for Ammiano, Katz, and allies to launch the domestic partners initiative both as a local policy innovation and as a new weapon in the broader culture war then swirling around the national presidential election campaign.

THE NEW DOMESTIC PARTNERS ORDINANCE

On November 4, one day before the 1996 general election, the Board of Supervisors unanimously approved the Non-Discrimination in City Contracts and Benefits Ordinance. Four days later, with Supervisors Ammiano, Katz, and Leal standing at his side, Mayor Willie Brown signed it into law effective June 1, 1997. Detailed guidelines for implementing the law would be announced in April, presumably giving city vendors ample time to comply. According to Ammiano, Mayor Brown had hesitated signing after the Roman Catholic Archdioceses and some business owners lobbied vigorously against the bill. He had already publicly endorsed universal coverage in principle, however, and the political momentum favoring passage was unstoppable.

Described in the media as "landmark" legislation, the new ordinance made San Francisco the first city in the nation to require that all city contractors offer the same benefits to employees' domestic partners (gay or straight) and to spouses of married employees. "This is a great day," said Supervisor Ammiano. "Let's face it: If it's good enough for Mickey Mouse, it's good enough for San Francisco" (Bowman, 1996). The ink was barely dry before Seattle, West Hollywood, Boston and New York asked Katz for copies of the ordinance (Lewis, 1996b). Once again, San Francisco had lived up to its reputation as the country's vanguard progressive city and "early riser" of social reform.

IMPLEMENTATION: PROBLEMS OF COMPLIANCE AND ISSUES OF LAW

With an estimated billion dollars worth of city business at stake (Shioya, 1997:15), most vendors were prepared to comply with the new ordinance. Others were gearing up to resist it or to seek exemptions. There was a lot of uncertainty about how the new law would work, however, and a number of thorny issues to resolve. Small business owners and managers were anxious because no insurance providers at the time were willing to sell domestic partners coverage to small employers and thus made compliance impossible (DeBare, 1997a). Another widely shared concern was that the new law was vulnerable to legal challenge and was likely to be overturned, sooner or later, in the courts. One potential legal obstacle was the Employee Retirement Income Security Act (ERISA), a federal statute that pre-empted cities and states from regulating benefits provided by private firms to their employees. Another federal statute, the National Labor Relations Act, prohibited state and local governments from interfering with collective bargaining agreements between private employers and unionized workers (Shioya, 1997:18). And there was the key question of whether large employers, particularly multinational corporations, would be willing to revamp their worldwide employee benefit plans at the behest of a single city. To some observers it seemed that even six months might not allow sufficient time to educate the city's vendors about the new law, test its legality in the courts, and clarify how it would be enforced in practice.

The task of writing guidelines to facilitate implementation of the new ordinance fell to the Gay, Lesbian, Bisexual, Transgender, and HIV Discrimination Unit of the city's Human Rights Commission. Commission chair Martha Knutzen said, "We have a model we can use for businesses that are apprehensive. But we want to show them that the equitable granting of benefits can be a positive" (Lewis, 1996b). In formulating and negotiating detailed guidelines over the next few months, the Commission, the Board of Supervisors, and Mayor Brown were flexible on some issues but unyielding on others.

On the side of compromise, the new law exempted other local governments and sole-source contractors and subcontractors from the equal benefits requirement. City officials were willing to certify compliance if a vendor could demonstrate that it had taken "reasonable" measures to secure equal benefits coverage for employees but had failed. They allowed vendors to offer employees with domestic partners a lump-sum-benefits cash equivalency in lieu of adopting a new insurance plan. They approved a variety of certification procedures and domestic partners registries (Blackwood, 1997; Gordon, 1997).

City officials also proved receptive to the creative use of alternative language in describing domestic partnerships. The Roman Catholic Archdioceses strongly objected to the new ordinance on religious grounds because it would force the church to recognize the domestic partnerships of workers employed by Catholic Charities, a church-affiliated nonprofit organization that received $5.6 million a year in city service contracts (Slind-Flor, 1997). City officials negotiated a compromise that allowed Catholic Charities employees to designate one member of their household (a spouse, a relative, or an unmarried partner) as eligible for "spousal-equivalent benefits." Once agreement was reached on this "don't ask, don't tell" policy and the offending "domestic partners" phraseology was excised, the archbishop ceased his public defiance of the law (Fernandez, 1997; Gordon,

1997a). It is worth noting that Kors, Sheehy, and Stuart, the architects of the new policy, applauded this pragmatic compromise. "The intention of the legislation was to end discrimination," they wrote, "not to force companies or churches to recognize our relationships" (Sheehy et al., 1997).

City officials were much less compromising on other issues, particularly in the face of lobbying efforts to dilute the new law, restrict its scope, and localize its impacts. Based mainly on cost considerations, the Committee on Jobs and other business lobbying groups pressed hard to restrict coverage to same-sex couples and to exclude unmarried heterosexual partners and extended family members from equal benefits rights. Supervisors Katz and Leal initially endorsed that change and tried to make revisions, but Ammiano adamantly opposed such tinkering, branding it "an attempt to nickel and dime civil rights" (Gordon, 1997e). His concern was that the proposed change would assign heterosexual couples second-class status. Siding with Ammiano, former mayor Agnos noted that when he signed the city's 1990 domestic partners law for city workers, it was with "the explicit hope that the city would eventually recognize all extended family members of workers." He also cited a 1990 survey of city employees showing that 47 percent of those who would add a domestic partner were in heterosexual couples (Agnos, 1997). After making one last attempt to restrict coverage (Gordon, 1997h), Katz and Leal retreated in the interest of gay and lesbian solidarity.

The single most controversial provision in the new ordinance required city vendors to provide equal benefits to all of their employees no matter where they worked or lived. This mandate boldly asserted San Francisco's regulatory authority beyond the city limits and attacked business prerogatives even in firms located thousands of miles away. San Francisco officials were adamant about enforcing this provision. The requirement of equal benefits for all employees posed no obstacle to smaller companies that hired mainly local workers. It did create a potential problem, however, for large corporate vendors that employed most of their workers outside the city. Many such firms complied fully with the new law and offered equal benefits to all of their employees everywhere. Other companies responded with only partial compliance limited to local employees. Still others, most notably United Airlines and Federal Express, opposed the new law on principle, challenged its validity in the courts, and in some cases threatened the city with disinvestment.

INVADING THE PRIVATE SECTOR: THRESHOLDS AND CHAIN REACTIONS

Despite its political outlier reputation, and out of proportion to its physical size and economic clout, San Francisco occupies a prominent location in regional and national business networks and in the global hierarchy of cities. Blessed by "place luck" and a "natural monopoly" over assets that make their city so attractive to business (Molotch, 1990:187; Peterson, 1995:29), San Franciscans have grown accustomed to dictating the terms for doing business on their turf. Expressing an attitude toward San Francisco shared by many corporate executives, the senior vice president of LS Transit Systems, a New Jersey company under contract with the city's public transit system, said: "This city does have a way of challenging vendors, whether it's this or a ban on doing business in South Africa or Burma. But we are committed to continuing to work with San Francisco. And, like many other companies with global operations, we are used to dealing with local customs" (DeBare, 1997a). A similar mix of business rationality and political pragmatism motivated other large corporate firms to comply with San Francisco's new domestic partners law. As this initial wave of compliance propagated through various business networks, market competition activated ripple effects that achieved nearly total saturation of policy coverage in some industries while encountering blockage in others.

As noted earlier, the lack of health insurance providers was a major obstacle confronting thousands of small business vendors. This problem was solved in March 1997, when the San Francisco Chamber of Commerce offered the city's small businesses an affordable health plan that included domestic partners coverage. The plan required months of negotiations with Kaiser Permanente, United Healthcare, and Blue Shield of California (Ginsburg, 1997). With the entry of this troika into the small business market, one broker predicted that other health plan organizations would soon join them. Another said, "The marketplace perspective will force all carriers to get into line. You can't do business in Northern California without doing business with San Francisco" (Rauber, 1997). By late May, as predicted, Blue Cross, Health Net, and PacifiCare had all jumped in with their own domestic partners coverage for firms with fifty or fewer employees. Along with Blue Shield and Kaiser, these insurers held more than 75 percent of the individual/small group market. These developments, in turn, led one business analyst to predict nearly complete saturation of the market over the months ahead (DeBare, 1997c).

San Francisco's ordinance triggered swift chain reactions and threshold effects throughout the entire health insurance industry. Once activated by entrepreneurial instigation, it took only weeks for market mechanisms to create an entirely new infrastructure of insurance options and pathways that made domestic partners coverage possible for small businesses not only in San Francisco but everywhere. Impressed by these developments, editors of the *San Francisco Business Times* (1997a) commented that "domestic partners insurance has gone from controversy to nonissue within a couple of weeks" and acknowledged that "sometimes a little government regulation can work wonders." The ground was thus quickly and quietly prepared within the private sector for an epidemic of social reform to take place. Even if political and religious conservatives had wanted to mobilize a protest, there simply was no time to do so.

In March 1997, Bank of America announced that it would extend health benefits to the domestic partners of its eighty thousand employees living throughout the United States. "We feel the San Francisco ordinance was a factor in our decision-making process," said BofA spokesman Dennis Wyss, "but only one factor" (Gordon, 1997d). According to reporter Ilana DeBare, the bank's decision was the result of a "mix of internal and external pressure." The city's new ordinance applied the external pressure, while BofA's gay and lesbian employees lobbied for equal benefits from the inside.

When news of BofA's decision reached the Reverend Louis Sheldon, chairman of the antigay rights Traditional Values Coalition, he said "it looks like I'm going to have to do my banking somewhere else" and warned that "the backlash from the moderate to conservative parts of California will be quite significant" (DeBare, 1997b). These threats from the cultural right did not dissuade Wells Fargo Bank and Union Bank of Calfornia from following BofA's example four months later by adopting domestic partners benefits (*San Francisco Business Times,* 1997b).

Prompted in part by San Francisco's new ordinance, PG&E announced in early May that it would provide domestic partners benefits to its twenty thousand California employees (Gordon, 1997f). In addition, Chevron, the Bay Area's top revenue-generating firm and its eighth-largest employer, announced in late April that it would extend domestic partners benefits to most of its twenty-six thousand employees in the United States. Leaders of Chevron's Lesbian and Gay Employees Association celebrated the decision (Hatfield, 1997). Chevron was "pushed along" in extending benefits by San Francisco's ordinance, said Chevron spokeswoman Alison Jones. In October, Houston-based Shell Oil announced that it too would begin offering domestic partner benefits in January, and Chicago-based Amoco followed by declaring its intention to give the policy strong consideration. Neither Shell nor Amoco did business with San Francisco, but the impact of arch-rival Chevron's announcement on their decisions was clear. Both companies compete with Chevron for geologists and petroleum engineers. "The market is very, very tight for good people," said Jones, and it requires that "we do anything we can to retain and attract them" (Jones, 1997). As happened in the health insurance and banking industries, the city's new law helped to trigger the adoption of domestic partners benefits by an industry leader, which in turn activated a chain reaction of similar adoptions by industry rivals.

Other corporate vendors, particularly those headquartered outside the region, felt much less internal and external pressure to comply with the city's new law. Even with $3 million in contracts at stake, for example, Consolidated Electrical Distributors, a Southern California-based corporation with four hundred branches across the country, attempted to limit compliance with the city's ordinance by directing its San Francisco branch to offer benefits cash equivalency to its thirty-five local employees. City officials rejected this proposal. Jeff Eagle, the branch manager, expressed the frustration of many vendors whose businesses were only small local units of larger corporate organizations: "Locally we want to comply, and the people who made this law should be most concerned with the people of San Francisco. Instead, they want to change the world. . . . Not everyone in the country is as liberal as San Francisco" (Gordon, 1997k).

UNFRIENDLY SKIES: THE CITY GOES TO WAR WITH THE AIRLINES

Although many corporate vendors complied fully with San Francisco's domestic partners ordinance and others tried to localize compliance and thus minimize its impact, United Airlines and Federal Express were in the vanguard of firms that mobilized business and political opposition to fight the new law tooth and nail.

United Airlines (UA), by far the largest carrier at San Francisco International Airport, has eighty-six thousand employees worldwide, including seventy-five hundred at the airport (Epstein, 1997a). The city's battle with UA began in January 1997, when the company's $13.4 million twenty-five-year lease for a new flight kitchen and an equipment repair facility at the airport came before the Board of Supervisors (Epstein, 1997b). The supervisors initially refused to approve the lease because it lacked language indicating that UA would comply with the new domestic partners law. UA executives responded that the law would not take effect until June and that the issue had not been raised in earlier negotiations with the Airport Commission.

Faced with this impasse, Board members and UA officials began talks that eventually produced what the supervisors thought was a deal. The twenty-five-year lease would be split into a short-term two-year lease and a long-term twenty-three-year lease that would be signed later if UA complied with the law. The Board then approved the two-year lease with the understanding that UA would use the time available to establish a domestic partners program (Epstein, 1997c). At least that much time would be needed, everyone agreed, because UA had to renegotiate twelve labor agreements with its unions in six countries (Gordon, 1997b).

On May 13, United Airlines, Federal Express, and twenty other airlines represented by the Air Transportation Association (ATA) sued in a U.S. District Court to block implementation of the city's domestic partners law. Carol Hallett, ATA's president, justified the law suit by arguing that "airlines have always been governed by federal, not local, laws because it would be impossible to operate in hundreds of communities with different and possibly contradictory local ordinances." According to the ATA lawsuit, the city's law was preempted by the Airline Deregulation Act and other federal laws governing airline operations (Holding, 1997). Hallett emphasized that issues of morality or sexual orientation were not motivating the lawsuit. "If another community passed an ordinance requiring that airlines could not provide benefits to domestic partners," she said, "we would file the same lawsuit" (Gordon, 1997g). She might also have mentioned that UA had adopted domestic partners benefits for employees in Canada, Brazil, New Zealand and the Netherlands under compulsion of national law (Aquino, 1997).

Reacting to ATA's lawsuit, city officials vowed to fight in court to save the law. Supervisor Katz disagreed with ATA's charge that San Francisco was meddling in the industry. "We're not meddling in the industry, " she said. "The ordinance does not dictate what kinds of benefits must be provided. The ordinance requires that [contractors] cannot discriminate" (Gordon, 1997g).

Claiming that UA had promised only to conduct a good-faith review of the ordinance, a UA spokeswoman said that the review was done and "we came to the conclusion that it was illegal." The locals vehemently disagreed. "What they have done is duplicitous," declared an angry Tom Ammiano (Gordon, 1997i). San Francisco's chief assistant attorney noted that other companies accepted the law without major difficulties. "Chevron, Bank of America, PG&E and the Catholic Charities have all agreed to provide these equal benefits to domestic partners," he said. "The airlines have decided to declare war. So much for the friendly skies" (Holding, 1997). "They lied to us," said the Milk Club's Jeff Sheehy (Gordon, 1997g). Sheehy later led a demonstration by gay activists outside a UA office. The protesters burned frequent flier cards, chanted "Liar, liar, pants on fire," and called for a boycott of UA (Irvine, 1997).

On June 2, the Board of Supervisors officially sponsored a boycott of UA and directed the city's agencies to fly United only as a last resort. Gay and lesbian groups around the country joined the boycott. As the boycott took off, however, David Tomb, founder of UA's gay and lesbian employee organization and a strong supporter of the city's new ordinance, surprised everyone by pleading for it to stop. He argued that the boycott would do "considerable damage to the relations we've established with our colleagues and management" and would have "a negative impact on those you are actually trying to help" (King, 1997).

On another front, city officials informed Federal Express, a party to the ATA law suit, that it had to comply with the city's ordinance or vacate its cargo storage facilities at San Francisco International Airport. In response, the delivery service giant declared that it would consider spending $18 million to move its cargo operations from San Francisco to the Oakland International Airport simply to avoid complying with the law. Despite the threatened loss of $2 million annually in lease revenues, city officials stood firm. When San Francisco Airport director John Martin learned about FedEx's possible move to Oakland, he said: "If they decide to [move to Oakland], that's fine. We are not going to back down. . . . There are plenty of other tenants that would love to have that cargo space." Despite the tough talk, city officials decided to delay enforcement until final resolution of ATA's lawsuit against the city (Ness, 1997).

On October 10, 1997, U.S. District Judge Claudia Wilken heard arguments from both sides in the case of *Air Transport Association of America v. City and County of San Francisco* (97-1753). The hearing attracted national media attention and also a blizzard of amicus curiae briefs from the National Center for Lesbian Rights, the American Civil Liberties Union's Gay and Lesbian Rights Project, the Lambda Legal Defense and Education Fund, and other organizations. ATA's attorneys argued that San Francisco's ordinance violated ERISA and also the Airline Deregulation Act, the Railway Labor Act, and the commerce clause of the U.S. Constitution's Fourteenth Amendment. The city's new law, they contended, had "transgressed into a federal regulation" and was "a blatant, intentional and improper incursion into federally protected territory." According to one legal reporter, Judge Wilken's line of questioning seemed to favor the city by raising a problem with ripeness and standing to sue. Her summary judgment on the dispute is expected sometime in December 1997 (Elias, 1997).

The ATA's arguments did score some points with the *San Francisco Examiner,* however, and the newspaper's editors warned that the city had "set itself up for a fall." Contending that the city's domestic partners ordinance "can work only if it is limited to companies from which the city buys goods and services," they did not see the logic in requiring businesses that pay the city millions of dollars for leases to comply with the law. "It punishes the city more than it punishes any corporate skinflint." They also argued that the new law "threatens the establishment of domestic partners laws elsewhere. If San Francisco's experience isn't smooth, other cities will be discouraged" (*San Francisco Examiner,* 1997a).

BUREAUCRATIC FRICTION AND THE COSTS OF REFORM

By late October 1997, the administrative complexities and financial costs of enforcing San Francisco's new domestic partners ordinance were becoming clear. As of October 30, 5,042 vendors had applied for certification. Of this total, the Human Rights Commission had reviewed 2,664 applications and approved 2,427—a compliance rate of 91 percent. The remaining 2,378 applications were still awaiting review by the overwhelmed and understaffed commission. This backlog frustrated contractors, complicated bureaucratic routines, and stalled the city's efforts to purchase a wide range of needed goods and services (Gordon, 1997k). Another backlog developed as the Board of Supervisors fell behind in reviewing numerous requests from vendors for exemptions. Realizing that they had become a bottleneck, the supervisors moved to give the Human Rights Commission authority to grant such waivers and considered allowing department heads to recommend individual contractors for exemption (Gordon, 1997j).

Because many established vendors refused to change their benefits packages, city department managers were forced to contract with more expensive alternative suppliers or to devise expedient temporary exemptions. The Department of Public Works, for example, had to pay a new certified vendor 17 percent more for a case of toilet paper after its old vendor refused to comply with the law. Prohibited by the law from using Federal Express or UPS, city departments were directed to use the regular mail even though the U.S. Post Office itself does not offer equal benefits to domestic partners. Some noncertified companies began using the names of certified firms as intermediaries in bidding on contracts.

These kinds of problems are a "big pain," Supervisor Ammiano admitted, but "any time you have something groundbreaking and new, it's difficult." Supervisor Katz agreed, adding: "It's hard to put a price tag on avoiding discrimination" (McCormick, 1997). City officials thus seem determined to implement the city's new domestic partners law no matter what the cost. Despite its high priority, however, the cause for gay rights is only one of many social justice movements that compete in San Francisco for popular support, government attention, and taxpayers' money. As the price tag for enforcing the domestic partners ordinance becomes more visible and precise, it remains to be seen whether most San Franciscans will continue to support its more ambitious objectives.

CONCLUSION

Building on this case study of domestic partners in San Francisco, three broad conclusions can be drawn that have theoretical import and also some relevance to political action in the culture war.

First, all politics is local, and culture war politics is no different. But not all politics is strictly local, and some localities are more equal than others in determining the course of national policy. In San Francisco, the culture war is essentially over at the local level. Leaders of the gay rights movement, in particular, are preaching to the converted in San Francisco. No longer a contested city on such issues, San Francisco has become an institutional combatant in the culture war on a much wider field of battle. That field consists of overlapping and interacting social, economic, and political networks that link people, groups, firms, governments, and cities to one another. At its core is a national network of "aligned political identities" (Bailey, 1998:40) created by the gay rights movement and strategically anchored in prominent nodal cities. San Francisco is embedded in and constrained by this field, but the city can also reshape it in the vicinity of its local turf and can radiate considerable influence through it by its actions. The case of San Francisco's domestic partners initiative demonstrates the cultural force a single city can exert through this field on business practices and the workings of capitalism.

Second, culture war issues are often interpreted as different in kind from the economic issues that typically dominate the agenda of local politics and the attention of regime theorists and other urban scholars. Elaine Sharp, for example, writes that "the symbolic politics and morality issues that are at the heart of local culture wars are not readily treated as divisible benefits, and the compromise and coalition-building that are central to regime theory are less relevant for understanding the uncompromising social conflicts of interest here" (Sharp, 1996: 742). In San Francisco, however, morality issues and economic issues are not treated as separate spheres by leaders of the city's progressive regime. Symbolic politics and morality issues suffuse and often dominate public economic decision making. Indeed, as illustrated by this case study, the cultural agenda and moral vanguardism of the regime's governing coalition are the driving force behind many policy initiatives (e.g., growth controls, neighborhood preservation, domestic partners) that would be regarded as contrary to economic logic in most cities. It is dumbfounding to some observers that the Chamber of Commerce—a partner in the city's governing coalition—would play such an active and important role in facilitating implementation of domestic partners. If regime theorists cannot comprehend that scenario, it is only because there are very few cities in which noneconomic cultural values have been institutionalized at the level of regime. San Francisco is one such city, and the theory needs to grow from the data.

Finally, looking ahead, it is fair to ask, Has San Francisco risked and committed economic suicide by arrogantly reaching too far and provoking business wrath? Facing a field of corporate Goliaths and armed only with its local legal slingshot, has the city, in the *Examiner*'s words, "set itself up for a fall"? Definitive answers might be forthcoming in early 1998 when the ATA lawsuit is settled and the city has had more time to convert its policy into action. It is possible, however, that San Francisco's new law will transform the context of intercity competition by empowering other cities, even poor ones, to pass such laws too. Logan and Molotch write (1987:294–95):

> The best way for the hands of the weak to gain strength is for the privileged places to get tougher. By squeezing capital's locational options from the top, residents can force firms to move down the place hierarchy in their search for satisfactory sites. This will strengthen the bargaining position at each place below, and each place, by imposing its own tougher criteria, will have the same effect on places still lower. All places will gain through this process, even places at the bottom of the hierarchy that must make the most deleterious deals.

To translate this argument into a prediction, if Federal Express does in fact move to Oakland to avoid complying with San Francisco's domestic partners law, then Oakland will be economically stronger and its leaders politically tougher the next time FedEx makes demands. And if FedEx then threatens disinvestment, where will it threaten to go? San Francisco? In time, as the Federal Expresses of the world pinball down the urban hierarchy, mobile capital will become placeless and nomadic. At that point, homeless corporate executives might decide to sink local roots and invest in social justice. Many have done so already in San Francisco, and the city can afford to let the recalcitrant ones go.

REFERENCES

Agnos, A. 1997. "Don't Erode Partners Coverage." *San Francisco Chronicle,* 18 April, p. A25.

Aquino, J. 1997. "Domestic Disturbance." *Recorder,* 19 September, p. 4.

Bailey, R. W. 1998. *Gay Politics, Urban Politics: Identity and Economics in the Urban Setting.* New York: Columbia University Press.

Blackwood, F. 1997. "Business Learns to Live With Domestic Partners." *San Francisco Business Times,* 28 March–3 April, p. 19.

Bowman, C. 1996. "Brown Signs Law on Partner Benefits." *San Francisco Chronicle,* 9 November, p. A15.

Brazil, E. 1996. "S.F. Leaders Set to Snub Clinton." *San Francisco Examiner,* 8 June, p. A1.

Button, J. W., B. A. Rienzo, and K. Wald. 1997. *Private Lives, Public Conflicts: Battles Over Gay Rights in American Communities.* Washington, D.C.: Congressional Quarterly Press.

Cohen, M. 1992. "Rooted Cosmopolitanism." *Dissent,* Fall, pp. 487–93.

DeBare, I. 1997a. "Small Firms Find S.F. Partner Law Hard to Handle." *San Francisco Chronicle,* 29 January, p. A1.

———. 1997b. "BofA Heeds S.F. Law, Offers Domestic Partners Benefits." *San Francisco Chronicle,* 11 March, p. A15.

———. 1997c. "Big Help for Small Firms: Large Insurers to Offer Domestic Partner Coverage." *San Francisco Chronicle,* 28 May, p. B1.

DeLeon, R. E. 1992. *Left Coast City: Progressive Politics in San Francisco, 1975–1991.* Lawrence: University Press of Kansas.

———. 1997. "Progressive Politics in the Left Coast City: San Francisco." In R. Browning, D. Marshall, and D. Tabb, eds., *Racial Politics in American Cities,* 2d ed. White Plains, N.Y.: Longman, pp. 137–59.

Elias, Paul. 1997. "City Partners Law Up in the Air." *Recorder,* 13 October, p. 1.

Epstein, E. 1997a. "Domestic Partner Law Showing Up in S.F. Contracts." *San Francisco Chronicle,* 30 January, p. A13.

———. 1997b. "S.F., United Cut Deal on Partners." *San Francisco Chronicle,* 8 February, p. A1.

———. 1997c. "S.F. Airline Trade Barbs Over Law: Charges Fly on Benefits for Domestic Partners." *San Francisco Chronicle,* 2 July, p. A13.

Fernandez, E. 1997. "Archbishop Tackles S.F. Politics." *San Francisco Examiner,* 9 February, p. C1.

Ginsburg, M. 1997. "Chamber Offers Health Plans." *San Francisco Examiner,* 12 March, p. D1.

Gordon, R. 1997a. "Partners: Catholics Offer a Trade-Off." *San Francisco Examiner,* 1 February, p. A1.

———. 1997b. "Supervisors OK United Deal." *San Francisco Examiner,* 11 February, p. A4.

———. 1997c. "Detailing Domestic Partners Benefits." *San Francisco Examiner,* 1 March, p. A5.

———. 1997d. "BofA to Offer Partners Benefits: New S.F. Law Pushed Banking Giant to Act." *San Francisco Examiner,* 11 March, p. A1.

————. 1997e. "Straight Couples Still 'Partners.'" *San Francisco Examiner,* 9 April, p. A7.

————. 1997f. "Domestic Partners to Get Benefits." *San Francisco Examiner,* 2 May, p. A3.

————. 1997g. "Airlines Sue S.F. over Domestic Partners Law." *San Francisco Examiner,* 14 May, p. A1.

————. 1997h. "Katz Revives Idea to Drop Straights from Partners Law." *San Francisco Examiner,* 16 May, p. A1.

————. 1997i. "United: No Promise of Benefits to Partners." *San Francisco Examiner,* 2 July, p. A1.

————. 1997j. "Partners Law Amendment Outlines New Waiver Rules." *San Francisco Examiner,* 29 October, p. A3.

————. 1997k. "Partners Approval Process Is Clicking." *San Francisco Examiner,* 31 October, p. A1.

Hatfield, L. 1997. "Chevron to Offer Partner Benefits." *San Francisco Examiner,* 1 May, p. A1.

Himelstein, L. 1997. "Going Beyond City Limits?" *Business Week,* 7 July, p. 98.

Holding, R. 1997. "Airlines Sue S.F. Over Benefits: Trade Group Balks at Domestic Partners Law." *San Francisco Chroncle,* 14 May, p. A15.

Hollinger, D. 1995. *Postethnic America.* New York: Basic Books.

Hunter, J. D. 1991. *Culture Wars: The Struggle to Define America.* New York: Basic Books.

Irvine, M. 1997. "Gays Protest at United Airlines." *San Francisco Examiner,* 25 May, p. C4.

Jones, Del. 1997. "Domestic Partner Benefits on Rise: San Francisco Policy Spreads," *USA Today,* 14 October, p. 8B.

King, J. 1997. "Boycott Plan Called Misguided." *San Francisco Chronicle,* 8 July, p. A11.

Lewis, G. 1996a. "Domestic Partner Rule May Hurt Small Business." *San Francisco Examiner,* 30 October, p. A11.

————. 1996b. "Benefits Bill Signed." *San Francisco Examiner,* 8 November, p. A1.

Logan, J. R., and H. L. Molotch. 1987. *Urban Fortunes: The Political Economy of Place.* Berkeley and Los Angeles: University of California Press.

Lynch, A. 1996. "Gay Couples Joyously Exchange Vows in S.F." *San Francisco Chronicle,* 26 March, p. A1.

McCormick, E. 1997. "Partners Law Has Price Tag for City." *San Francisco Examiner,* 12 September, p. A1.

Molotch, H. L. 1990. "Urban Deals in Comparative Perspective." In J. R. Logan and T. Swanstrom, eds., *Beyond the City Limits: Urban Policy and Economic Restructuring in Comparative Perspective.* Philadelphia: Temple University Press, pp. 175–98.

Ness, C. 1997. "City to FedEx: Deliver on Partners Law or Get Out." *San Francisco Examiner,* 16 September, p. A1.

Peterson, P. E. 1995. *The Price of Federalism.* Washington, D.C.: Brookings Institution.

Raine, G. 1997. "More Firms Give Gay Partner Benefits." *San Francisco Examiner,* 24 June, p. A1.

Rauber, C. 1997. "Insurers Start to Feel at Home with Domestic Partners." *San Francisco Business Times,* 21–27 March, p. 6A.

San Francisco Business Times. 1997a. "Supes Help Business Find Domestic Bliss." 28 March–3 April, p. 38.

————. 1997b. "Wells Fargo, Union Jump on Benefits Bandwagon." 18–24 July, p. 22.

San Francisco Chronicle. 1996. "Bad Advice from the Political Master." 7 June, p. A24.

San Francisco Examiner. 1996. "Benefits for Gay Partners at IBM." 20 September, p. B1.

————. 1997a. "The Domestic Partners Flaw." 16 May, p. A20.

————. 1997b. "Taking on the World: Sovereign State of San Francisco Swings its Avenging Fist." 18 June, p. A20.

Schneider, M., and P. Teske. 1992. "Toward a Theory of the Political Entrepreneur: Evidence from Local Government." *American Political Science Review* 86 (September): 737–47.

Sharp, E. B. 1996. "Culture Wars and City Politics: Local Government's Role in Social Conflict." *Urban Affairs Review* 31 (July): 738–58.

————. 1997. "A Comparative Anatomy of Urban Social Conflict." *Political Research Quarterly* 50:261–80.

Sheehy, J., G. Kors, and C. Stuart. 1997. "Legislative Intent." *San Francisco Chronicle,* 21 March, p. A28.

Shioya, T. 1997. "In Sickness and in Health? The Promise of Equal Benefits for Domestic Partners is Uncertain under S.F.'s New Law." *SF Weekly,* 8–14 January, pp. 15–18.

Slind-Flor, V. 1997. "Church, Airlines Balk at Benefits Law." *National Law Journal,* 17 February, p. A6.

Stone, C. 1989. *Regime Politics: Governing Atlanta 1946–1988.* Lawrence: University Press of Kansas.

Tarrow, S. 1994. *Power in Movement: Social Movements, Collective Action and Politics.* Cambridge: Cambridge University Press.

Unger, R. M. 1987. *False Necessity: Anti-Necessitarian Social Theory in the Service of Radical Democracy.* Cambridge: Cambridge University Press.

Zukin, S., and P. DiMaggio. 1990. "Introduction." In S. Zukin and P. DiMaggio, eds., *Structures of Capital: The Social Organization of the Economy.* Cambridge: Cambridge University Press.

8
Values in Conflict: Local Government Response to Hate Crime

Donald P. Haider-Markel and Sean P. O'Brien

In the 1980s, bias-motivated crime began to be recognized as a social problem in the United States (see McDevitt and Levin, 1993). Bias or hate crimes are defined as crimes that are committed, wholly or in part, on the basis of a victim's physical characteristics or group affiliation, which include race, ethnicity, religion, physical or mental disability or handicap, gender, sexual orientation, and nationality (U.S. Department of Justice, 1995:1). By 1995, more than fifty state and local governments had passed legislation to address hate crimes in one form or another (see Berrill, 1992; Freeman and Kaminer, 1994). The increase in the salience of hate crime as a policy issue, however, has largely been ignored by social scientists (but see Jenness and Grattet, 1996; Haider-Markel, 1998) and research on local hate crime policy is virtually nonexistent.

Hate crime, at least in the abstract, is a simple crime issue. Most people are generally opposed to crime in any form and look to government to punish and reduce crime. When majority opinion is skewed in this way, politicians often propose public policy to curry electoral favor. But it is in the details of addressing hate crime that controversy can erupt.

Under Dillon's Rule, public officials may dispute the notion that local governments have the authority to address the issue.[1] Other opponents may become concerned over the constitutional issues involved, including freedom of speech. In addition, the symbolic value of hate crime laws for lesbians and gays may mobilize opposition. Political opposition occurs most often when proposed hate crime ordinances cover sexual orientation.

Given these aspects of the hate crime issue, local governments face the complex task of ensuring that hate crime is taken seriously without invoking the possible culture war issues that may be raised.

* * *

GOVERNMENT ACTIVITY ON HATE CRIMES

Most research on hate crime policy, like most of the public law on hate crime, is with reference to the state or national level (see Jenness and Grattet, 1996; Haider-Markel, 1998). The 1990 federal Hate Crime Statistics Act (HCSA), which cleared Congress in 1989, requires the U.S. Department of Justice to collect statistics on crimes motivated by race, ethnicity, religion, and sexual orientation. The law requests that states and localities voluntarily collect and report statistics on hate crime incidents. Although few organized interests opposed the bill, HCSA was originally opposed by the Justice Department and some members of Congress made unsuccessful attempts to remove the sexual orientation clause (Berrill, 1992:17–19).

The voluntary nature of the HCSA leaves considerable space for states and localities to maneuver on the issue. State and local hate crime policy often takes one of three forms: general laws that prohibit interference with an individual's civil rights, provisions that enhance penalties for bias-motivated crimes, and laws that distinguish between specific bias-motivated crimes. Hate crime policy frequently addresses specific categories or groups of persons, enables victims to file civil lawsuits, requires police training on hate crimes, and requires government agencies to collect statistics on hate crimes. Most state hate crime policies follow the sample legislation proposed by the Anti-Defamation League, and most have been reaffirmed through court challenges (see Freeman and Kaminer, 1994).[2]

Although there are few inherent limitations to state hate crime policies, local governments may perceive weaknesses that can be addressed more readily through local policies. For example, state laws may exclude certain groups or may fail to provide for law enforcement training on hate crimes. Local governments, however, may be constrained by their charters or the activities of county and state governments. Local government activity on hate crime, therefore, can in part be understood within an intergovernmental context.

EXISTING RESEARCH AND A THEORY OF LOCAL GOVERNMENT ROLES

Two models of local government activity offer useful insights in the analysis of local hate crime policy: a social regulatory model of policy adoption and a typology model of local government roles on divisive culture war issues. We suggest a hybrid model that combines elements of both to explain local government responses to the issue of hate crime.

Hate Crime Laws as Social Regulatory Policy

Tatalovich and Daynes (1988:2–4) argue that some public polices can best be classified as *social regulatory policy*. Social regulatory policy regulates a social relationship rather than an economic transaction and is linked to a normative debate over the morality of individual actions and the subsequent consequences of those actions for the rest of society. Social regulatory policies are often, therefore, attempts both to regulate behavior and to redistribute values in society. Social regulatory policy therefore intersects the traditional categories of regulatory policy and redistributive policy, resulting in a pattern of politics that combines elements of both.

Like other types of social regulatory policy, such as abortion, pornography, and gun control (Tatalovich and Daynes, 1988), hate crime policies are expected to regulate a societal harm and place a normative value on that harm, as well as compensate victims and punish offenders. Proponents of hate crime legislation argue that hate crimes harm not only the immediate victims, but also the community as a whole by attaching a positive value to bias-motivated behavior (Ward, 1986:46; McDevitt and Levin, 1993:137).

A key component of social regulatory policy involves the distribution of values, an area requiring little expertise. Therefore, governments need not consult with social "industry" experts before they act on the issue. Instead, social regulatory policies may largely arise out of the political demands of citizens and interest groups, the preferences of politicians, and bureaucratic structure and behavior (Gray and Williams, 1980:155–57; Wirt, 1983; Tatalovich and Daynes, 1988; Nice, 1992).

As with redistributive policies, the enactment of social regulatory policy is often influenced by the level of issue salience. If issue salience is high, information costs will be low, allowing for high citizen participation and the mobilization of interest groups. Attentive interest groups are likely to include citizen, single issue, minority, and religious groups, such as pro-life, African American, or lesbian and gay groups. Salient issues also frequently attract the attention of political elites, including politicians and bureaucrats (Meier, 1994:4–7; see also Polsby, 1984:393).

The social regulatory policy framework, therefore, suggests that hate crime laws are more likely to be adopted by local governments when supportive interest groups are strong, the salience of the issue is high, political elites (both politicians and bureaucrats) are sympathetic, and opposition forces are weak (see Haider-Markel, 1998). The framework, however, does not explicitly discuss the variation in roles that governments might adopt should controversy over the adoption or implementation of hate crime policy ensue. Implicit in the framework is the assumption that success or failure in policy adoption is sufficient to understand the dynamics of public policy (see Haider-Markel, 1998). This assumption underestimates the importance of government actions ranging from immediate responsiveness to repression of the demands of challengers of the status quo.

A Typology of Local Government Roles

In her work, Sharp (1996) views the specific role of government in culture war conflicts as a fundamental question rather than an implicit assumption. Sharp

(1996:747) identifies six roles played by local governments in culture wars: evasion, repression, hyperactive responsiveness, responsiveness, entrepreneurial instigation, and unintentional instigation. The typology of local government roles provides a framework for understanding how local governments address controversial social issues, but the framework does not explain how those roles become politically possible. Implicit within the framework is the notion that local political culture, institutions, and social composition will influence how a government responds to culture war issues (Sharp, 1996:755). How these factors influence government response, however, is not incorporated as an explicit part of Sharp's framework.

A Hybrid Framework

By combining the Tatalovich and Daynes and Sharp frameworks, we can construct a rich model of the pattern of urban politics surrounding controversial social issues. In this section, we describe the contours of a hybrid framework that combines the social regulatory policy framework with the typology of local government roles.

Table 8.1 outlines the main aspects of Sharp's (1996) typology of government roles. Government roles are shown as either first or second order. Beneath the possible roles, we specify the factors that are likely to influence government roles as suggested by Tatalovich and Daynes (1988). The predicted strength of each factor is listed to the right. Hyperactive responsiveness, responsiveness, and entrepreneurial instigation represent positive government responses to challengers of the status quo, and evasion and repression characterize negative responses to challengers.

Local government's role is likely to vary according to the level of each of the political factors. For example, we expect government to adopt a responsive posture toward challengers when interest-group activation and issue salience are at least moderate, elites are somewhat sympathetic, and opposition forces are not strong. When these factors are even stronger (i.e., interest groups are strong; issue salience is high; elites are uniformly sympathetic; and opposition forces are weak), a more dramatic posture—hyperactive responsiveness—is hypothesized. By contrast, negative postures such as evasion and repression are to be expected when interest groups representing a status quo challenge are weaker, elites are not sympathetic, issue salience is relatively low, and opposition forces are strong. Entrepreneurial instigation is somewhat of a distinct case. Although this role is certainly possible, the strength of each political factor is less likely to be certain. For example, although we know that at least one elite should be sympathetic in this case, interest groups may or may not be strong, salience may be moderate or low, and so forth. Second-order government roles—the unintentional instigation of challengers or supporters of the status-quo—are more complex. How the po-

Table 8.1. The Hybrid Framework: Determinants of Local Governent Response to Hate Crime

	Status Quo Challengers	
	Supportive	Not Supportive
First Order	*Hyperactive responsiveness*	*Evasion*
Interest groups	Strong	Weak to moderate
Salience	High	Low to moderate
Elites	Sympathetic	Nonsympathetic or mixed
Opposition forces	Weak	Strong to moderate
	Responsiveness	*Repression*
Interest groups	Strong to moderate	Weak
Salience	High to moderate	Low
Elites	Sympathetic to mixed	Unsympathetic
Opposition forces	Weak to moderate	Strong to moderate
	Entrepreneurial instigation	
Interest groups	Weak to moderate	
Salience	Low to moderate	
Elites	Mixed	
Opposition forces	Unclear	
Second Order	*Unintentional instigation*	*Unintentional instigation*
Interest groups	Weak to moderate	Weak to moderate
Salience	High	High
Elites	Sympathetic or mixed	Nonsympathetic or mixed
Opposition forces	Weak to moderate	Strong to moderate

litical factors suggested by Tatalovich and Daynes (1988) influence second-order response is not readily apparent, but the main constant in these cases should be relatively high levels of issue salience.

Schattschneider (1960) argues that the factors important in a political conflict are likely to change if one side is able to mobilize new actors or alter the venue of political conflict. Similarly, Sharp's (1996) description of second-order roles can be viewed as an expansion of the scope of the conflict. In fact, Sharp implicitly assumes that if one coalition is dissatisfied with the government's response (and has the requisite resources), it will expand the scope of the conflict. Furthermore, as Haider-Markel and Meier (1996) demonstrate, issue salience is a key factor in conflict expansion. As salience increases, conflict expansion becomes more likely and visa versa. Once a conflict expands, the influence of existing political forces on government response becomes less certain. In fact, if the scope of conflict can be expanded on culture war issues, disagreement is even more likely to occur over core moral values. In this case, the advocacy coalition that shares core values with the majority of the populace is more likely to succeed (see Haider-Markel and Meier, 1996). The hybrid model sketched here attempts to make these points explicit.

LOCAL GOVERNMENT ACTIVITY ON HATE CRIME

Local government response to hate crime has exhibited considerable diversity. Only a scattering of localities have passed hate crime ordinances, but many local police departments have established policies related to hate crimes (see Kelly, 1993). For example, neither San Francisco nor New York City has local hate crime ordinances, but law enforcement officials in both cities have established bias crime task forces and aggressively collect statistics on hate crime (Kelly, 1993).

Several factors are likely to account for the relatively low number of local hate crime ordinances. First, the passage in over thirty-six states of statewide laws against bias-motivated crimes may have decreased the need for local laws. Second, many cities simply lack the authority, as outlined by their incorporation charter, to pass laws to create or enhance criminal penalties; an issue that the case studies below make clear.[3] Finally, localities may simply find it easier, and less controversial, to establish bias crime task forces rather than pass legislation to satisfy challengers of the status-quo.

Case studies were identified by first constructing a list of all known localities that have been pressed to consider legislation on hate crime.[4] Although some potential cases were inevitably overlooked, the list is fairly comprehensive.[5] From our main list, we selected cities based on state and regional distribution. The cities in this nonrandom sample also vary considerably by population size, size of minority population, and, to a lesser extent, by local political culture. The amount of variation in the sample should allow for a reasonable exploration of the hybrid framework in addition to providing a basis from which to generalize the findings.

Albuquerque, New Mexico

Albuquerque has a growing population exceeding 385,000, over 40 percent of whom are nonwhite.[6] Local government consists of a mayor and a nine-member city council elected from separate districts to four-year terms. Although New Mexico does have a hate crime law requiring law enforcement to collect statistics for hate crimes based on race and ethnicity, the law is extremely narrow and does not increase criminal penalties, allow for civil action, or provide for law enforcement training (Haider-Markel, 1997: Appendix I). The narrow scope of the state law has provided the impetus for activists to push for more expansive state and local laws.

In the early 1990s, a coalition of Latino, Native American, African American, women's, religious, and gay and lesbian organizations formed in New Mexico around the issue of hate crimes. By 1993, the coalition's efforts led to the passage of the New Mexico Hate Crimes Bill in both legislative houses.[7] The bill was subsequently vetoed by the Republican governor, who would also veto a similar version in 1995. Republican legislators and antigay lobbying groups offered significant opposition to the bill, and the effort to override Governor Johnson's veto fell two votes short.

Faced with an evasive state government, the coalition trained its focus on local hate crimes initiatives. On December 16, 1996, after an intense lobbying effort on behalf of the coalition, the Albuquerque Hate Crimes Ordinance (0-56) was passed 7–2 by the Albuquerque city council. The ordinance, sponsored by the mayor and council member Bregman provided for penalties of ninety days in jail and a fine of no more than $500 for the commission of bias-motivated crimes. Because felonies are subject to state jurisdiction, only misdemeanor crimes are covered by the penalty enhancer. Covered under the ordinance were crimes committed out of animus on the basis of ancestry, gender, disability, national origin, religion, and sexual orientation. An amendment aimed at stripping the bill of coverage of sexual orientation failed by a vote of 6–3.

Albuquerque Police Chief Joe Polisar testified in favor of the ordinance, characterizing it as needed legislation. Although the issue was highly salient, opposition forces were not significantly mobilized. Those speaking in opposition to the bill included members of the New Mexico Militia, a right-wing minister, and the New Mexico Christian Coalition. Faced with a highly mobilized hate crime coalition, the opposition forces held little sway with local officials.

Although hate crime activists had originally focused their attention on passing state legislation and virtually ignored local government, continued evasion by the governor mobilized activists in Albuquerque. Local officials responded almost immediately. Had the comprehensive state hate crime legislation passed, it seems unlikely that local activists and officials would have taken action on the issue.

Chicago, Illinois

Its population exceeding 3 million, Chicago is the largest city in the sample.[8] Over 50 percent of the population is nonwhite; nearly 40 percent of those are African American, and 20 percent are Latino. Chicago is covered by a state hate crime law, a limited form of which was enacted in 1986. The city is also covered by Cook County's narrow hate crime law (Haider-Markel, 1997: Appendix I). Chicago uses a mayor-council form of government, with council members elected from fifty wards.

In November 1989, the thirty-one-member Hate Crimes Prosecution Council, composed of politicians, legal experts, community organizers, and government officials, undertook initiatives to combat hate crime. The council's purpose was to train prosecutors to litigate hate crime cases, provide assistance to hate crime victims, and recommend local and state legislation (Davis, 1990; Tomaso, 1993:99). The increased saliency of the issue resulted from the legislature's expansion of the state hate crime law and the passage of a similar law in Cook County. Although each of these laws was similar in content, the county law excluded sexual orientation.

In a keen display of entrepreneurial instigation, Alderman Bernard Hansen (44th) sponsored a local hate crime ordinance on December 6, 1990. The proposal covered crimes motivated by gender, age, or sexual orientation bias (Kass, 1990a). Hansen argued that his bill supplemented state and county law by adding more categories, requiring police to keep statistics on hate crime, mandating police training on hate crimes, and providing counseling to victims of hate crime (Kass, 1990a).[9] Persons convicted of violating the ordinance faced a maximum $500 fine and/or six months in jail. Hansen chose to announce the proposal against a backdrop of supportive aldermen, minority groups, and lesbian and gay activists. Few individuals and groups testified in opposition to the proposal, and there was no immediate mobilization by potential opposition groups (Kass, 1990a,b).

The proposal moved easily through the full council on December 19 and was quickly signed by the mayor. In large measure because of the existence of a state hate crime law, there was little negative reaction to Chicago's ordinance. Chicago and Cook County police and prosecutors have aggressively enforced the city, county, and state hate crime laws and have been reasonably attentive to minority and lesbian and gay concerns (Tomaso, 1993; Morales, 1995). In fact, the state's attorney in Cook County wrote *The Prosecutor's Guide to Hate Crime*, a 153-page book on convicting persons accused of committing hate crimes (Morales, 1995:34–35).

Louisville, Kentucky

Louisville is a medium-sized Southern city with a population of 270,000.[10] More than 30 percent of the population is nonwhite, and a majority of these residents are African Americans. Louisville is not covered by a state hate crime law, but a failed attempt was made to pass such a law in 1990 (Haider-Markel, 1997: Appendix H). The city uses a mayor-council form of government with council members elected from twelve wards.

In January 1990, two white men burned a six-foot cross and left a threatening note on the lawn of a black family that had recently moved into a predominately white Louisville neighborhood. Community leaders expressed outrage over the incident, and local activists from the Kentucky Rainbow Coalition formed a coalition of groups to call for a local hate crimes ordinance. Alderman Bather took up the cause of the activists, and on February 10, 1990, introduced a proposal that, among other things, would make it illegal to harass or intimidate anyone on the basis of their race, gender, religion, sexual orientation, or ethnic origin (Matthews, 1990a).

On March 7, the first council hearing on the proposed ordinance drew a coalition of gay, Jewish, disabled, and black groups, each arguing that sexual orientation should be retained in the proposal. Those opposed to the proposal argued that gays should not be covered under the ordinance because homosexual sodomy is illegal under Kentucky law. The Reverend James Bevel of Washington,

D.C. presented the harshest argument, linking homosexual behavior to the decline of civilization (Cunningham, 1990a).

By early July, law enforcement officials began to support the proposal publicly. Jefferson County officials pledged to be more attentive to bias-motivated crimes and promised to provide special bias-crime training to county police (Cunningham, 1990b; Stewart, 1990). On July 10, the city council passed the ordinance 8–4 in the presence of over two hundred onlookers, few of whom represented opposition groups. The hate crimes coalition lobbied successfully to defeat (7–4) an amendment to strip sexual orientation from the law. The law was also amended to delay implementation for ninety days to give the state Attorney General time to offer an opinion on its constitutionality (Miller, 1990). Before the law took effect in October, the Attorney General issued an opinion declaring the law unconstitutional. The main sticking point appeared to be that a person would have to first violate a state or federal law in order to violate the new law. Such a concept was argued to violate state law (McDonough, 1990).

In the fall, Alderman Bather introduced a revised law that removed all criminal penalties but gave the Louisville–Jefferson County Human Relations Commission the power to investigate and impose monetary penalties against any person who, out of bigotry, harms another.[11] Support for the new measure had increased over the summer as the media provided intense coverage of at least twenty-one incidents in which four young black men beat and robbed randomly chosen whites (McDonough, 1991a).

Aldermanic support for the revised law, however, was stymied by an increasingly mobilized opposition force of religious groups. On September 24, approximately fifty opponents of the hate crime law protested in front of city hall against the inclusion of sexual orientation in the law. One group, Citizens for Decency (CFD), argued that if the ordinance was passed "it would be seen as an invitation to homosexuals nationwide to converge on our community, creating another San Francisco" (McDonough, 1991b).

On October 4, the city council held a public hearing on the new measure. The hearing was packed with supporters; opponents filed in after holding a protest outside. Members of CFD spoke against the measure, arguing that the law might prevent ministers from teaching, in accordance with the Bible, that homosexuality is wrong (Muhammad, 1991a). The salience of the issue intensified as newspapers published multiple stories, editorials, and columns on the legislation and hate crime incidents (see, e.g., Pearce, 1991; Stanley, 1991).

On November 12, the city council passed the hate crime measure 7–4–1 before a crowd of over two hundred (Muhammad, 1991b). The state attorney general reviewed the law and declared that it would pass constitutional muster, thereby derailing religious groups who had planned to challenge the law in court. Overall, local sources suggest that there would have been little or no opposition to the Louisville hate crime law if sexual orientation had not been included. They attribute passage to the efforts of the bill's sponsor, Alderman Bather, and heavy lobbying efforts on the part of the hate crime coalition. Some law enforcement officials, including the Chief of Police, did express support for the measure and cited hate crime as a problem, but most rank-and-file officers remained silent on the issue.

When the issue of hate crime was first raised in Louisville, local government action verged on the hyperactively responsive. Hate crime activists were able to push legislation through the council fairly quickly, even though constitutional problems were raised. However, the inclusion of a delay that allowed for constitutional review meant that the legislative process did unfold at a normal pace and that Louisville city government's role was simple responsiveness to challengers of the status quo.

Oklahoma City, Oklahoma

Oklahoma City is covered by a narrow and relatively weak state hate crime law that was passed in 1988 (Haider-Markel, 1997: Appendix I).[12] Of its roughly 444,000 residents, 25 percent are nonwhite. Minority groups have very little influence on Oklahoma City politics, but gay influence increased with the formation of a lesbian and gay PAC. The city government comprises a city manager (appointed by the mayor and council), the city council (elected from eight wards), and the mayor.

In 1988, a series of acts of vandalism against local churches and synagogues brought the issue of hate crimes to the attention of Oklahoma City residents. On his own initiative, Councilman Mark Schwartz (Ward 2) proposed a hate crimes ordinance that would create criminal penalties for those convicted of bias-motivated crimes.[13] Schwartz's proposal also established a human rights commission to ensure enforcement of the law (see Berrill, 1992). The initial proposal did not provide coverage for crimes perpetrated on the basis of a victim's sexual orientation. Local gay groups, however, convinced Schwartz to include the clause by reminding him of their role in his election.

Opposition to the measure, from both citizens and council members, was largely diminished because no public hearings were held on the issue and local newspapers largely avoided editorializing until after the law had passed. Without media attention, the salience of the issue remained fairly low. Although activists were unable to elicit active support from the law enforcement elites, law enforcement officials did not voice public opposition to the ordinance.

In the absence of mobilized opposition, and with the support of the mayor, the hate crime proposal passed easily through the council on March 15, 1988. One council member did voice opposition to the inclusion of sexual orientation in the bill. Instead of voting, however, he opted to take a stroll while the votes were taken and tallied. Although the ordinance appeared strong in theory, time has shown that it is largely symbolic. The police have yet to collect any hate crime statistics or make an arrest under the ordinance. Furthermore, the human rights commission—the body named to track hate crimes in the city—was defunded in 1994.

The Oklahoma City case, one of entrepreneurial instigation, suggests that issue salience need not be high for local government to act. If issue salience had been higher, local gay groups may have been unable to use what little influence they had to expand the scope of the law after it was introduced because heightened issue salience likely would have sparked a more highly mobilized opposition.

Springfield, Missouri

Springfield is a medium-sized city of just over 147,000 residents.[14] The city's minority population is rather small; African Americans make up less than 2 percent of the population. Springfield is covered by a state hate crime law, but the law is narrow in scope and limits coverage to race and ethnicity (Haider-Markel, 1997: Appendix I). The municipal government is of the council-manager variety, with four council members elected by district and five elected at-large. Springfield's charter has a home-rule clause, which provides the government with a fair amount of local autonomy.[15]

From the beginning, the issue of hate crime in Springfield was framed as a "gay issue." In 1993, an arsonist targeted the home of a local gay actor who held a role in a controversial play at the University of Missouri. A newly formed group called Citizens Organized to Oppose Hate and Bigotry (COHAB) joined forces with the local chapter of the National Association for the Advancement of Colored People and convinced the mayor to quickly establish a Task Force on Bias Crimes. On the basis of the initial task force findings, council members Wilson, Wolff, and Rhodes sponsored a bias crimes ordinance (Council Bill 93-277). The proposal provided criminal penalties for those convicted of bias-motivated crimes based on race, color, gender, religion, national origin, disability, or sexual orientation (Leonard, 1994a).[16]

Gay groups were instrumental in ensuring that the ordinance quickly passed its first Council reading on September 20 and its final reading on October 4. Local law enforcement officials were indifferent to the measure. Opposition forces were unable to mobilize in time to block its passage, but once the ordinance did pass, a local group formed to collect signatures for a ballot repeal of the measure (Keen, 1994). The repeal was organized by Citizens for Decent Standards (CDS). To mobilize the community, CDS held public screenings of the antigay videos *Gay Rights, Special Rights,* and *The Gay Agenda.* CDS also sponsored visits by the Reverend Lou Sheldon and Paul Cameron, two national antigay activists (Keen, 1994; People For the American Way, 1994:51).

In January 1994, CDS presented the council with a petition, signed by twelve hundred citizens and calling for a referendum on the ordinance. The city council voted to add the item to the February 8 local election ballot (Leonard, 1994a).

After the vote, CDS forces continued their antigay campaign, arguing that the ordinance was a mini-gay rights bill that would protect pedophiles (Keen, 1994; Leonard, 1994b). Having successfully expanded the scope of the conflict, CDS forces succeeded in their efforts to outmaneuver ordinance proponents, and the ballot measure passed by a margin of 71 to 29 percent, repealing the hate crime law (Keen, 1994; Leonard, 1994b).

This case clearly demonstrates that local government may have a first-order role that differs from its second-order role, even when the resources of proponents and opponents remain fairly stable. Springfield's first-order role was hyperactively responsive, largely because the mayor and council members acted unusually quickly without allowing opposition forces to vocalize fully the extent and depth of their concerns. Had politicians pursued a process that allowed for a full airing of community sentiment, the task force might not have been formed and the ordinance probably would have failed. The hyperactive first-order role unintentionally instigated opposition forces in the form of CDS. Once opposition forces mobilized, they proceeded to expand the conflict to the broader public and successfully appealed to citizen fears and bias against homosexuality. This case suggests that local governments can unintentionally instigate opposition forces when they are hyperactively responsive to the demands of challengers.

Tulsa, Oklahoma

Tulsa's population of nearly 390,000 is 15 percent black, 3 percent Latino, and 5 percent Native American.[17] Tulsa is covered by a narrow and relatively weak state hate crime law (Haider-Markel, 1997: Appendix I). Although the city is not known for progressive stances on civil rights issues, African Americans, Native Americans, Latinos, and lesbians and gays have had moderate influence on local politics. Tulsa government is organized in the mayor-council form, with nine council members representing their own districts.

The debate on discrimination and bias-motivated crime in Tulsa can be traced back as far as 1977. Over time, the existing city Human Rights Commission became more aggressive in addressing minority concerns and reaching out to Tulsa's gay community. Throughout most of the 1980s, however, opposition from Mayor Inhofe stymied government consideration of minority issues, including hate crimes. In 1987 the Say No to Hate Coalition was formed by local activists.[18] The coalition's principal objective was to pass a statewide hate crime law. It made parallel efforts to pass a local ordinance.[19] At minimum, the coalition wanted the Tulsa city council to adopt a resolution calling for a state hate crime bill. About the same time, the Tulsa Police Department formed a unit to track hate crimes.

In 1993, the coalition convinced the Tulsa Human Rights Commission to conduct a study and complete a report on hate crimes in Tulsa, a move supported by the new mayor. During the course of its study, the commission focused on the fact that, even though most Tulsa hate crimes were committed against gays and lesbians, sexual orientation was not covered in the state hate crime statute. The commission recommended that the city call for the state statute to be amended to include sexual orientation. It also asked Tulsa police to comply voluntarily with the Federal Hate Crimes Statistics Act of 1990 and, to that end, begin reporting hate crimes committed on the basis of sexual orientation. The city council ignored these recommendations and failed to discuss in council sessions the issues raised in the report. This inaction occurred despite media coverage of several hate crimes, including the murder of a gay man in 1993.

In 1994, the hate crime issue became increasingly intertwined with homosexuality. During the course of a new study by the Human Rights Commission, local conservative and religious groups attended a number of public hearings to voice their displeasure at the discussion of sexual orientation. As opposition forces mobilized, most members of the city council indicated that they would not even consider the hate crime issue. Nonetheless, the commission's 1994 report made the same recommendations as the 1993 report (see Human Rights Commission, 1994).

The city council, along with the mayor, refused to act on the relatively weak recommendations contained in the 1994 report. No further public hearings were held or resolutions introduced thereafter. This evasion was largely due to the commission's focus on sexual orientation, a focus which caused politicians to veer away from the hate crime issue entirely.

Wichita, Kansas

With a population of just over 300,000, Wichita is not covered by a state hate crime law.[20] In fact, the state legislature did not even consider a hate crime law until 1996 (see Haider-Markel, 1997: Appendix H). Wichita uses a mayor-council form of government, but also has a city manager. The city council is composed of six members, each elected by district.

In October 1989, local activists from minority and gay groups began calling on the city to address the issue of hate crimes. Although local black leaders initiated the debate, the Wichita Gay and Lesbian Alliance lobbied heavily for the passage of a local ordinance that would include penalties for crimes motivated by sexual orientation bias (Lynn, 1990a,b). In drafting the initial proposal, local black leaders consulted with activists in St. Louis who had passed a hate crime law in February 1989 (Lynn, 1990c).

The mayor and several council members came out in favor of an ordinance early in the debate. The first draft of the ordinance covered crimes based on race, color, gender, religion, national origin, age, ancestry, disability, or handicap. Sexual orientation was included during a closed meeting that took place after the city council's first review of the ordinance. Revealing their anger over the inclusion of sexual orientation, some council members blocked an October 2 vote on the ordinance by invoking a series of rarely used parliamentary maneuvers (Lynn, 1990a).

Once the decision was made to delay the vote, the battle for the hate crime law revolved solely around the question of recognizing gays and lesbians as a minority group. Indeed, one city official speculated that "without the phrase 'sexual orientation' the ordinance would have been approved without delay" (Lynn, 1990a). The main opposition group, the Wichita Alliance of Evangelical Churches (WAEC), mobilized heavily against the hate crime ordinance and called for the removal of the sexual orientation clause (Lynn, 1990a). Members of WAEC argued that the law would ban ministers from preaching against homosexuality from the pulpit (Lynn, 1990b). Local police stayed out of the political fray, but did announce that they would begin collecting hate crime statistics under the 1990 Federal Hate Crimes Statistics Act (Lynn, 1990b).

The final draft of the bill provided penalties of up to $2,500 and/or one year in jail for misdemeanors motivated by bias. Sexual orientation was included, but the bill was amended to read "nothing in the ordinance should be construed to promote, encourage or condone any organization, group or religion" (Wichita ordinance no. 41-204). The amendment was accepted by the council in a unanimous vote. Although the amendment did not completely satisfy the groups lobbying on either side of the bill, the ordinance passed 5 to 2 on October 16, 1990 (Lynn, 1990c).

Little negative aftermath followed in the wake of the law's passage, but many characterized the law as a symbolic effort (Lynn, 1990c). Local police have enforced the law, but have yet to establish a special task force to deal with hate crimes beyond the collection of statistics. The Wichita case suggests that even when local governments are responsive to challengers, they can also be responsive to opposition forces through weak policy implementation and enforcement.

Summary

Although the cities examined here exhibit variation in their history of progressive politics, size of minority population, and in the structure of government institutions, these factors appear to have little influence on how each local government addressed the hate crime issue. For example, the size of the nonwhite population in each city varied by as much as 50 percent, but higher minority populations ensured neither a quick nor a comprehensive response by local government. Despite their contrasting structures of government, both Chicago and Oklahoma City yielded cases of entrepreneurial instigation, and, although Wichita has a council-manager form of government and Louisville and Albuquerque do not, all three sites were responsive to activists favoring hate crime ordinances.

The cases demonstrate that although local governments vary in the roles they play on culture war issues, hate crime in particular seems to elicit roles that are favorable to challengers of the status quo. As shown in Table 8.2, these cases reveal several examples of entrepreneurial instigation, responsiveness, and even hyperactive responsiveness; but only one example of evasion and no instances of repression were detected in these case-study cities. This suggests that hate crime, like the issue of crime in general, tends to be an issue with only one politically acceptable side—the side pushing for more help for victims and more aggressive action against offenders.

In the only case involving a first-order role unfavorable to challengers of the status quo, Tulsa's local government eschewed the demands of local activists and refused to pass resolutions calling for the expansion of the state hate crime law. Tulsa's evasion of the issue appears to be due to the relative weakness of challenger groups, unsympathetic politicians, low issue salience, and a fairly well mobilized opposition.

Albuquerque is somewhat of a unique case, both because it passed its ordinance well after the other localities and because local government action, although responsive, was largely a reaction to evasion on the issue by the state government. If the state government had been responsive to hate crimes, it is unlikely that Albuquerque officials would have addressed the issue. Increased issue salience, combined with the mobilization of local challengers, led sympathetic elites to respond affirmatively to hate crime activists. In fact, one might even describe the Albuquerque case as a first-order role of evasion by the state and a second-order role of unintentional instigation of local challengers of the status quo.

The Albuquerque and Tulsa cases may also suggest a minor revision of the Sharp (1996) framework. Recall that Sharp (1996:747) defines the evasion role as a lack of policy responsiveness. In our cases, Tulsa officials virtually ignored the hate crime issue; by contrast, New Mexico legislators tried to be responsive

Table 8.2. Local Government Roles in Response to Hate Crime: The Cases in Comparison

First Order	Hyperactive responsiveness	Evasion
	Springfield, Mo.	Tulsa, Okla.
	Responsiveness	Repression
	Albuquerque, N.M.	(none)
	Louisville, Ky.	
	Wichita, Kans.	
	Entrepreneurial instigation	
	Chicago, Ill.	
	Oklahoma City, Okla	
Second Order	Unintentional instigation	Unintentional instigation
	(none)	Springfield, Mo.

but were blocked by the governor. The cases are different, but would be classified as instances of evasion under Sharp's conceptualization. Given the importance of sympathetic political elites in our model, perhaps the evasion role should be refined into two categories: government officials ignore the issue (evasion); or elites are divided, with some attempting to be responsive while others block the policy initiative (nonresponsiveness). Symbolic actions, such as Oklahoma City's unenforced ordinance and defunded implementing commission, also might be classified as nonresponsive roles.

Localities such as Louisville and Wichita, faced with forces mobilized on both sides of the issue, reacted slowly, but were decidedly responsive to hate crime activists. Louisville represents an interesting case because, although government response was slow during the second round, the first ordinance passed even though the council was cautioned it might be unconstitutional. Furthermore, during consideration of the revised ordinance, opposition forces mobilized (around the inclusion of gays) more forcefully. In this sense, the first-order response in Louisville might be thought of as hyperactive, whereas the second-order response, after unintentional instigation of opposition forces, was merely responsive. The key appears to be issue salience centered around the inclusion of gays. As salience increased, opposition forces mobilized but were unable to block the initial proposal. This finding suggests that general issue salience may increase the likelihood of government action, but increased salience concerning gays may diminish the influence of hate crime activists.

In Chicago and Oklahoma City, hate crime activists faced little organized opposition, and hate crime policies were adopted fairly quickly. Government action in both cities, however, appeared driven by the entrepreneurial activities of political elites rather than hate crime activists. Even though Chicago's minority and gay interest groups were stronger and elites more sympathetic than those in Oklahoma City, entrepreneurial instigation in both cities explains why both governments addressed hate crimes. This finding suggests that the activity of entrepreneurial politicians can compensate for the absence of other supportive political forces. But, the strong enforcement of hate crime laws in Chicago, in contrast to that in Oklahoma City, may demonstrate that political entrepreneurs cannot ensure strong policy enforcement without the support of other political forces, such as interest groups.

Government action in Springfield, while initially exhibiting a role of hyperactive responsiveness, unintentionally mobilized opposition forces that were able to repeal the hate crime ordinance by ballot initiative. The case illustrates the dynamic nature of culture war politics; even when government is responsive, losers in the legislative arena may be able to expand the scope of the conflict to include an audience more receptive to their perspective. In this particular case, opposition forces were able to reverse local government action by ballot initiative, but the losers on any culture war issue can also reverse government action by electing politicians sympathetic to their perspective.

SUMMARY

In general, local government's role in dealing with the hate crime issue is contingent on the strength of challenger interest groups, the salience of the issue, the support of politicians, and the strength of opposition forces. However, interest-group strength and issue salience did not help to account for cases of entrepreneurial instigation.

Furthermore, the influence of bureaucratic political elites (in this case, law enforcement officials) is less clear. Sometimes police officials lend their support to drives for hate crime ordinances, but it is not clear whether that support was instrumental in gaining responsiveness. The ability of bureaucratic institutions to influence government activity on culture war issues merits further study.

Although the structure of local political institutions appeared to have little influence in our cases, the cases did reveal that there is an intergovernmental dimension to culture war politics. In several cases, the activities of challengers of the status quo and local government were, in part, structured by the actions of county and state governments. For example, if New Mexico officials had not been evasive on hate crime, Albuquerque probably would not have considered the issue. In Chicago, a political entrepreneur was able to gain support for his hate crime proposal by pointing out the limitations of the Illinois hate crime law. In Louisville, Oklahoma City, and Tulsa, challengers sought state and local government action simultaneously with mixed results.

State government action does not necessarily prevent local governments from adopting a role on these issues, and state inaction does not ensure local government responsiveness. Instead, factors specified in our hybrid model, such as interest-group strength and sympathetic elites, are more likely to determine local government roles. At a minimum, however, state government responsiveness or evasion may serve to increase the salience of culture war issues and thereby mobilize attentive publics at the local level.

Finally, the results of this analysis suggest that local politics concerning hate crime and other culture war issues can best be understood by adopting a theoretical framework that incorporates both the role of local government and the factors that are likely to influence those roles. Specifically, government roles ranging from hyperactive responsiveness to repression can best be explained within a framework that incorporates the influence of groups on both sides of the issue.

NOTES

1. Dillon's Rule refers to the relationship between states and cities. A city's legal authority is limited by its charter, which is passed by the state government. The Home Rule movement, which began in the late 1800s, increased the authority of cities when some states passed laws that allowed cities to draft and amend their own charters.

2. In *R.A.V. v. City of St. Paul,* the U.S. Supreme Court ruled that a local hate crime ordinance violated the freedom of speech (Freeman and Kaminer, 1994:5). The Supreme Court upheld Wisconsin's hate crime law, which was modeled on the ADL statute, in *Wisconsin v. Mitchell.* The Court ruled that the law focused on conduct motivated by bias and therefore did not threaten free speech (Freeman and Kaminer, 1994:6–7). Hate crime laws have also been upheld in state and circuit courts in California, Florida, Idaho, Illinois, Iowa, Michigan, Missouri, New Jersey, New York, Ohio, Oregon, Vermont, and Washington (Freeman and Kaminer, 1994:13–18).

3. One interesting case, not included in the analysis, is Orange County, North Carolina. County commissioners wrote an ordinance in 1992 that would create bias crime protections for several minority groups. The ordinance, however, had to be cleared by the state legislature. To avoid controversy, the state assembly removed sexual orientation. The law passed and went into effect in 1993. In 1995, Orange County petitioned the state legislature to expand the ordinance to include sexual orientation but the measure failed in the assembly (Schultz, 1997).

4. The following localities have considered legislative action on hate crime: Albuquerque, N.M.; Atlanta, Ga.; Burlington, Ia.; Chicago, Ill.; Columbus, Ohio; El Cerrito, Calif.; Henderson, Ky.; Independence, Mo.; Lacey, Wash.; Louisville, Ken.; Montgomery County, Md.; Oklahoma City, Okla.; Olympia, Wash.; Orange County, N.C.; St. Louis, Mo.; St. Paul, Minn.; Seattle, Wash.; Springfield, Mo.; Tulsa, Okla.; Tumwater, Wash.; Wichita, Kans. (see Haider-Markel, 1997: Appendices H, I).

5. For example, see Berrill's (1992) list which only includes enacted laws that also cover sexual orientation.

6. Unless otherwise noted, the information on Albuquerque is from correspondence with Bob Summersgill, publisher of the *New Mexico Rainbow.*

7. The bill would have enhanced criminal penalties for hate crimes based on race, ethnicity, religion, and sexual orientation.

8. Unless otherwise noted, information on the Chicago case was obtained through correspondence with Rick Garcia of the Illinois Federation for Human Rights.

9. In the late 1980s, the Chicago Police Department had adopted its own policy of collecting statistics on bias crimes relating to race, national origin, religion, and sexual orientation. This policy, however, was not required by law (Kass, 1990a).

10. Unless otherwise noted, information on Louisville was obtained through interviews and correspondence with local activists Jane Hope and Carla Wallace.

11. The revised law covers victims of attacks motivated by race, religion, sexual orientation, ethnicity, health-related conditions, or disability (McDonough, 1991a).

12. Unless otherwise noted, information on Oklahoma City is from an interview with Bill Rogers, a local gay community activist.

13. The criminal penalties for a violation of the law include a fine not to exceed $500 and/or imprisonment not to exceed ninety days (see Oklahoma City ordinance number 18,949).

14. Unless otherwise noted, information on Springfield is from local lesbian activists Blaize Malone and Leah Edelman.

15. Information from Springfield city charter, made available to the authors by the Springfield City Clerk's Office.

16. Information based on Assistant City Attorney internal memo dated September 9, 1993.

17. Unless otherwise noted, information on Tulsa was obtained from interviews with local activist Kelly Kirby.

18. The coalition comprised representatives of many groups including the NAACP, the Jewish Federation, Tulsa Metropolitan Ministry, Tulsa Oklahomans for Human Rights, and the Tulsa Police Department, among others.

19. The activists were successful in the state legislature in 1988. The resulting hate crime law, however, only covers race, ethnicity, and disability.

20 Unless otherwise noted, information on Wichita is from correspondence with Scott Curry of the Land of Awes, a local gay activist group.

REFERENCES

Berrill, Kevin T. 1992. *Countering Anti-Gay Violence through Legislation.* Washington, D.C.: National Gay and Lesbian Task Force Policy Institute.

Cunningham, Rob. 1990a. "Aldermen Hear Speakers Plead for Louisville Hate-Crime Law." *Louisville (Ky.) Courier-Journal,* 8 March, sec. B.

———. 1990b. "Aldermanic Panel Approves Proposed Hate-Crime Law." *Louisville (Ky.) Courier-Journal,* 29 June.

Davis, Robert. 1990. "New Program to Aid 'Hate Crime' Victims in Suing Tormentors." *Chicago Tribune,* 31 January, sec. 2.

Freeman, Steven M., and Debbie N. Kaminer. 1994. *Hate Crimes Laws: A Comprehensive Guide.* New York: Anti-Defamation League.

Gray, Virginia, and Bruce Williams. 1980. *The Organizational Politics of Criminal Justice.* Lexington, Mass.: Lexington Books.

Haider-Markel, Donald P. 1997. "From Bullhorns to PACs: Lesbian and Gay Politics, Interest Groups, and Policy." Ph.D. diss. University of Wisconsin-Milwaukee.

———. 1998. "The Politics of Social Regulatory Policy: State and Federal Hate Crime Policy and Implementation Effort." *Political Research Quarterly* 51(1): 69–88.

Haider-Markel, Donald P., and Kenneth J. Meier. 1996. "The Politics of Gay and Lesbian Rights: Expanding the Scope of the Conflict." *Journal of Politics* 58:352–69.

Human Rights Commission. 1994. Report and Recommendations of the Committee on *Sexual Orientation Discrimination.* Tulsa, Okla: Human Rights Commission.

Jenness, Valerie, and Ryken Grattet. 1996. "The Criminalization of Hate: A Comparison of Structural and Polity Influences on the Passage of 'Bias-Crime' Legislation in the United States." *Sociological Perspectives* 39:129–54.

Kass, John. 1990a. "City 'Hate Crime' Law Would Add Women." *Chicago Tribune,* 7 December, sec. 3.

———. 1990b. "No Love Lost as Foes Assail Daley at Hate-Crime Talks." *Chicago Tribune,* 15 December, sec. 1.

Keen, Lisa. 1994. "Missouri Voters Repeal City's 'Mini-Gay Rights Bill.'" *Washington (D.C.) Blade,* 18 February.

Kelly, Robert J., ed. 1993. *Bias Crime: American Law Enforcement and Legal Responses,* rev. ed. Chicago: University of Illinois at Chicago.

Leonard, Arthur S. 1994a. "Lesbian/Gay Legal News." *Lesbian/Gay Law Notes,* February.

———. 1994b. "Lesbian/Gay Legal News." *Lesbian/Gay Law Notes,* March.

Lynn, Jim. 1990a. "Delay in Vote Ignites Gay-Rights Fight." *Wichita (Kans.) Eagle,* 3 October.

———. 1990b. "Gay Rights Focus of Hate-Crime Fight." *Wichita (Kans.) Eagle,* 15 October.

———. 1990c. "Wichita Adopts Extra Penalty for Hate Crimes." *Wichita (Kans.) Eagle,* 17 October.

Matthews, Clarence. 1990a. "Alderman Proposes Outlawing Harassment Based on Race, Religion." *Louisville (Ky.) Courier-Journal,* 9 February.

———. 1990b. "Residents Come Together from Diverse Backgrounds to Try and Lessen Prejudice." *Louisville (Ky.) Courier-Journal,* 29 June.

McDevitt, Jack, and Jack Levin. 1993. *Hate Crimes: The Rising Tide of Bigotry and Bloodshed.* New York: Plenum Press.

McDonough, Rick. 1990. "State Opinion Calls City's Hate-Crimes Law Unconstitutional." *Louisville (Ky.) Courier-Journal,* 3 October, sec. B.

———. 1991a. "Attacks Boost Support for Hate-Crimes Measure." *Louisville (Ky.) Courier-Journal,* 7 September, sec. B.

———. 1991b. "Demonstrators Urge Aldermen Not to Pass Hate Crimes Ordinance." *Louisville (Ky.) Courier-Journal,* 25 September, sec. B.

Meier, Kenneth J. 1994. *The Politics of Sin: Drugs, Alcohol, and Public Policy.* Armonk, N.Y.: M. E. Sharpe.

Miller, Calvin. 1990. "Board of Aldermen Passes Law Making 'Hate Crimes' Illegal." *Louisville (Ky.) Courier-Journal,* 11 July, sec. B.

Morales, Jorge. 1995. "Cities of Light." *Advocate,* July (11.34–35).

Muhammad, Lawrence. 1991a. "Homosexuals Support Hate-Crime Ordinance at Hearing; Foes Assail it." *Louisville (Ky.) Courier-Journal,* 5 October.

———. 1991b. "Hate-Crimes Bill Passes; Ordinance Includes Protections for Gays." *Louisville (Ky.) Courier-Journal,* 13 November, sec. B.

Nice, David C. 1992. "The States and the Death Penalty." *Western Political Quarterly* 45:1037–48.

Pearce, John. 1991. "Moral Zealots." *Louisville (Ky.) Courier-Journal,* 10 November.

People For the American Way. 1994. *Hostile Climate.* Washington, D.C.: People for the American Way.

Polsby, Nelson. 1984. *Political Innovation in America.* New Haven, Conn.: Yale University Press.

Schattschneider, E. E. 1960. *The Semi-Sovereign People.* New York: Holt, Reinhart, and Winston.

Schultz, Mark. 1997. "County Panel Rewrites Civil Rights Code for Gays, Lesbians." *Chapel Hill (N.C.) Herald,* 2 March, sec. A.

Sharp, Elaine B. 1996. "Culture Wars and City Politics: Local Government's Role in Social Conflict." *Urban Affairs Review* 31:738–58.

Stanley, T. L. 1991. "Violence is Increasing, Activists Say." *Louisville (Ky.) Courier-Journal,* 10 November, sec. A.

Stewart, Kay. 1990. "Hate Crimes to Get More Scrutiny in County." *Louisville (Ky.) Courier-Journal,* 4 July.

Tatalovich, Raymond, and Byron W. Daynes, eds. 1988. *Social Regulatory Policy: Moral Controversies in American Politics.* Boulder, Colo.: Westview Press.

Tomaso, Al. 1993. "Hate Crimes." In Robert J. Kelly, ed., *Bias Crime: American Law*

Enforcement and Legal Responses, rev. ed. Chicago: University of Illinois at Chicago, pp. 93–104.

U.S. Department of Justice. 1995. *Hate Crimes Statistics, 1994.* Washington, D.C.: Federal Bureau of Investigation, Criminal Justice Information Services Division.

Ward, Benjamin. 1986. "Hate Crimes: The Police Response in New York City." *Police Chief* 53 (December): 46–47.

Wirt, Fredrick M. 1983. "Institutionalization: Prison and School Policies." In Virginia Gray, Herbert Jacob, and Kenneth N. Vines, eds., *Politics in the American States,* 4th ed. Glenview, Ill.: Scott, Foresman/Little, Brown.

9
Fred Phelps versus Topeka

Rick Musser

It was a remarkable declaration of hostilities. The *Topeka (Kans.) Capital-Journal,* the metropolitan daily serving the Kansas state capital, was calling down the wrath of a whole community on a crusading, antigay Baptist preacher and his family. "The Phelps family has declared war on Topeka," the lead editorial read on November 20, 1994 *(Topeka (Kans.) Capital-Journal,* 1994c). "It must stop, and it will stop, if this community rises up and unites in opposition to this tyranny." The newspaper promised to attempt to bring together the entire community "to formulate specific strategies" to put a stop to the Phelps family's demonstrations. "They want a fight, and they've got it," the editorial concluded. Since the summer of 1991, the Phelps family, Fred, wife Marge, nine of their thirteen children, and forty grandchildren had laid moral siege to the city—picketing homes, churches, and public events with their antihomosexual message while spewing out a fax machine campaign so virulent and so relentless that the state legislature had passed a statute against fax harassment (Gowen, 1995).

Operating under the religious banner of his Westboro Baptist Church (whose small congregation mostly comprised members of his extended family) the Reverend Fred Phelps had drawn national media attention with his message of damnation for homosexuals and anyone else who got in his way. The Phelps message was neither subtle nor refined. "God Hates Fags" (Gowen, 1995) was a sign common at his picket lines on Topeka's sidewalks and in its parks. He and his pickets had shown up at the funerals of those who had died from AIDS complications. The signs they carried proclaimed: "Fags Burn in Hell" and "Gays Deserve to Die" (Bull 1993). Phelps had been profiled by the *Washington Post* (Gowen, 1995) and the *Chicago Tribune* (You, 1994). Phelps had been a guest on a number of afternoon syndicated television talk shows, and Hugh Downs, cohost of ABC's news magazine *20/20* (Gospel, 1994), called Phelps "one of the most outrageous people we have ever met on this show."

158

But it was the people and officials of the City of Topeka who lived daily with Phelps's insults. His fax machines rolled out messages calling the district attorney a "Jezebelian Self-Confessed Whore" (March 9, 1993, Westboro Baptist Church, Kansas State Library Fax Collection) and the mayor the "antichrist" (December 1992, Westboro Baptist Church, Kansas State Library Fax Collection). The Reverend Phelps had managed to concoct a brew of religious fights, public assembly fights, free speech fights, and media fights that, one journalist observed (Gowen, 1995), had turned the city of Topeka into "a First Amendment laboratory and a constitutional scholar's dream." It is a situation that also makes the controversy between the Reverend Phelps and the city of Topeka ripe for study as one of James Davison Hunter's "culture wars" (Hunter 1991) and, in particular, a case study of the dynamics of local government repression in the face of culture war controversy.

THEORETICAL PERSPECTIVES ON REPRESSION

The dynamics of citizen rebellion or protest and governmental response to dissent are subjects of a by now substantial line of inquiry, including numerous cross-national studies (Gurr, 1986; Della Porta, 1995; Lichbach, 1995; Booth and Richard, 1996; Rasler, 1996; Davenport, 1997). The theoretical frameworks behind that work have not been adequately integrated into the study of urban politics in the United States, however. This investigation of a local governments' repressive tactics in response to culture war activists provides an important occasion to attempt that integration. This section outlines some key theoretical perspectives concerning citizen activism and state repression that will be applied in the analysis of the case.

In particular, the Phelps case draws attention to theoretical explanations that portray both protest and repression as cycles that wax and wane with changes in costs or political opportunities. One key theoretical perspective is Sydney Tarrow's (1994) concept of the "political opportunity structure" shaping the interaction between the state and dissidents. Tarrow contends that social movements form when ordinary citizens respond to changes in opportunities that lower the cost of collective action. These changes in opportunity may result from increased access to power, shifts in ruling alignments, availability of influential allies, or schisms among political elites. The costs of collective action can range from concrete financial penalties and legal sanctions to less quantifiable emotional and social debits. Tarrow also notes that political opportunities produce complementary forces that can be hostile to protesters. As collective action succeeds, it creates cycles that bring in the state. As the cycle of protest widens, challengers make demands for changes that would have seemed foolhardy earlier and governmental forces respond with reform, repression, or both.

But costs and opportunities exist on both sides of the protest and repression equation. Mark Lichbach (1995:26, 257) has been particularly explicit in theorizing that the costs and mobilizing problems that constitute the "rebel's dilemma" are mirrored by a similar "state's dilemma." Costs and mobilizing problems also confront governing elites as they attempt to control rebellious citizens. From this perspective, it is not necessarily easy for government officials to repress protesters. Weak states face particular problems in this regard. The very elements that make it difficult for weak states to mount a repressive response also make the need for repression greater, because "weak states invite collective dissent" (Lichbach, 1995:68). For example, government "may be divided among itself" with differing factions contending for power. Under such circumstances, repression is complicated, and the "state is therefore most vulnerable to collective dissent" (Lichbach, 1995:69). Likewise, governments that have irresponsible leaders or face financial crises are vulnerable to collective dissent, yet less capable of controlling that dissent through repression.

By acknowledging the constraints on repression that governing officials face, Lichbach's work suggests that some regimes will be much less likely than others to succeed when using repression as a strategy to deal with protest. In looking at the Phelps case, Lichbach's work provides theoretical support for the notion that repression is a relatively high-cost strategy for governments. If we couple Lichbach's notions of governmental constraints with Cobb and Ross's (1997) notion of a cycle in governments' responses to challengers of the status quo, the actions of both Phelps and the Topeka city government are theoretically interpretable. Cobb and Ross describe a cycle in which low-cost strategies for containing challenges are used first, whereas higher-cost strategies are used less frequently and typically only after low-cost strategies have failed. Governmental responses to culture wars might therefore be hypothesized to be cyclical, with evasion constituting an early stage of governmental response when dissident forces seem so innocuous that the costs of a repressive action seem not worthwhile. Repression can be expected at a later stage in the cycle when the circle of protest widens and the costs of not responding seem higher than the costs of repressive measures.

The case study in this chapter examines the relationship between political opportunities and costs for both the Reverend Phelps and his protesters, on the one hand, and the city of Topeka, on the other, and how those shifting opportunities and costs created a dynamic that led the community from a strategy of evasion to one of repression. Information for the case study is derived primarily from analysis of 643 *Topeka Capital-Journal* articles covering the years 1992 to 1997.

CONTEXT FOR THE CONTROVERSY

Topeka is the capital of a state which, until recently, posted signs welcoming travelers crossing its miles of prairie to "The Land of Ahs," a play on the state's prevailing image as home to Dorothy and Toto. It is a city of 120,000 (Hall and Gaquin, 1997) that is a little less well off than the national average (with a household median income of $26,774) and a little whiter than the national average (with 84.7 percent Caucasians, 10.6 percent blacks, and 5.8 percent Hispanics). All things considered, it would not be unusual to hear Topeka used as a synonym for Everytown, U.S.A.

Prior to 1985, Topeka had a commission form of government (Topeka, 1997), in which legislative and executive functions are held in the hands of the same elected officials. In 1985, however, Topeka adopted a new set of governing arrangements that include a strong mayor, a city council, and a chief administrative office. Topeka's mayor is elected at-large and serves as titular head of the city and presiding officer of the city council. He recommends actions to the city council; and, although he cannot vote, holds general veto power. The city council is composed of nine members elected from nine districts. Besides legislative powers, they assist the mayor in hiring the chief administrative officer and can override a mayoral veto with six votes. The chief administrative officer functions at the mayor's discretion and, at present, holds full delegated administrative responsibility.

Topeka does have a place in the nation's history of moral crusades and crusaders. Abolitionist John Brown stands astride a huge Kansas history mural in the statehouse, his eyes burning with the zeal that some would say sparked a civil war. Carry Nation began her saloon-smashing days in this town and in a state that still banned liquor by the drink until the 1980s. And it was the Topeka school board that was "The Board" in the landmark civil rights case of *Brown vs. The Board of Education.* But now Topeka faces Fred Phelps, who labels it "Sodom City" and has sued it for $7 million (Fry, 1997b) for what he calls a pattern of persecuting him and his followers and failing to protect them in a number of incidents dating back to 1991.

Fred Waldron Phelps was born in 1929 in Meridian, Mississippi and had a typical Southern upbringing in a respected Southern family. In 1947, while waiting to turn seventeen so that he could begin attending the U.S. Military Academy, Phelps "felt the call" at a small Methodist revival meeting, abandoned a West Point appointment, and enrolled in Bob Jones University then located in Tennessee. He changed his denomination to Baptist and became zealous, devout, a fiery orator and an eccentric, according to the Southern Baptist minister who ordained him (Taschler and Fry, 1994e). Phelps was taking his religion to the street corners as early as 1951 in Pasadena, California, where he railed at fellow students at John Muir College about petting, profanity, teachers' filthy jokes, and pandering to the lusts of the flesh (*Time,* 1951).

Phelps arrived in Topeka in 1954 on the day the U.S. Supreme Court handed down its *Brown v. The Board* decision. He was hired as an associate pastor at the East Side Baptist Church and soon was chosen to set up a new, west side congregation. Westboro Baptist Church opened its doors for its first service in 1955. The beliefs of the Westboro Church are aligned with the Primitive Baptist Religion. Primitive Baptists believe a predetermined number of people were chosen for redemption before the world was created and only they will be saved on judgment day. He and his congregation will be among those saved, Phelps believes (*Topeka Capital-Journal,* 1994b).

While serving as pastor, the Reverend Phelps also sold vacuum cleaners, baby strollers, and insurance, but Taschler and Fry document (1994d) how it was the law that became Phelps's source of secular income. He combined his college hours from other schools, finished an undergraduate degree from Washburn University in Topeka in 1962, and earned a law degree from the same school in 1964. Phelps has contended that his law school years were difficult because a delegation of Topeka lawyers had tried to block his admission to law school. According to Phelps, they did not like his sermons on a local radio show where he had preached before applying to law school. When it came time to be admitted to the bar, Phelps could not find any judge in town to swear to his good character, a routine formality with most young attorneys. Instead, he provided the bar with affidavits of his Eagle Scout and American Legion awards from his days in Mississippi .

Phelps developed a reputation as a tough and knowledgeable courtroom adversary and won several honors for his work on civil rights cases (Taschler and Fry, 1994b). There is also evidence (Taschler and Fry, 1994d) that Phelps used the law aggressively. In 1977, the state sought to have him disbarred in connection with a case in which he used the courts to punish a court reporter who had failed to have a transcript ready for him when he wanted it. The Kansas Supreme Court condemned his conduct, and Phelps was disbarred in Kansas in 1979. He surrendered his license to practice law in a federal court in 1989 after a complaint questioned the way Phelps used letters to make demands of the cities of Wichita and Hutchinson and two divisions of Boeing Co. The complaint charged the letters threatened law suits unless the parties paid money or took other actions to satisfy his clients.

Fred Phelps may no longer practice law, but his legal legacy lives on in his children. The children earned law degrees, married, and moved in around the site of the church, purchasing property in a city block that is sometimes referred to as the "Phelps complex" (Taschler and Fry, 1994c). Of his thirteen offspring, eleven became lawyers, and many of them still practice as part of the Phelps family law firm. Phelps managed to gather around him an extended family that was at once a congregation and a law firm, both of which marched to the vision of their patriarch.

SUNDAY IN THE PARK WITH FRED

In the summer of 1991, the Phelps family began their antihomosexual crusade by picketing Gage Park, which contains the Topeka Zoo, a small-gauge train ride, and ample picnic space. The park was targeted by Phelps because of its reputation for being a cruising spot for local homosexuals (Fry, 1995a). The picketing gained momentum, spreading to residential neighborhoods and businesses while Phelps also spread his antigay message through faxes to a network of media outlets, state offices, and individuals.

Substantiating the community's early evasion of a confrontation with the Westboro pickets amounts to submitting evidence that nothing happened, always more difficult than proving something occurred. But the words of those involved in the Phelps battle clearly indicate that turning a blind eye to his outrageous signs and faxes, taunts and jeers was the early reaction of both governing officials and the community more generally. The Reverend Robert Layne of St. David's Episcopal Church, who would later become deeply embroiled with Phelps, told the press: "We ignored them for a year. We prayed that God would temper their hatred with love. It didn't work" (Fry, 1994b). That sentiment was confirmed by another Phelps foe, District Attorney Joan Hamilton, who said, "A lot of people used to say if we just ignore them, they'll go away. The trouble is they haven't. They sort of developed this attitude that they can do whatever they please to whomever they please" (Gowen, 1995).

The reasons behind the evasion strategy appear to have been rooted in a belief that the best way to counter Phelps was to ignore him. That reasoning was coupled with a healthy fear of the emotional, legal, and financial consequences of challenging Phelps's behavior. Nowhere was the evade-and-ignore strategy better articulated than among the editors and publishers who were responsible for Phelps's access to the media. In personal conversations and in the pages of their publications, many journalists explained that it was publicity and a forum that Phelps sought and that the best way to deal with him was to deny him that publicity and that forum. "We've been told Phelps thrives on publicity, that he will go away if we'd only ignore him," the *Capital-Journal* wrote (1994a). Also inherent in the evade-and-ignore strategy was the realization that taking action against Phelps was taking action against everyone's right to protest. In another editorial (*Topeka Capital-Journal,* 1993a), the newspaper used the metaphor of Phelps as a nagging insect bite, arguing that picking at the irritation would do more harm than good. "Scratch an itch long enough and first you produce an open wound, then a scar," the paper wrote.

There is also ample evidence that individuals in the community were simply intimidated by Phelps, frightened of what he would do to them if they spoke out against him. Residents of the neighborhoods affected by the Westboro pickets told reporters (Taschler, 1993) that they were afraid to have their names used in stories about the picketing, and several Phelps opponents said that the protesters had tried to get them fired from their jobs. Phelps's litigious nature had a chilling influence on the press, as well. Preparations for a student-authored article (Lewis, 1993) on the children of the Westboro Baptist Church included a detailed review of the piece by legal counsel on the presumption that Phelps would file suit.

Perhaps the most dramatic evidence of the fear that Phelps could generate appeared in the report of a city team assigned to investigate why the Topeka

Police Department had failed to arrest Phelps's pickets for city code violations dating back to 1991. "During personal interviews," the report said, "one high-ranking officer stated emphatically a no-arrest order regarding the WBC pickets exists. This order was verbally given to him by Chief Beavers in the following statement: 'Commander, the Phelpses are not going to live in my house. Don't these officers know the Phelpses can sue us and take our houses? Commander, do you understand my order?'" (Hall, 1996c).

The evade-and-ignore strategy did not effectively deter the Phelps group. Phelps's faxes continued to trumpet the Gage Park protests, counting off the weeks with headlines that evoked network news coverage of the Iran hostage crisis. "Week 51 of the Great Gage Park Decency Drive," proclaimed Westboro's fax of June 5, 1992. All that was missing was the tag line: "Topeka Held Hostage."

A COMMUNITY RESPONDS

No single event marks the change in how Topeka and its citizens dealt with Phelps; but, by 1992, events transpired that appeared to be aimed at hindering and repressing the Reverend. Citizens began to organize anti-Phelps groups. One of the earliest called itself Sunday in the Park without Fred (Sodders, 1993a). During the 1992 session of the Kansas legislature, a law banning funeral picketing and an amendment adding faxes to the state telephone harassment statute passed, laws later challenged by Phelps in court (Fry, 1993a). During the fall of 1992, Joan Hamilton ran for Topeka district attorney on a platform that included the promise she would faithfully prosecute the Phelps family for any criminal activity (Gowen, 1995). Hamilton, regarded by some as a dark-horse candidate, won the post and was credited with being the first politician brave enough to take on Phelps (Gowen, 1995).

By the spring of 1993, Phelps was clearly becoming a Topeka political issue. In the race for city council, some candidates rushed to deny charges that they had connections to Phelps, while two Phelpses ran for office themselves (Hall, 1993b). Fred Phelps entered the mayoral primaries, and the vote there provided a quantitative snapshot of his standing in the community. Of 15,613 votes cast, Phelps got 285 (Hall, 1993a). Phelps's son, Jonathan, ran for a city council seat and garnered only 62 votes, losing a spot in the general election runoff to Jim Kelly, with 1,512 votes, and Dennis Dobson, a founder of Sunday in the Park without Fred, with 373 votes (Sodders, 1993a). After incumbent mayor Felker was re-elected, he admitted (Blankenship, 1993a) that he had taken a political risk by not being perceived as being tough on Phelps and his followers.

Hanging over the elections was the fact that the council had already begun to consider ordinances that would limit and control picketing within Topeka's city limits. Topeka's efforts to inhibit Phelps by regulating picketing stand at the center of any case that city government attempted to repress his antigay activity. By

February 1993, on a 9–0 vote, the council adopted an ordinance banning picketing of a residence, limiting a favored Phelps tactic of showing up in force at the homes of those who opposed him. That ordinance was only the beginning of a drawn-out effort to control Phelps's picketing. A tougher law that would have required a $25 picketing permit and would have created "picket-free zones" near building entrances languished in committee until September 1993. Then council members rewrote the ordinance after several Topeka churches organized a petition drive to ban picketing within 250 feet of a place of worship from thirty minutes before until thirty minutes after a service.

The action came after an incident on Labor Day weekend of 1993. By that time, the Phelps family had moved the focus of its Sunday picketing from Gage Park to the sidewalks in front of churches throughout the community. The churches targeted were seldom gay churches or churches with gay pastors. Rather, they were mainstream churches that Phelps contended supported homosexuality because they did not condemn it. In the Labor Day incident, Phelps's followers engaged in a confrontation with the Reverend Weeks outside his First Lutheran Church—a confrontation that led to a scuffle with the gray-haired Reverend Weeks being pinned to the ground by four picketers claiming to be making a citizens' arrest. Eventually, two of Phelps's sons along with two other Westboro Baptist Church members were charged with battery and unlawful restraint in connection with the incident; the two Phelpses and one other picketer were acquitted in January 1996, and the other protester was found guilty (Naseer, 1996).

This incident sparked the unification of the church congregations of Topeka into a force that drove the ensuing picket ordinance debate. In October 1993, the council adopted a picketing ordinance limiting pickets to a hundred-foot setback from church grounds. Phelps and his supporters, along with some antiabortion activists, opposed the ordinance. A week later, Mayor Felker vetoed the ordinance, saying it was unconstitutional. The council reworked the ordinance with help from the state attorney general's office and passed it again in December 1993. Before the week was out, the mayor vetoed the ordinance again. No attempt was made to override the second veto.

In April 1995, Interfaith of Topeka, representing about fifty Topeka congregations, tired of waiting for the council to act and voted to organize an initiative petition for a stronger picketing ordinance (Hall, 1995b). Under Kansas law, if a petition for an ordinance has the required, valid signatures, the city council has twenty days to adopt the ordinance or call for a special election. The Interfaith ordinance, drafted by Topeka attorney and Phelps foe Jerry Palmer, limited pickets to within ninety feet of a church. But in July 1995, the council, on a 7 to 2 vote, passed a more moderate version of the ordinance, voting down the petition initiative version of the ordinance on a 4 to 5 vote. The more moderate version, supported and signed by the mayor, reduced the picket buffer distance to fifty feet and kept the pre- and post-service half-hour picketing curfews while requiring churches to publicly post the times of services (Blankenship, 1995a). Not satisfied with those restrictions, the Interfaith petition drive gathered about forty-nine hundred signatures (Blankenship, 1995b) and, rather than put the city through a special election, the council, on a 5 to 4 vote, adopted the Interfaith version of the ordinance in September 1995 (Hall, 1995d). In a wide-ranging ruling in January 1997, a Shawnee County District Court judge struck down the ninety-foot buffer zone, held that at least portions of the funeral picketing law were constitutional, and ruled that a requirement to post service times and several other portions of the 1995 picket law were unconstitutional (Fry, 1997a).

Legal wrangling over the picketing ordinances continues, but none of the picketing ordinances has stopped the Phelpses. The Westboro pickets can still be seen all over Topeka, including during morning rush hours on the overpass that crosses the busiest section of the downtown freeway. The legislative pressure on pickets also continues. In late 1997, the city council considered an ordinance limiting the size of "held, worn or carried" signs—meaning picket signs—to eighteen by twenty-four inches. The Phelpses contended (Hall, 1997) that they had $124,000 tied up in the signs they use for antihomosexual picketing and threatened to sue if the ordinance were passed.

ARRESTING THE PROBLEM

Phelps and his followers faced other skirmishes along nonlegislative lines. His faxes were unsuccessfully challenged when Phelps's foes asked the Kansas Corporation Commission to investigate whether existing laws protected telephone customers from Phelps's brand of harassment (Myers, 1994a), and a newspaper editorial (*Topeka (Kans.) Capital-Journal,* 1995a) urged Southwestern Bell to "end the torrent of scornful and libelous fax messages sent by Westboro Baptist Church." Shawnee County Sheriff's officers even raided Phelps's law offices and temporarily seized fax machines and computers in connection with a series of charges filed by the district attorney (Sodders, 1993c). Legal pressure from the community also led local radio station WREN to halt temporarily weekly broadcasts by Phelps because of potentially defamatory remarks he made on the air (Myers, 1994b). But, if the picketing ordinance campaign comprised one front in Topeka's culture war with Phelps, it was District Attorney Joan Hamilton who led the attack along the second front: the battle to charge Phelps with criminal conduct.

While running for district attorney, Hamilton had pledged to enforce the laws covering the Westboro pickets' actions. Before her election, she had helped author some of those laws, serving in the Kansas legislature and sponsoring an amendment that had added faxes to the state's telephone harassment codes (Fry, 1993a). Once in office in Topeka, she set about bringing charges against Phelps and his clan. Her first efforts sought to punish Phelps's name-calling tactics under the Kansas criminal defamation statute, a law that had been on the books since 1970 but had not been tested. She filed a series of charges based on faxes and fliers in which Phelps targeted a Topeka City Council member, a police officer, other citizens and survivors of people who had died (Funk-Fleischer, 1993). (A sample of a Phelps fax: "Soon now, these two apostate Jews will join their looney dopehead daughter ANITA in Hell, she'll spit in their face for helping send her there." The fax was referring to Irv and Beth Sheffel, whom the fax called "Antichrist Hawkers of a Satanic Sodomite Gospel" [December 1992, Westboro Baptist Church, Kansas State Library Fax Collection]). When a federal district judge ruled the state's defamation law "substantially overbroad" and unconstitutional (Funk-Fleischer, 1993), Hamilton appealed the ruling and approached the legislature about passing a revised law, which it did in 1995 (Myers, 1995). While the defamation charges were held up by constitutional challenges, Hamilton proceeded along other lines. In March 1995, she charged Phelps and five of his followers with misdemeanor assault and battery, battery, and criminal restraint for actions linked to street scuffles and name-calling during picketing in the summer of 1994 at a local restaurant (Fry, 1995b). In a series of seven trials played out over an intense four weeks in neighboring Lyon County, church members were acquitted on nine counts and convicted of three (Boczkiewicz, 1997), including the Reverend Phelps's conviction (Fry, 1995d) for calling people in an eighty-six-year-old woman's birthday party entourage "pimp" and "queer faggot" (Fry, 1995c).

There is no doubt that Phelps saw Hamilton's actions as a direct assault on his tactics and his message. Westboro faxes charged that criminal law was being used to circumvent their First Amendment rights (Fry, 1995c), and the pickets' defense attorney, Emporia attorney Don Krueger, called Hamilton's prosecutions of Phelps "the most egregious exercise of prosecutorial power I've ever seen" (Boczkiewicz, 1997). He added that Hamilton's platform when she ran for district attorney was one of eliminating Phelps's and his church's right of free speech and that she was "using the district attorney's office in an attempt to accomplish that end" (Boczkiewicz, 1997).

A number of other citizens swore out complaints against Phelps—people like attorney Jerry Palmer (Myers, 1993) or gay city council candidate Russ Ptacek (Sodders, 1993b), whom Phelps had "outed." Individual off-duty, law enforcement officers were also willing to press charges when Phelps called them a "son of a bitch" (Fry, 1993c). In stark contrast with the growing efforts in a number of quarters to repress Phelps, Topeka police action against Phelps was noticeably absent. Police were regularly assigned to stand by at picket sites and certainly had witnessed name-calling and what most people would have classified as abusive behavior by the Westboro pickets. Topeka Police Chief Gerald Beavers admitted to District Court Judge Franklin Theis (Fry, 1995e) that one of the most common complaints he got from Topekans about the Westboro pickets was, "Why won't the police department take action when pickets call people 'whore',' 'bitch' and 'fag lover'?" Beaver's November 1995 testimony came during a hearing to determine whether Theis would sign orders blocking enforcement of the city's and state's picketing ordinances. Beaver's explanations as to why police did not act, and his courtroom denial that there was any police no-arrest policy for pickets, set in motion a chain of events leading to his resignation less than three months later.

In December 1995, Concerned Citizens for Topeka, Inc., a group of what only could be described as leading citizens who had emerged as a counterforce against Phelps, called a press conference at which their president, former secretary of state Jack Brier, produced two Topeka police officers who told reporters that they were under orders to ignore misdemeanor crimes committed by Phelps and members of his Westboro Baptist Church (Hays and Ernst, 1995). Both the city and the Sheriff launched probes into the matter and, by February 1996, amid growing evidence that he did, indeed, order the Phelps's violations ignored, Beavers resigned at the request of the Topeka mayor (Hall, 1996a). His successor immediately discontinued assigning officers to Westboro picket sites (Hall, 1996b). Whether Beavers' "no-arrest policy" was actually at the heart of the mayor's request for his resignation is unclear (Hall, 1996b). What did clearly emerge from the incident were two reports that firmly established that Topeka police had a "no-arrest" policy for Phelps dating back to 1991, two years before Beavers took office. The city's report also indicated that it appeared that "the stridency of the church's picketers increased as it became evident that they wouldn't be arrested for their actions" (Hall, 1996c).

When the sheriff was asked if he knew why Beavers had initiated the no-arrest policy, Dave Meneley said the chief had fallen in with city council members and county commissioners who were in league with Phelps. The police chief also cited possible legal reprisals that the Phelpses might take against him and other members of the police department if officers interfered with the picketing (Hall, 1996c). Beavers' explanations to Judge Theis in November 1995 indicated that police found it difficult to interpret what words qualified as "fighting words," words covered by the statute that would "arouse alarm, anger, or cause resentment" (Fry, 1995e).

FROM CASE CONCLUSIONS TO THEORY

Imputing the motivations of individuals, organizations, or whole communities based on analysis of news coverage has drawbacks. Media statements rarely reflect the complete, or sometimes even true, feelings of their speakers. However, the record of what has been said over the years in the culture war between Phelps and the city of Topeka provides some evidence for understanding the motivations and constraints facing the participants in this struggle.

That evidence is largely consistent with theories of dissent and repression that focus on the costs and opportunities to rebels and to the state apparatus. This case also suggests two important extensions of that theoretical perspective. First, while acknowledging the important ways in which repression is a costly strategy for a regime, the case also highlights the important costs that accrue to a regime that *avoids* repression for an extended period of time. When the costs of evasion accumulate, repression may be expected even though it is costly. As the following section indicates, the costs of evading rather than repressing a dissident group can include damage to the community's image, threats to its economic development plans, and loss of regime legitimacy as the general public loses patience with dissident action. Second, the Phelps case suggests that, instead of the symmetry between the rebel's dilemma and the state's dilemma that Lichbach (1995) posits, there is an interesting lack of symmetry in situations where dissidents have unique resources for overcoming collective-action problems. In the case at hand, these resources included the extensive legal capacity of Phelps's group and the advantages of small group size and familial ties as the basis for mobilization. The case also illustrates how certain elements of repression can be converted from costs to benefits for some dissident groups. In other words, attempts at repression may make it easier rather than more difficult for dissidents to sustain collective action.

The State's Dilemma: Costs of Repression and Costs of Evasion

In the conflict between Topeka and Fred Phelps, the community was goaded into action by public pride, economic threats, and a growing exasperation with the street corner and facsimile machine tactics used by Phelps and the Westboro pickets. The image as "the town that tolerates hate speech" is an image that most cities would rather avoid. The national media attention that Phelps drew certainly did little to help Topeka's image and its pride. It is not easy to explain or to defend tolerance of protected speech when the message is as crude and as hurtful as Phelps's. Relief followed worry when ABC's *20/20* profiled Phelps in July 1993. "Before the Phelps sequence aired last Friday," wrote the *Topeka (Kans.) Capital-Journal* (1993b), "Topekans were worried that our community would be besmirched in eyes of millions of viewers certain to watch." But the editorial writer was pleased that the town emerged with a "a positive image of understanding and tolerance—even for those who choose to spread divisive messages."

Other major media portrayals were not so sure of Topeka's tolerance. *Washington Post* reporter Annie Gowen wrote in November 1995 that Phelps's tirades and the public reaction to them had "raised an uneasy issue" in Topeka. "Almost no one in Topeka claims to approve of Fred Phelps's methods," she wrote, "but public officialdom in this conservative prairieland has been at times curiously slow to condemn his message" (Gowen, 1995).

The city and the *Capital-Journal* seemed galvanized into action when Phelps pickets confronted poet Maya Angelou and frightened her into canceling an appearance in nearby Emporia. In its bellicose editorial quoted at the beginning of this chapter, the *Capital-Journal* cited the incident. The paper wrote, "Our honored guests have been made to confront his ugliness—and at our invitation. Beloved inaugural poet Maya Angelou is the latest of many high profile visitors to leave Topeka with the filth of Phelps on their shoes" (*Topeka (Kans.) Capital-Journal,* 1994c). City Hall columnist Mike Hall probably provided the clearest evidence of the link between image and government tactics when he explained in April 1995 that those on the city council who favored a stronger picketing ordinance argued that some action needed to be taken before the international exhibit "Treasures of the Czars" opened in the city. "Having picketers out there every day would do more damage to the city's image than the benefit from the czar's exhibit," Hall explained (Hall, 1995a).

Others in Topeka saw the connection between the damage Phelps could do and economic development. Drawing new industry, new jobs, and top-level business talent to a town where Fred Phelps stalked visitors was clearly a tough sell. Another incident that appeared to galvanize public reaction was a Phelps letter to union representatives working with the Burlington Northern and Santa Fe Railway in St. Paul, Minnesota. A railroad merger held out the prospect of six hundred new clerical jobs being moved to Topeka. When Phelps wrote that Topeka was "well known as Sodom City, U.S.A., the homosexual Mecca of the world" and that leading churches of Topeka were paralyzed "because the leading ministers are openly gay and lesbian" (Chilson, 1995), the ranks of Concerned Citizens for Topeka swelled from sixty to five hundred in a matter of weeks (Gowen, 1995). "I think when you try to destroy the city's economic potential, you have really stepped over the line," said the Topeka Chamber of Commerce president (Chilson, 1995).

It was not Phelps's message that seemed to bother Topeka so much as how and where and to whom he delivered it. Topeka Mayor Felker's liaison to the gay community told national gay and lesbian newsmagazine *The Advocate* (Bull, 1993) in 1993 that "Everyone is disappointed that so few people outside the (gay) community are willing to speak up against Phelps." Added the lesbian manager of a local restaurant targeted by Phelps protesters, Sharon York, "If Phelps had done this to the city's Blacks or Puerto Ricans you would have a very different reaction. I'm beginning to think that the lack of action is due to homophobia" (Bull, 1993). The actions that the city did take seem to have come when Phelps called members of the larger community vile names, when Phelps picketed homes, funerals, weddings, and churches, or when the Westboro Church pickets embarrassed the community in front of national and international audiences and threatened to undermine economic prospects.

Even beyond the venues he chose and the language he used, Phelps seemed determined to pick a fight. He was relentless, tenacious, even gleeful, in his efforts to affront people with his message. "As long as it's a gay issue, it doesn't matter," said Judy Miller of Topeka's Gay and Lesbian Task Force. "But he crossed the line" (Gowen, 1995). On the other hand, a more subtle interpretation of Phelps's impact does appear from time to time. Gay and lesbian forums did produce observations that Phelps and his actions could be, in the end, a positive thing for the gay community, if not for Topeka. "I think Fred is an asset to our cause," said one audience member at an October 14, 1997 meeting in Lawrence, Kansas, sponsored by the National Gay and Lesbian Task Force to chronicle hate crimes. "All of these people, though they are not gay, feel as if they have been a victim of Phelps. People are much more aware (of hate crime) because of Phelps."

In short, the city and its leaders ultimately were pressed into more aggressive action against Phelps by the accumulating force of public opinion, reinforced by the threats that this culture war posed for community image and for the community's economic development hopes. The accumulating costs of evasion, costs in the form of threats to legitimacy, image, and economic development, eventually outweighed the prospective costs of repression and propelled local officials to eschew the evasion role in favor of repressive action.

On the Possibility of Nonsymmetrical Dilemmas for Rebels and the State

The case of Topeka's response to Fred Phelps fully illustrates the many costs and constraints that constitute the state's dilemma (Lichbach, 1995) in responding to dissident forces. And the case reminds us that, in addition to the many problems of collective action that any regime would face, local governments in a democratic society are also constrained by First Amendment law and the specter that governmental actions will not be upheld in court.

But if the legal rights embodied in the First Amendment generally serve as a constraint on governmental action, they provide an especially potent constraint when government deals with certain types of dissident groups, that is, those with the resources and expertise to make use of the law and the reputation of aggressive litigation. The Phelps church and legal firm possesses a holy war resolve and has met virtually every effort to regulate their behavior with protracted litigation. The cost of facing Phelps in court can be enormous and certainly has acted to curb the city's actions. As early as 1993, city officials were warning that cracking down on the Westboro picketers would carry a heavy price tag, even if the city prevailed. The cost of passing an unconstitutional picketing ordinance could be as much as $250,000 in legal fees owed by the city to Phelps and his church, Mayor Felker pointed out before he vetoed the city council's early effort to keep pickets a hundred feet away from a church (Blankenship, 1993b). Phelps has always been fond of making good on the threat of costly legal action and, when he sued district attorney Hamilton (seeking to halt her prosecutions against him for conducting what he called her personal vendetta against him for his religious beliefs), the state attorney general's office budgeted $25,000 for private lawyers to defend her (Fry, 1994a). When Interfaith of Topeka pushed forward its initiative for stronger picket laws, opponents again raised the issue of the expense to defend the city's ordinance. The man behind the petition drive, attorney Jerry Palmer, countered that it was going to cost the city $50,000 for a special election if it did not adopt the Interfaith ordinance. One of the most publicized actions of Concerned Citizens for Topeka was to enlist the aid of twenty lawyers to provide free legal assistance to any "victim" sued by Phelps and his group (*Topeka (Kans.) Capital-Journal,* 1995b).

The biggest counterweight to the city's actions may be that Phelps could easily win more than he loses in his numerous legal appeals. He has already had one Kansas criminal defamation law declared unconstitutional (Funk-Fleischer, 1993) and has convinced the court to dismiss four counts of criminal defamation against him under new statutes because those charges were based on language that is protected speech (Fry, 1997c). He stopped prosecutions under the state's funeral picketing law when a federal judge declared it unconstitutionally vague (Hall, 1995c) and had parts of the city's picketing ordinance set aside on First and Fourth Amendment grounds (Johnson, 1997).

Phelps has not always been the legal victor. He has been unable to beat some criminal charges, but he has appealed the verdicts. The city and state have learned from earlier Phelps victories and have passed laws and ordinances that better meet constitutional tests. Phelps did fail to prevail when one of his cases reached the U.S. Supreme Court, which rejected Westboro requests to overturn a temporary restraining order limiting picketing outside a Topeka church (Morrison, 1997). But Topeka has often given Phelps the First Amendment high ground and, in a culture war, moral high ground is ground worth holding.

Under normal circumstances, the threat of legal action against a repressor state might easily be fit into a theoretical interpretation that views dissenters and the governing regime as players in a symmetrical game. The governing regime uses repressive tactics to raise the costs of collective action for dissenters, and the dissenters use legal challenges to raise the cost of repression for the regime; and, just as it is costly for the regime to mount a repressive response, so also is it costly for dissenters to mount legal challenges in order to counter repression.

But the costs of mounting a legal challenge were minimized for the Westboro pickets because so many of the members of the Phelps family are practicing lawyers. Furthermore, the relatively small size of this protesting group, combined with the family ties that bind many of them together, mean that these dissidents exemplify a special category, a "privileged group," in terms of overcoming collective-action problems (Olson, 1971).

Indeed, the Westboro pickets were remarkably immune to other kinds of constraints and problems that normally constitute costs and obstacles to group mobilization. In theoretical frameworks like those offered by Tarrow (1994) and Lichbach (1995), repressive actions by the state, or even the threat of repressive actions, are defined as costs imposed on the organizers of protest movements—costs that can seriously disrupt the capacity to mobilize for protest. The behavior of the Westboro pickets suggests that repressive acts can, if anything, energize some protest groups and that such protest can be sustained over the long haul despite the traditional insights of collective-action theorizing. This is because, as Hirschman (1982) points out, what might appear to be costs of collective action are, at least to certain types of participants, actually benefits. The striving and struggling are actually part of what some participants get out of collective action, not simply costs that they must bear in order to achieve a collective good. This characterization seems particularly apt in the Phelps case. It is not an exaggeration to note that Phelps and his family have spent their lives preparing for their confrontation with the city of Topeka. The arrests and litigation in which they have been involved are part of the raison d'être of this group. Even if this is not true, Dennis Chong (1991) argues that protest groups can convert what would otherwise be costs of collective action into benefits by acting as if it were true. By choosing jail over bail, for example, activists erase a potent cost that would-be repressors normally can impose.

In short, this case study of the Westboro pickets versus the city of Topeka exemplifies a particular kind of repression scenario: a David and Goliath encounter in which a tiny and apparently resource-poor protest group nevertheless has characteristics that make it much more difficult for government to repress it effectively. This scenario heightens the costs of repression for government and, at least for a time, deters government officials from attempting repression.

Ultimately, however, city government moved from a role of evasion of a group challenging the status quo to a role of repression. What factors about the city and about Phelps created that dynamic?

In this case, it appears that actions to repress Phelps had their roots in a rising community political will that would no longer tolerate the group's message or, even more likely, would not tolerate the way that message was delivered. Once aroused, that community will expressed itself in the election of public officials, like District Attorney Hamilton, who saw voter support as a mandate to take action. The rising political will also manifested itself in community initiatives that bypassed elected officials who were not repressive enough fast enough, as in the case of the Interfaith petition drive for stronger picketing statutes.

Evasion itself can also carry the seeds of later repression when it emboldens those who challenge the status quo, as it seemed to do when Topeka police followed a no-arrest policy for the Westboro picketers. As the pickets became bolder by picketing churches and harassing people at picket sites, the level of political will against them ratcheted up, hastening the slide toward repression and, eventually, precipitating other community actions. Concerned Citizens for Topeka, aroused by an evasion policy, produced evidence that helped bring down the chief of police and change the policy.

For their part, Phelps and the Westboro pickets were a group that simply refused to be ignored and evaded. Given their desire for media attention, the evade-and-ignore strategy might have been ultimately a more effective and less expensive option for dealing with a group like the Westboro pickets. But the forces in the Topeka confrontation seemed to pull each other toward a repressive government response.

Also contributing to a more repressive response were the linked elements of community image and community economic development. As Phelps threatened those resource bases, embarrassing national figures like Maya Angelou and contacting those who could influence economic growth, he embarrassed the city's leaders and brought the resources they controlled into play against him.

REFERENCES

Blankenship, B. 1993a. "Policeman Disciplined for Leaving Picketers." *Topeka (Kans.) Capital-Journal,* 7 April, p. D1.

———. 1993b. "Topeka Clergy Denounce Hate Tactics." *Topeka (Kans.) Capital-Journal,* 12 October, p. 1A.

———. 1995a. "Moderate Picketing Law Passes." *Topeka (Kans.) Capital-Journal,* 12 July, p. 1A.

———. 1995b. "Interfaith Presents Petition. *Topeka (Kans.) Capital-Journal,* 22 July, p. 1A.

Boczkiewicz, R. 1997. "Court Orders Westboro Suit Against D.A. Reopened." *Topeka (Kans.) Capital-Journal,* 13 August, p. 1A.

Booth, John A., and Patricia Bayer Richard. 1996. "Repression, Participation and Democratic Norms in Urban Central America." *American Journal of Political Science* 40 (November): 1205–32.

Bull, C. 1993. "Us vs. Them." *The Advocate,* 2 November, p. 43.

Chilson, M. 1995. "Railroad Union Leader Shocked by Phelps Letter." *Topeka (Kans.) Capital-Journal,* 7 October, p. 1A.

Chong, Dennis. 1991. *Collective Action and the Civil Rights Movement.* Chicago: University of Chicago Press.

Cobb, Roger, and Marc Howard Ross. 1997. "Conclusion: Agenda Denial—The Power of Competing Cultural Definitions." In R. Cobb and M. H. Ross, eds., *Cultural Strategies of Agenda Denial.* Lawrence: University Press of Kansas, pp. 203–20.

Davenport, Christian. 1997. "Movements, Countermovements and Political Domination." Paper prepared for presentation at a conference, Comparative Human Rights and Repression: Theory, Explanatory Variables and Persisting Paradoxes, Boulder, Colo., 20–21 June.

Della Porta, Donatella. 1995. *Social Movements, Political Violence, and the State: A Comparative Analysis of Italy and Germany.* Cambridge: Cambridge University Press.

Fry, S. 1993a. "Phelps Aims at New Laws." *Topeka (Kans.) Capital-Journal,* 2 July, p. 1E.

———. 1993b. "Suit by Phelps Targets Funeral Law." *Topeka (Kans.) Capital-Journal,* 20 July, p. 3C.

———. 1993c. "Judge Finds Phelps Sr. Innocent." *Topeka (Kans.) Capital-Journal,* 31 August, p. 5A.

———. 1994a. "Private Lawyer to Help Defend D.A." *Topeka (Kans.) Capital-Journal,* 10 January, p. 5A.

———. 1994b. "Church to Respond to Picketers." *Topeka (Kans.) Capital-Journal,* 23 February, p. 1A.

———. 1995a. "Phelps." *Topeka (Kans.) Capital-Journal,* 1 January, p. 14A.

———. 1995b. "Prosecutor Denies Case against Phelps Tied to Stephan Trial." *Topeka (Kans.) Capital-Journal,* 10 March, p. 7A.

————. 1995c. "Witnesses Disagree over Remarks." *Topeka (Kans.) Capital-Journal,* 11 August, p. 1A.

————. 1995d. "Phelps Guilty; Appeal Planned." *Topeka (Kans.) Capital-Journal,* 12 August, p. 1A.

————. 1995e. "Chief Testifies on Picket Policy." *Topeka (Kans.) Capital-Journal,* 7 November, p. 1A.

————. 1997a. "State Funeral Picketing Law Upheld." *Topeka (Kans.) Capital-Journal,* 17 January, p. 1A.

————. 1997b. "Phelps Sues City for $7 Million." *Topeka (Kans.) Capital-Journal,* 22 March, 11A.

————. 1997c. "Charge against Phelps Dismissed." *Topeka (Kans.) Capital-Journal,* 18 November.

Funk-Fleischer, A. 1993. "D.A. to Appeal Fax Decision." *Topeka (Kans.) Capital-Journal,* 7 July, p. 1A.

"Gospel of Hate—Topeka Preacher's Crusade against Gays." 1994. 2 September. 20/20, American Broadcasting Corporation. Transcript #1435.

Gowen, A. 1995. "Holy Hell." *Washington Post,* 12 November, p. F5.

Hall, G. E., and D. A. Gaquin, eds. 1997. *1997 County and City Extra; Annual Metro, City and County Data Book,* 6th ed. Lanham, Md.: Bernan Press.

Hall, M. 1993a. "Felker, Van Slyke to Face Off." *Topeka (Kans.) Capital-Journal,* 3 March, p. 1A.

————. 1993b. "Where Was Phelps Factor in Primary?" *Topeka (Kans.) Capital-Journal,* 6 March, p. 8a.

————. 1995a. "Picketing Issue May Have Cost Mechler, Schimmel in Races." *Topeka (Kans.) Capital-Journal,* 10 April, p. 2C.

————. 1995b. "Interfaith Plans Anti-Picketing Petition." *Topeka (Kans.) Capital-Journal,* 26 April, p. 7A.

————. 1995c. "Interfaith of Topeka Joins Petition Drive for City Ordinance." *Topeka (Kans.) Capital-Journal,* 29 April, p. 1E.

————. 1995d. "Picketing Restriction OK'd." *Topeka (Kans.) Capital-Journal,* 13 September, p. 1A.

————. 1996a. "Beavers Resigns as Chief." *Topeka (Kans.) Capital-Journal,* 2 February, p. 1A.

————. 1996b. "Sources: Beavers Didn't Show Respect." *Topeka (Kans.) Capital-Journal,* 15 February, p. 1A.

————. 1996c. "Probes of Chief Released." *Topeka (Kans.) Capital-Journal,* 17 February, p. 2A.

————. 1997. "Proposed Sign Ordinance under Fire from Phelpses." *Topeka (Kans.) Capital-Journal,* 3 November, p. 11A.

Hays, K. L., and T. Ernst. 1995. "Special Treatment Alleged for Picketers." *Topeka (Kans.) Capital-Journal,* 14 December, p. 1A.

Hirschman, Albert O. 1982. *Shifting Involvements.* Princeton, N.J.: Princeton University Press.

Hrenchir, T. 1996. "Menely Inquiry Points to Beavers." *Topeka (Kans.) Capital-Journal,* 15 February, p. 1A.

Hunter, J. D. 1991. *Culture Wars.* New York: Basic Books.

Johnson, F. 1997. "Judge Orders City to Pay Fees to Phelps Attorneys." *Topeka (Kans.) Capital-Journal,* 31 May, p. 1A.

Lewis, W. 1993. "Children on the Line for God." *University Daily Kansan,* 17 February, p. 1.

Lichbach, Mark. 1995. *The Rebel's Dilemma.* Ann Arbor: University of Michigan Press.

Morrison, S. 1997. "Supreme Court Rejects Westboro's Request." *Topeka (Kans.) Capital-Journal,* 22 January, p. 8A.

Myers, R. 1993. "Phelps Arrested for Slurs." *Topeka (Kans.) Capital-Journal,* 18 February, p. 1A.

———. 1994a. "Regulators Asked to Investigate Telephone Laws." *Topeka (Kans.) Capital-Journal,* 19 August, p. 7B.

———. 1994b. "WREN Cancels Weekly Phelps Show." *Topeka (Kans.) Capital-Journal,* 2 September, p. 1A.

———. 1995. "Legislature Passes New Defamation Statute." *Topeka (Kans.) Capital-Journal,* 2 May, p. 6A.

Naseer, M. 1996. "1 Guilty, 3 Innocent in Trial of Picketers." *Topeka (Kans.) Capital-Journal,* 24 January, p. 1A.

Olson, Mancur. 1971. *The Logic of Collective Action: Public Goods and the Theory of Groups.* Cambridge, Mass.: Harvard University Press.

Rasler, Karen. 1996. "Concessions, Repression, and Political Protest in the Iranian Revolution," *American Sociological Review* 61 (February): 132–52.

Sharp, E. B. 1996. "Culture Wars and City Politics." *Urban Affairs Review* 31(6): 738–58.

Sodders, L. M. 1993a. "Incumbents Garner Most Votes in Districts 5, 7, 9." *Topeka (Kans.) Capital-Journal,* 3 March, p. 2D

———. 1993b. "Fliers Spur Ptacek to File Complaint against Phelps." *Topeka (Kans.) Capital-Journal,* 6 April, p. D1.

———. 1993c. "Sheriff Raids Phelpses." *Topeka (Kans.) Capital-Journal,* 23 June, p. 1A.

Tarrow, S. 1994. *Power in Movement: Social Movements, Collective Action and Politics.* Cambridge: Cambridge University Press.

Taschler, J. 1993. "Residents Say Picketers Make Them Prisoners." *Topeka (Kans.) Capital-Journal,* 15 January, p. 1A.

Taschler, J., and S. Fry. 1994a. "Allegations of Abuse Denied." *Topeka (Kans.) Capital-Journal,* 3 August, p. 4

———. 1994b. "As a Lawyer, Phelps Was Good in Court." *Topeka (Kans.) Capital-Journal,* 3 August, p. 5.

———. 1994c. "No Sparing of the Rod, Sons Recall." *Topeka (Kans.) Capital-Journal,* 3 August, p. 5.

———. 1994d. "Phelps Law Career Checkered." *Topeka (Kans.) Capital-Journal,* 3 August, p. 5.

———. 1994e. "The Transformation of Fred Phelps." *Topeka (Kans.) Capital-Journal,* 3 August, p. 2.

Time. 1951. "Repentance in Pasadena." 11 June, p. 57.

Topeka (Kans.) Capital-Journal. 1993a. "Watch Your Fax!" [editorial]. 4 July, p. 4D.

———. 1993b. "Triumph of Community" [editorial]. 14 July, p. 4A.

———. 1994a. "The Good, Bad, Ugly" [editorial]. 15 July, p. 4A.

————. 1994b. "Pure Happiness Can Leave Phelps Sleepless." 3 August, p. 5.

————. 1994c. "Enough Is Enough" [editorial]. 20 November, p. 4A.

————. 1995a. "Bell, It's Your Call" [editorial]. 22 January, p. 4A.

————. 1995b. "Intimidation Insurance" [editorial]. 21 September, p. 4A.

Topeka Office of Public Affairs. 1997. *The Evolution of Topeka's City Govt.* [Brochure] Topeka, Kans.: Topeka Office of Public Affairs.

You, B. 1994. "A Holy War Against Gays."*Chicago Tribune,* 26 April, Tempo section p. 1.

10
The Politics of Needle Exchange

David L. Kirp and Ronald Bayer

Throughout much of Western Europe and in Australia, users of heroin and other injection drugs have had ready legal access to clean needles since the mid-1980s. Pharmacies sell needles over the counter, much like aspirin, and some cities run needle exchanges where addicts can swap used needles for new, sterile ones. Most public health experts in these countries believe that providing clean needles is an effective strategy for reducing the risk of transmitting the human immuno-deficiency virus (HIV) among drug addicts and those with whom they have intimate contact (Kirp and Bayer, 1992).[1] So widespread is this belief and so consistently supportive is the research that needle exchange increasingly is regarded as a routine standard of care, akin to providing insulin to people with diabetes. Indeed, the failure to ease access to clean needles, whether through market availability or subsidized exchange, is increasingly regarded as medical malpractice.

Some of the strongest support for this policy comes from American research. Preliminary findings in a study by researchers at Yale University suggest that the needle exchange in New Haven, Connecticut, which has been operating since 1990, has slowed the spread of HIV without causing the rise in drug use that some had feared (Kaplan and Heimer, 1992). Similar findings were reported in Tacoma, Washington (Hagan et al., 1991), which has the nation's longest-running program. This evidence, combined with data from abroad, prompted the National AIDS Commission (National Commission on AIDS, 1991) and the National Academy of Science (Institute of Medicine, 1986) to endorse a broad trial of needle exchange.

Reprinted by permission of the Henry J. Kaiser Family Foundation from *Dimensions of HIV Prevention: Needle Exchange,* eds. Jeff Stryker and Mark Smith (Menlo Park, Calif., 1993). The Kaiser Family Foundation is an independent health care philanthropy and is not associated with Kaiser Permanente or Kaiser Industries.

The research indicates that widespread adoption of needle exchange in the United States could save tens of thousands of lives. Increasingly, acquired immune deficiency syndrome (AIDS) in America is a needle-borne epidemic centered in predominantly African American and Latino ghettos and affecting intravenous drug users, their sexual partners, and their children. Injection-drug users account for about one-third of the 250,000 cases of AIDS, and they constitute the fastest-growing risk group. Sharing needles is the main reason. Before the advent of AIDS, researchers typically described this practice as a ritual of solidarity for a widely despised segment of the population that has few other ways to show solidarity. Sometimes it amounts to a tacit suicide pact among those who will give up anything for the formidable, if fleeting, pleasure of a fix. But, as users have become knowledgeable about how AIDS is transmitted, needle sharing is mostly an act of desperation by those without ready access to clean needles.

Nonetheless, mainstream American politicians still mostly dismiss the idea of making clean syringes available to drug users as misguided and dangerous, as "sending the wrong message" in the midst of the official war on drugs. American law reflects this hostility. A doctor's prescription is necessary to buy needles in many states, including those where drug injection is most common. And in almost every state, needle possession for the purpose of illegal drug use is outlawed by drug paraphernalia statutes (Gostin, 1991). The United States unintentionally has become the control group in an international investigation of the effectiveness of needle exchange.

With the notable and recent exception of New York City, few of the needle exchanges in the United States are situated at epicenters of the twin scourges of AIDS and intravenous drug use. Though the estimated number of exchanged needles tripled between 1990 and 1992, to a cumulative total of nearly two million, that statistic needs to be placed in perspective. In 1992, more needles—seven hundred thousand for an estimated three thousand injection drug users—were exchanged in Amsterdam (population 750,000) (Des Jarlais and Friedman, 1992) than in any American city.

THE ROOTS OF OPPOSITION

It is easy enough to understand why needle exchange in this country is so generally unacceptable. It has been opposed on deep-rooted ideological grounds by the unusual and powerful coalition of "just say no" conservatives, law enforcement agencies, and establishment figures in the black community.

Presidents Reagan and Bush rejected needle exchange, even when effective AIDS prevention appeared to hang in the balance, because they saw it as undercutting the national message of zero tolerance for drug use. Although Health and Human Services Secretary Dr. Louis Sullivan kept an open mind on the subject, his was not the official voice of the administration. In a July 1992 bulletin, drug czar Robert Martinez insisted that the nation must not "sound a retreat in the war against drugs by distributing clean needles to intravenous drug users in the hope that this will slow the spread of AIDS. . . . There is no getting around the fact that distributing needles facilitates drug use and undercuts the credibility of society's message that using drugs is illegal and morally wrong" (Executive Office of the President, 1992). Former Los Angeles Police Chief Daryl Gates was more blunt: "We should take users and shoot them." Although Gates's statement is hyperbolic, it does reflect a widespread police hostility toward heroin addicts. Urban police departments could have discouraged needle sharing by aggressively shutting down the shooting galleries where much of the sharing has occurred, but this has not happened—a course of inaction that Harvard drug policy expert Mark Kleiman believes to be deliberate. Shooting galleries, Kleiman contends, have not been closed precisely because they are such effective vectors of AIDS transmission (Kleiman, 1992).

The public debate about needle exchange has been mostly a whites-only affair, but many African American politicians and ministers, whose constituents have been decimated by the twin plagues of drugs and AIDS, have been vocal opponents. Legislation that prevents cities from spending federal dollars on needle exchange or even the distribution of bleach was promoted in Congress by a political odd couple: conservative Republican Sen. Jesse Helms of North Carolina and Rep. Charles Rangel, a progressive African American Democrat whose New York City district has one of the nation's highest rates of HIV infection.

Blacks' deep distrust of social experimentation, which looks like experimentation on them, is a major explanation for this hostility. Benjamin Ward, a former New York City police commissioner, told the *New York Times* that "as a black person, I have a particular sensitivity to doctors conducting experiments, and they too frequently seem to be conducted against blacks" (Lambert, 1988). According to surveys conducted by Stephen Thomas, director of the Minority Health Research Laboratory at the University of Maryland in College Park, only one black person in five—compared with two-thirds of all Maryland households—trusts federal reports on AIDS. Two of every three blacks think there might be some truth to reports that AIDS was developed in a germ-warfare laboratory. Although 85 percent of Maryland households generally dismiss the idea that AIDS is a form of genocide against blacks, some two-thirds of black church members entertain that possibility (DeParle, 1990).[2] So do some black leaders. Needle exchange is "genocide," said Harlem City Councilman Hilton Clark who, damning the New York City experiment, added that its promoters "should be arrested for murder and drug distribution" (Anderson, 1991). Similar sentiments have been expressed by black spokesmen in such typically liberal locales as San Francisco and Boston.

To be sure, the black community is divided on the wisdom of needle exchange. Those African Americans, mostly young and mainly gay, who identify more with the style of AIDS activism favored by the AIDS Coalition to Unleash Power (ACT UP) than with black churches, regard opposition to needle exchange by establishment black leaders as an instance of literally deadly denial; they too have sometimes turned to the language of genocide. That charge is usually a conversation-stopper—and a policy-stopper too.

To say that all needle exchange supporters could be crammed into a phone booth is an exaggeration—but not much of an exaggeration. Needle exchange is promoted by AIDS activists; by some public health officials, AIDS researchers, and political liberals; and by some members of the largely disenfranchised community of intravenous drug users. These groups do not make for a politically powerful coalition. Therefore, the infrequently asked question about the politics of needle exchange is, Why has the program been implemented at all, given such formidable obstacles? In its contentiousness, needle exchange does not stand alone among public health issues; others include the distribution of condoms in schools and, historically, fluoridation of the water supply. This effort to explain why needle exchange has been successful in some locales but not others thus increases our understanding of the trajectory of this policy—and also of the possibilities and limits of radical public health reform generally.

CHARISMA MATTERS

Nearly everywhere that a needle exchange is operating, a single activist or a handful of individuals has served as the catalyst. In this initial phase, charisma matters. The names of these contemporary Johnny Appleseeds are well-known in the needle exchange world: Dave Purchase in Tacoma, Washington; Jon Parker in New Haven, Connecticut and Boston; Robert Elovich and Yolanda Serrano in New York City; George Clark in San Francisco; and Aaron Peak of Honolulu, Hawaii, who now runs an exchange in Nepal. Usually, an act of civil disobedience—the willingness to court arrest for distributing clean needles illegally—has been necessary to attract the attention of public health officials, the press, and particularly politicians and police, all of whom must eventually acquiesce if needle exchange is to be sustained.

These individuals have used different strategies, or, more precisely, differences in personality have led to different strategies. Sometimes, as with Elovich and Parker, a cadre such as an ACT UP chapter or the AIDS Brigade has formed around them. In other instances, as with Purchase and Peak, the individual *is* the program, at least at the outset. Because these typically are activists who have come to needle exchange with a history of organizing, their initial inclination is to be confrontational. Some have opted to remain outsiders, seeing themselves as organizers in the Saul Alinsky mold rather than as members of the community (Alinsky, 1971). Parker, for example, prefers an us-versus-them approach, and he wears his dozens of arrests in eight states as a badge of courage. Others—including Kathleen Oliver in Portland, Oregon; Purchase in Tacoma; and Patrick Haggerty in Seattle—more closely fit the Jane Addams tradition of social-work activism. They have relied on their long-standing membership in a community to counter the charge that they are carpetbaggers, to shame the opposition (Oliver once declared: "What you're really saying is that these people are expendable, that you'd rather have them die of AIDS than give them needles"), and, vitally, to win support for their initiative by drawing on connections they have developed over the years.

Outsiders gain real power from their remarkable willingness to take personal risks. In Portland, Bill Reese, Ph.D., known as "Dr. Bill," who legally sold needles to local drug users, saw his store firebombed by antagonists. Despite complaints from store owners in Tacoma, authorities were unwilling to jail veteran drug counselor Purchase when he set up his one-man operation, a card table on a downtown sidewalk, and that gave him influence over public decision making. Public health officials in Hawaii sought to avoid the embarrassment that would follow if Peak distributed needles on the streets, as he threatened to do, and were arrested; they enlisted his participation in a coalition that supported state legalization of needle exchange. In New York City, Elovich and other activists were arrested and tried under the state's drug paraphernalia law. A jury acquitted them on grounds of public health "necessity," which gave them a moral authority they could rely on for broader political purposes.

But charisma is an inherently unstable base for a continuous social enterprise. Needle exchange requires an organization to arrange regular staffing of sites, to obtain clean needles, and to dispose of used needles. Although volunteers often operate the exchanges, needles cost money, and there is not a reliable private source of support. The generally held view is that clients cannot subsidize the service, that their participation and the personal responsibility it evinces are a sufficient contribution.

In some cities, notably San Francisco, contributions from private donors have kept needle exchanges operating. The American Foundation for AIDS Research (AmFAR) has delivered the support essential to run needle exchanges in several cities, including Portland and Boulder, Colorado, and to expand New York City's program. In this sense, AmFAR has been an agent of change, much as the Ford Foundation nurtured community action through its "gray areas" program in the late 1950s, developing a model that the federal government could draw on in the war on poverty.

But these efforts cannot survive for very long on grants alone. Private money is scarce for something as controversial as needle exchange.[3] In San Francisco, for instance, corporate donors such as Levi Strauss & Co. have not been eager to publicize their involvement. And though foundations such as AmFAR are enthusiastic about launching new ventures and are even willing to fund needle exchange where it is illegal, they have neither the resources nor the interest to deliver aid in perpetuity. The Portland program, the first one launched in this country, still depends on private largesse; it has been in constant danger of closing because of a lack of funds.

In the not-so-long term, then, public endorsement is essential to maintain needle exchange. It ensures, at the least, an end to police harassment of those handing out needles; it may also bring money, legitimacy, and the institutionalization of these programs under the umbrella of public health services. But securing public funds is another matter. Indeed, the limited prospect of finding such support has prompted many needle-exchange proponents to advocate changes in the nation's drug paraphernalia laws so that drug injectors can easily purchase needles in pharmacies. Yet advocates of needle exchange often stress that changing the behavior of drug users by linking them to treatment requires the personal contact and the development of trusting relationships that only programs can provide—"open arms more than open doors [to pharmacies]," as one program director phrased it.

PUBLIC HEALTH SUPPORT

Since the early days of the AIDS epidemic, many leading public health officials in America have supported the concept of needle exchange. Nearly a decade ago, David Sencer, then New York City's health commissioner, publicly warned that failure to distribute clean needles meant "condemning large numbers of addicts to death from AIDS" (Bayer, 1991). His successor, Steven Joseph, who pushed for a needle-exchange clinical trial, told the *New York Times* in 1988 that "we don't have that much time" (Anderson, 1991). These officials perceived the issue not as a moral or law-enforcement concern but as a straightforward, if politically volatile, public health concern. They did not believe, as many politicians did, that providing needles would invite a new contagion of drug use. "I never heard of anybody starting drugs because needles were available or stopping because they couldn't find a clean one" (Anderson, 1991), declared Mervyn Silverman, president of AmFAR and former health director in San Francisco. Many public health officials visited Amsterdam, and even more attended the annual international AIDS conferences, so that they learned of needle-exchange successes in Western Europe and Australia. Although these experts never saw needle exchange as a panacea, intuitively it has seemed to be a promising strategy for harm reduction, an approach that could accomplish in the realm of drug use what condom campaigns were meant to achieve in the domain of sex.

The endorsement of public health officials is essential to bring needle exchange into being. Although private ventures can survive where, as in Portland, the public health department has largely distanced itself from the enterprise, no community has embraced needle exchange as public policy without more explicit official backing. For health officials, however, endorsement can be personally costly. It means testing the credibility and clout of public health authorities in confronting such powerful antagonisms as law enforcement officials; politicians at all levels of government who see the issue from a law-enforcement or moral perspective; well-organized members of the "moral majority"; and some leaders of the very communities—African American and Latino—whose members apparently stand to gain most from needle exchange. Endorsement also means developing ties with activists who may be difficult allies because they instinctively distrust "the system" and who lack experience operating within it. Interestingly, such support has come from across the ideological spectrum, including health officials identified with a more traditional public health approach to the AIDS epidemic, such as public health directors Stephen Joseph in New York City, Christine Gebbie in Oregon and then Washington state, and Molly Coye, first in New Jersey and then in California.

On occasion, endorsement of needle exchange has come directly from the top of the public health hierarchy. In New York City, health commissioners Sencer and Joseph spoke out early, despite opposition from the state health director, David Axelrod. In Philadelphia, the public health director, with the mayor's support, expressed his willingness to distribute needles—and risk arrest if necessary—to defy the governor. Elsewhere, as in Seattle, Tacoma, and Hawaii, the needle exchange idea filtered up the organizational ladder—from the street-level bureaucrats who have daily contact with drug users to those who manage the drug-treatment or AIDS program, and eventually to department heads, who took up the matter with their counterparts in law enforcement and with politicians. Public health officials do not always win these contests. Coye, California's health director, could not convince Gov. Pete Wilson to sign legislation legalizing needle exchange,[4] just as she had failed several years earlier in New Jersey when Gov. Thomas Kean rejected her efforts to organize a needle exchange clinical trial (Bayer, 1991). Regardless of whether they succeed, such efforts demand leadership and risk taking not ordinarily associated with bureaucrats.

This crazy-quilt pattern of adoption and rejection of needle exchange in the United States reflects a diffusion—and confusion—of authority in a federal system. Sometimes reformers have taken advantage of this division of responsibility, despite what has been Washington's adamant opposition to needle exchange. Similarly, local autonomy has enabled county or municipal health officials to undertake needle exchange where state health departments have been cautious, reluctant, or unsympathetic.

But divisions of authority also can hinder innovation. In New York, for example, state health officials have been unwilling to endorse a needle exchange effort by a local coalition because New York City's mayor remains ambivalent. More often, states have checked local initiatives. Conservative Democratic governors in Pennsylvania and Maryland have opposed initiatives from Philadelphia and Baltimore. On several occasions, the socially conservative legislature in Massachusetts has rebuffed efforts by Boston Mayor Raymond Flynn to legalize needle exchange. Baltimore's police chief has threatened to arrest anyone who distributes needles, which has driven that city's effort underground. Washington, D.C., launched a ninety-day needle exchange clinical trial, rather than a full-scale program, only because the brief experiment did not require the approval of the capitol's congressional oversight committee; for District of Columbia officials, this episode offered another argument for statehood (Anderson, 1991).

IS THIS CONTROVERSY DATA-PROOF?

Efficacy research has been a source of support in the effort to launch needle swapping. Studies, particularly those in New Haven and Tacoma, have helped overcome policymakers' doubts, and in some places, needle exchange has been promoted as an experiment to be scientifically evaluated, not as a policy to be implemented generally. Not surprisingly, though, the strong ideological dimension of the issue means political considerations often trump the data. As science historian Warwick Anderson notes, the issue has become "so enmeshed in politics that no one can now say who was talking as a scientist and who as a politician: There was no room left for relatively autonomous science" (Bayer, in press).

New York City's experience, about which Anderson writes, is instructive. In 1988, when Health Commissioner Joseph received the go-ahead to start a needle-exchange experiment, opposition from the city's black and Latino leadership was vitriolic. The fact that this was just a study, not an entire program, mattered not at all. The black and Latino caucus on the city council denounced the scheme as "beyond all human reason." In a letter published in the *Amsterdam News*, the city's leading black newspaper, and signed by a number of luminaries,[5] the idea was assailed as "a very serious mistake" that would lead to the legalization of drugs (Lambert, 1990).

A little more than a year later, David Dinkins, who had become the city's first black mayor, fulfilled a campaign promise to black constituents and abruptly ended the experiment. Newly appointed Health Commissioner Woodrow Myers, an African American, announced that he was "ideologically opposed" to needle exchange and could "not imagine any data" that would change his mind (Bunch, 1990). Myers took his ideologically based antagonism even further when he sought to cancel a city contract to educate addicts on how to sterilize their works with bleach. The city's Black Leadership Coalition on AIDS, a politically powerful group, backed Myers, labeling bleach-and-teach a "Trojan horse for the African American community" (O'Keefe et al., 1991).

Within two years, however, Mayor Dinkins had changed his mind. The illegal but widely publicized needle exchange efforts of New York City's AIDS activists had put the item back on the public agenda. Another relevant factor was the Yale University-sponsored study, released in mid-1991, suggesting that a needle-exchange clinical trial had slowed the spread of HIV but did not increase drug use, as had been feared (Daniels, 1992). Those preliminary findings received a great deal of press attention, partly because they carried Yale's imprimatur. The fact that New Haven's black mayor, John Daniels, an opponent of needle exchange when he was a state legislator, had supported the trial and boldly announced its success put great pressure on Dinkins. Myers, the New York city health commissioner, had resigned and been replaced by Margaret Hamburg, a public health pragmatist; this made the mayor's shift easier to stage manage. Hamburg cited the New Haven findings in an analysis recommending a shift in policy.[6] Moreover, James Dumpson, a senior black figure in the city's social welfare circles who was the chairman of the Black Leadership Coalition on AIDS and a member of Hamburg's working group, announced that he favored distributing sterile injecting equipment to addicts. Even though many leading black politicians remained unconvinced, they recognized that Dinkins was politically vulnerable, and so agreed to let the mayor reverse himself without sparking a political explosion. When Dinkins announced in 1992 that he would permit needle exchange in New York City supported by state and private funds, it was vital for him literally to surround himself with a broad spectrum of black leaders.

Elsewhere, though, the efficacy studies have had less impact on policy. Advocates often have referred loosely to findings from Amsterdam, New Haven, and Tacoma, but this has been more rhetorical flourish amid political argument than a reexamination. The fact that Tacoma had a needle-swapping program was more pertinent to officials in nearby Seattle than the New Haven study was. A key legislator in Hawaii rejected all European research as irrelevant to the American experience.

The research project in Tacoma has regularly been redesigned in response to complaints from critics, whereas the New Haven study has been criticized for depending in part on mathematical projections rather than concrete data. That's to be expected, even though the empirical evidence supporting needle exchange is quite as strong as, say, the evidence for Head Start. But this has not kept opponents from dismissing the findings as unconvincing. The researchers, many of whom have become vocal enthusiasts of the programs they are investigating, claim they have been unfairly held to a higher standard of proof than the standard for other programs. That proposition, while true, is politically irrelevant. It is difficult to imagine *any* findings that would satisfy opponents such as federal drug czar Martinez and Governor Wilson of California because their skepticism rests on ideological concerns; for them, data are essentially beside the point. On the other hand, those who are more sympathetic to needle exchange often acknowledge privately that conclusive proof of the effectiveness of exchange would be difficult to establish. In the face of this uncertainty, they nonetheless consider the risks worthwhile—certainly less than the risk of inaction. Doug Sutherland, who as the mayor of Tacoma made an about-face on the issue and became a supporter of needle exchange, noted: "We cannot tell [how effective needle exchange is], and we will never be able to tell. We are trying to prevent something from happening. How can you know you've been successful?"

RACIAL POLITICS

As New York City's experience indicates, race has been a vital and volatile factor in the politics of needle exchange, at least in cities most devastated by the needle-borne AIDS epidemic. Concern about racial conflict may be one reason why the idea has not been taken seriously—indeed, has barely been mentioned in such major centers as Newark, New Jersey; Detroit, Michigan; Cleveland, Ohio; and Miami, Florida.

Yet there are signs that blacks' objections to needle exchange have lessened, and this creates new political opportunities for proponents. The policy-stopping talk of genocide is no longer so widely heard. The endorsement of needle exchange in the past few years by black mayors in New Haven, Philadelphia, Washington, D.C., and New York City has made it more difficult for minority community leaders to sound the charge of racism. Tacit acquiescence by the black establishment is increasingly replacing resistance as the norm. In Baltimore, for instance, needle exchange was rejected when Mayor Kurt Schmoke proposed it in 1988. The idea was dismissed in the outcry over Schmoke's call for an open discussion of drug legalization. Now the idea is quietly resurfacing. Schmoke backed away from legalization; a key state legislator, who is black and represents Baltimore, endorsed needle exchange; the state attorney general is supportive; and no vocal opposition is anticipated from the city's powerful black clergy.

Minority unhappiness with needle exchange has been much less evident in the western states, where many programs operate. There, with the instructive exception of Los Angeles, African American communities generally are smaller, and drug addiction is not viewed as a predominantly minority problem. Not that race has been irrelevant. Black leaders in Tacoma opposed situating a needle exchange in their neighborhood, and their wishes were honored. Seattle, which has had a program since 1990, waited three years and sought support from local African American leaders before it proposed expanding the effort into a predominantly black area.

Race has also shaped the discussion of needle exchange in a very different way—as a buttress for conservative and white opposition. Strong resistance from law-enforcement officials and politicians is likely in a state such as New Jersey, where race, drugs, and crime are perceived as closely linked phenomena and are particularly salient concerns. In contrast, in places such as Seattle, Portland, Boulder, and Hawaii, the belief that drug addiction has fueled a crime wave among nonwhites is less widely held. There is less fear of drug-related crime generally and less concern that needle exchange will boost the number of addicts. All of this translates into less opposition to needle swapping. Police in Tacoma saw the issue as a health concern, not a law-enforcement matter. Honolulu police initially were disinclined to testify against a needle-exchange bill and did so only when the state prosecutor pushed them to say something; in their testimony, the police expressed opposition to the legislation in pro forma terms that really bespoke their indifference. Hawaii's legislators were unimpressed when the U.S. attorney appointed by President Bush provocatively warned them that they risked creating a "needle park" in Honolulu. The opposition in Seattle and Portland has been so miniscule that now, several years after needle-exchange programs were adopted, local elected officials express some surprise that the issue still is controversial in other cities.

PERSUASIVE RATIONALES

When John Daniels was a member of the Connecticut Legislature, he was outspoken in his opposition to needle exchange. What changed his mind, he says, was a visit to the neonatal intensive care unit at New Haven's city hospital. The legislator-turned-mayor left the hospital sick at heart about the AIDS-blighted lives there, convinced that if needle exchange could save a single child from such a fate, it was worth implementing (Daniels, 1992).

Daniels's conversion story is not unusual. The primary selling point of needle exchange is not that it will slow the spread of HIV among drug users but rather the impact that needle-borne HIV transmission has had on the "innocents": women and especially children. In Hawaii, for instance, a septuagenarian pediatrician was a major force behind passage of state legislation. Concerning the effect of needle exchange on addicts, the most politically persuasive contention is that the exchanges are a bridge to treatment, not merely dispensaries for reducing the number of infected needles circulating among drug users (Joseph, 1989). The addict, it is said, comes to recognize that someone cares about his fate; from that contact, treatment for addiction, job training, housing support, and welfare—in short, full membership in the commonweal—can follow. This argument seeks to neutralize the charge that needle exchange represents a capitulation to addictive behavior. The argument is used even though advocates acknowledge that it is crucial to reach out even to people who are not interested in treatment.

The needle user who persists in maintaining his habit is socially problematic—an enemy deviant, as sociologists might say—whereas the addict who seizes on the needle exchange as a way to end his addiction is more acceptable because he is repentant. This explains the emphasis on treatment in rhetoric favoring needle exchange, even though everywhere there are waiting lists for methadone-treatment programs and no funds to expand those programs. Moreover, because of the perception that exchanges do only what their name implies (exchange needles), they have been regarded not as permanent arrangements but rather as public health "experiments" that must be carefully monitored.[7] The European concept of providing clean needles as a routine standard of care has not caught on in this country. Only in Seattle is the expansion of needle exchange being promoted with the public health argument that the targeted area "deserves" this state-of-the-art program.

THE PRICE OF PERSUASIVE RATIONALES

Choosing these arguments for needle exchange—emphasizing the benefits for women and children, the bridge to treatment, and the experimental nature of exchange—while de-emphasizing the problems of addiction may be necessary to secure adoption. These arguments intentionally neutralize the perceived social threat and make needle exchange (unlike, say, condom distribution in high schools) seem like a goodwill gesture from "us" to "them." Yet at the same time such arguments camouflage the reality that at the card table in Seattle's skid row and inside New Haven's mobile van, the government is using taxpayers' dollars to supply "works" to drug users. Although there are sound public health reasons for these ventures, politicians do not willingly discuss those reasons. New Haven Mayor Daniels still perceives needle exchange as a political millstone. "Don't ask for a signing ceremony," the governor of Hawaii told advocates when the bill authorizing a needle exchange reached his desk, expressing his wish to avoid calling attention to what had been done.

More locales are likely to launch exchanges during Bill Clinton's presidency. Predictably, the new administration will support such ventures, at least if they are styled as experiments, and strings on how federal drug-control funds are expended may well be loosened. Still, at the local level, where needle exchanges are operated, programs will live a fragile life after their inception. The political coalitions that brought many exchanges into existence were short-lived, their members having moved on to other issues. When the charismatic figure who launched a venture leaves, the program may suffer because it is not fully integrated into the public health bureaucracy. In Hawaii, needle exchange founder Peak departed for Nepal shortly after that state passed needle exchange legislation in 1990, worn out by politicking. The state, which has three thousand to twelve thousand intravenous drug users, exchanged only twenty thousand needles in 1992, making the new law mostly a symbolic accomplishment. Even if they stay on, those who advocate radical policy change are not necessarily capable of making the transition to program managers. There is little in the way of a national network to provide information or assistance to beleaguered programs, although efforts to create a network are afoot. Furthermore, while the media have been mostly supportive, the possibility of a media-genic scandal is always present; possibilities include the child who pricks himself with a used needle bearing the code of a needle exchange, the fifteen-year-old who overdoses with drugs using a needle supplied by an exchange, or the dealer who swaps hundreds of needles at the exchange and then resells them on the street.

One way that skeptical politicians have been persuaded to vote for needle exchange is by stressing how cheap it is, but this too is a problematic strategy. Politicians have typically been reluctant to provide more than token funding because invariably they perceive priorities that are more pressing or more politically attractive. In Portland, for example, where budgetary retrenchment has had a profound impact on the needle exchange program, exchange activist Kathleen Oliver points out the difficulty of asking for funds to buy sterile needles when libraries are being closed.

Meanwhile, those politicians who are searching for a reason not to increase support for methadone treatment and drug education will seize on needle exchange as a convenient rationale. "See, we're doing something," will be the claim. This argument confuses the part for the whole. More importantly, it invites a new epidemic of denial concerning the scope of the drug issue. To deal with these second-generation challenges to the implementation of needle exchange—which should be seen not as an end in itself but rather as part of a far broader drug education, treatment, and control policy—will require a type of politics quite different from what has thus far emerged.

EDITOR'S COMMENT

Because it was originally written for another purpose, this chapter does not explicitly use the terminology that is shared by other chapters in this volume; that is, there are no explicit references to the typology of governmental roles in culture war controversies that provides an overarching framework for the volume. The chapter is reprinted here, however, for several reasons. First, it provides an excellent, descriptive account of developments concerning an important issue in local culture wars: needle exchanges for intravenous drug users as a weapon in the war on HIV infection. Incorporation of this chapter thus enhances the diversity of topical coverage in the volume, extending it to an important public health issue. Second, the chapter offers excellent case examples of several of local government's culture war roles, most notably entrepreneurial instigation and responsiveness. The chapter is also of special interest because it offers a look at types of entrepreneurs that are not evident in other cases. The task of incorporating this chapter into the development of a theoretical perspective on local culture wars is taken up in the concluding chapter.

NOTES

1. Much of the unreferenced material in this chapter is based on the authors' site visits and personal discussions with key figures in the shaping of needle exchange policy at the state and local level.

2. See Thomas and Quinn (1993).

3. For a complete discussion of needle exchange funding, see Lurie and Chen (1993).

4. On September 30, 1992, Governor Wilson vetoed Assembly Bill No. 2525, which would have authorized a needle exchange pilot program in San Francisco.

5. Signatories included Congressmen Charles Rangel and Floyd Flake; Sterling Johnson, the assistant district attorney in charge of drug prosecutions; Wyatt Walker, the pastor of Harlem's Covenant Baptist Church; and Wilbert Tatum, the newspaper's publisher.

6. Hamburg had greater latitude than otherwise might have been the case because David Axelrod, New York state's chief health official, who was very cool to the idea of needle exchange, had been felled by a stroke and was out of the policy loop.

7. Some places, such as Hawaii, have succeeded in making their temporary programs permanent.

REFERENCES

Alinsky, S. D. 1971. *Rules for Radicals: A Practical Primer for Realistic Radicals.* New York: Random House.

Anderson, W. 1991. "The New York Needle Trial: The Politics of Public Health in the Age of AIDS." *American Journal of Public Health* 81:1506–17.

Bayer, R. 1991. *Private Acts, Social Consequences: AIDS and the Politics of Public Health.* New Brunswick, N.J.: Rutgers University Press.

———. In press. "The Dependent Center: The First Decade of the AIDS Epidemic in New York City." In D. Rosner, ed., *Epidemic!* New Brunswick, N.J.: Rutgers University Press.

Bunch, W. 1990. "AIDS Group Opposed Bleach Giveaway." *New York Newsday,* 16 June, p. 7.

Daniels, J. 1992. Speech at The Kaiser Forum, "Needle and Syringe Availability and Exchange for HIV Prevention." Menlo Park, Calif., 10–11 December.

DeParle, J. 1990. "Talk of Government Being Out to Get Blacks Falls on More Attentive Ears." *New York Times,* 29 October, p. A12.

Des Jarlais, D. C., and S. R. Friedman. 1991. "AIDS and Legal Access to Sterile Injection Equipment." *Annals of the American Academy of Political Science* 521:42–65.

Executive Office of the President. Office of National Drug Control Policy. 1992. "Needle Exchange Programs: Are They Effective?" *ONDCP Bulletin* 7:1–7.

Gostin, L. 1991. "The Interconnected Epidemics of Drug Dependency and AIDS." *Harvard Civil Rights-Civil Liberties Law Review* 26:113–84.

Hagan, H., D. C. Des Jarlais, D. Purchase, et al. 1991. "The Tacoma Syringe Exchange." *Journal of Addictive Diseases* 10:81–88.

Institute of Medicine. 1986. *Confronting AIDS: Directions for Public Health, Health Care, and Research.* Washington, D.C.: National Academy Press.

Joseph, S. C. 1989. "A Bridge to Treatment: The Needle Exchange Pilot Program in New York City." *AIDS Education and Prevention* 1:340–45.

Kaplan, E. H., and R. Heimer. 1992. "HIV Prevalence Among Intravenous Drug Users: Model-Based Estimates from New Haven's Legal Needle Exchange." *Journal of AIDS* 5:163–69.

Kirp, D. L., and R. Bayer, eds. 1992. *AIDS in the Industrialized Democracies: Passions, Politics and Policies.* New Brunswick, N.J.: Rutgers University Press.

Kleiman, M. 1992. *Against Excess: Drug Policy for Results.* New York: Basic Books.

Lambert, B. 1988. "The Free Needle Program Is Under Way and Under Fire." *New York Times,* 13 November, p. E6.

———. 1990. "Myers Opposes Needle Projects to Curb AIDS." *New York Times,* 10 April, p. B4.

Lurie, P., and D. Chen. 1993. "A Review of Programs in North America." In J. Stryker and M. D. Smith, eds., *Needle Exchange.* Menlo Park, Calif.: Kaiser Family Foundation, pp. 11–34.

National Commission on AIDS. 1991. *The Twin Epidemics of Substance Abuse and HIV.* Washington, D.C.: National Commission on AIDS.

O'Keefe, E., E. Kaplan, and K. Khoshnood. 1991. *Preliminary Report: City of New Haven Needle Exchange Program.* New Haven, Conn.: New Haven Health Department.

Slater, C. M., and G. E. Hall, eds. 1993. *1993 County and City Extra.* Lanham, Md.: Bernan Press.

Thomas, S. B., and S. C. Quinn. 1993. "Understanding the Attitudes of Black Americans." In J. Stryker and M. D. Smith, eds., *Needle Exchange.* Menlo Park, Calif.: Kaiser Family Foundation, pp. 99–128.

11
Moral Principles of Local Officials and the Resolution of Culture War Issues

Paul Schumaker

Urban policymakers are well aware of—and, for the most part, agree with—the precept that governments should not legislate morality. Thus, they normally prefer to avoid or evade culture war issues. Culture wars sometimes break out among groups in American cities, however, and urban officials have little choice but to adjudicate such conflicts, ultimately casting their votes with one side or the other. Less frequently, urban officials are motivated to be much more active participants on one side or the other of culture war issues, sometimes initiating or instigating them.

Drawing on interviews with city council and school board members in twelve American cities, this chapter describes how these policymakers cast themselves into such roles in urban culture wars. It describes their normal hesitancy to engage culture war issues in such a way as to put their governments on the side of legislating morality, but it goes on to consider why and when officials enact the very social controls that they normally regard as inappropriate and ill-advised. Some of their constituents claim that there are important justifications for legislating morality; they believe that people's actions should be controlled so that they better conform to religious precepts, to universal ethical principles, and/or to dominant community values, and they believe that laws are required to prevent people from harming themselves, or harming others, or depriving others of their equal rights. Officials sometimes find such justifications convincing, and sometimes not. This chapter examines the views of urban officials about such justifications and indicates the kinds of issues for which regulation and control are considered most and least justified.

Because of the pivotal roles that urban officials play in conflict resolution, theories about culture wars must be able to explain and predict their roles in these highly visible events. In the interviews, urban officials suggest that the outcomes of culture wars are determined by the attitudes and actions (and inactions) of officials like themselves, and that these, in turn, are determined by their moral principles and their values. Thus, an important step in developing a theory about urban culture wars is to analyze these principles and values, accounting for their interrelationships and determinants.

AN EXAMINATION OF URBAN OFFICIALS

This chapter is based on a larger study of urban justice, in which 120 elected officials were interviewed between March and August 1993. Because of the obvious connections among justice, morality, and culture wars, these interviews provide an abundance of information about officials' attitudes and actions in local culture wars, but the findings are exploratory because the culture war phenomenon was not its primary focus.

The interviews were conducted in twelve cities: Atlanta, Georgia; Austin, Texas; Baltimore, Maryland; Green Bay, Wisconsin; Kansas City, Missouri; Minneapolis, Minnesota; Orlando, Florida; Pasadena, California; Providence, Rhode Island; Salt Lake City, Utah; San Jose, California; and Seattle, Washington. The cities are major urban centers—generally in the hundred thousand to million population range—and they were selected to try to capture the diversity of urban life in America. Beyond obvious regional variations, these cities differ greatly in their racial and ethnic composition—ranging from largely white communities (Green Bay and Salt Lake City) to cities that have strong black majorities (Baltimore and Atlanta), substantial Hispanic populations (Pasadena, San Jose, and Austin), or a large number of Asian Americans (Seattle). These cities have diverse cultures, as the individualist, moralistic, and traditionalist aspects of political cultures emphasized and assessed by Daniel Elazar (1984) are evident to various degrees in our sample cities.[1] Interviews were sought with about five or six city council members and another five or six school board members in each city. Persons who had served in these capacities since 1980 were randomly called and asked if they would be willing to participate in two-hour interviews focusing on how they thought about "fairness" and how they applied their ideas of fairness to urban policymaking. Depending on the availability of potential interviewees and the logistics of getting from one interview to another, ten to twelve interviews were scheduled in each city. Thus, the sample is composed of the first ten to twelve people in each city who agreed to the interviews.[2] The resulting sample was evenly split between members of the city council and the school board: fifty-nine persons had served on city councils, fifty-six had served on school boards, and five had served in both capacities. Ninety-four persons (78 percent) were white, twenty-one black, two Hispanic, and three Asian American. Women made up 47 percent of the sample. More participants identified themselves as liberals (31 percent) than as conservatives (23 percent), and many respondents preferred to give themselves other labels, such as "moderates" (19 percent), "fiscal conservatives and social liberals" (13 percent), and "radicals" or "socialists" (8 percent).

Data concerning officials' attitudes and actions regarding culture wars were attained from three parts of the interview transcripts. To begin the interviews, officials were asked to tell at least one story about "issues, policy areas, or cases that arose while [they] were in office" that exemplified issues of "fairness" as they understood that term. Such stories were requested because stories provide rich research material reflective of human cognitive capacities (Schank, 1990) and because respondents are less likely to be influenced by the conceptual frameworks and perceived values of the researcher when they provide open-ended stories than when they respond to highly structured questions (Van Maanen, 1979). By telling stories about specific cases or issues, officials usually provide fairly accurate accounts of their own beliefs and activities regarding these issues, without distortions intended to make their attitudes and actions seem more socially acceptable. Respondents usually offered one or two stories at the beginning of the interview, although some told as many as five. Overall, officials told 221 stories during this portion of the interviews. Of these, 25 dealt with what can be regarded as culture war issues, addressing such matters as gambling, recreational drug use, smoking in public places, prayers in schools and at public meetings, abortions and access to family planning clinics, gay rights, regulating hate groups like the Ku Klux Klan (KKK), and promoting or restricting multiculturalism and bilingual education in public schools.

A second source of information regarding officials' attitudes and activities in culture war issues was the open-ended responses of officials to a probe at the end of the interview about their recurrent concerns while in public office and/or those things that others attributed to them as the central things they stood for while in office. Most officials provided comments that were irrelevant to culture wars (e.g., "I was an advocate for managed growth," or "I am an environmentalist"); however, at this point in the interview, twelve officials provided responses that situated themselves with respect to culture war issues. Six officials declared that they sought to curb discrimination: Some claimed to be advocates of civil rights generally, and some were advocates for equal rights for racial minorities and/or gays. Three officials declared that they stood for individual freedom and choice and that they opposed excessive governmental control in various social policy areas such as abortion. And three officials declared that they were spokespersons for multiculturalism. In short, no official claimed a core identity as an advocate for a particular morality or lifestyle. Insofar as officials perceived themselves as activists in culture war issues, they claimed to be advocates of nondiscrimination, freedom, and diversity—at least in this portion of the interview.

A third source of information regarding officials' attitudes and activities with respect to culture wars was their open-ended response to twenty-one principles of justice, presented to them during the middle of the interview. These principles focused on different criteria and procedures for the just distribution of social goods (Schumaker and Kelly, 1994) and did not directly invite commentary or stories regarding culture war issues. However, officials frequently spoke about culture war issues when responding to principles regarding the relevance of the ascriptive traits, moral merit, and social contributions of individuals to just distributions. And officials occasionally spoke to culture war issues when providing applications of equal rights principles, utilitarian principles, and the importance of democratic procedures in resolving urban conflicts. Thus, some additional information about officials' roles in culture wars was attained from this portion of the interview.

When reviewing these three portions of the interview transcripts, some decision rule was required for determining which information was pertinent to culture wars and which concerned other kinds of issues. To capture the issues that concern the analysts of culture wars, the comments and stories were sorted using a simple but critical distinction: Was the respondent addressing the nature of the good (or "human virtue") or the distribution of goods (or "justice")? In Greek antiquity, the Roman Empire, and the Christian Commonwealth that dominated Western Civilization through the Middle Ages, it was generally thought possible to give some universal account of the good and virtuous life for all, and that political life involved promoting virtuous beliefs and behavior in all members of the political community. However, the ideal of a universal conception of human goodness and virtue has been assaulted in modern times. Perhaps Thomas Hobbes laid the foundation for this assault by claiming that each individual is the best judge of his or her own good. Subsequent liberal thought during the modern era in the West has increasingly addressed the issue of the just distribution of those goods that people desire as a means to better achieve a personally defined conception of the good life. This does not mean that modern politics is unconcerned with promoting virtuous behaviors or prohibiting certain actions. The existence of culture wars is evidence of this concern. But modern politics deals with two fairly distinct moral questions: What kinds of restrictions should be imposed by governments on the pursuit of the good life by self-regarding individuals? How should social goods be distributed? Although these questions are related (Galston, 1980), culture wars can best be conceptualized as addressing the first question. For present purposes, moral issues regarding the just distribution of goods have been set aside, and attention is focused on those stories and comments that officials provided in the interviews dealing with "good" or "virtuous" human behavior and the kinds of social policies that are required to promote such behavior and curtail "bad" or "sinful" acts.[3]

Thus, the data here come from compilations of all comments and stories told by the interviewed officials pertaining to moral concerns about enhancing human goodness through social control policies. These compilations provide the qualitative data presented below and were the basis for constructing several indices used for a series of quantitative analyses as well.

Although 120 officials were interviewed for the larger study, 27 provided insufficient commentary on culture war issues to be included in the present analyses. Thus, the sample size for describing and analyzing the distribution of support for legislating morality is 93. The number of officials commenting on various justifications for legislating morality is smaller than this, often considerably so.

COMPETING PRINCIPLES REGARDING THE LEGISLATION OF MORALITY

Table 11.1 summarizes the attitudes of urban officials about legislating morality. Most officials oppose social regulations. Overall, 30 percent of the officials offered unprompted but quite explicit expressions of this principle, such as the following.

Government should be neutral with regard to morality.
Morality is not the concern of governmental officials; moral values are individualized and we should not insist on imposing our values on others.
Officials should not side with one set of cultural values over another.
Public officials should not be involved in areas of morality except to be role models.

Although most officials simply declared their opposition to the regulation of morality, some offered rationales for that opposition. The most common rationales were that the regulation of morality required officials "to make subjective value judgments"; that dealing with social regulation "diverts attention from more important issues"; that such policies are normally "ineffective at changing the offensive behavior"; and that such issues were highly conflictual, "tearing the city apart" and igniting political opposition against them. The most amusing rationale was offered by a member of the school board in Providence: "You can't legislate morality. Most public officials are devoid of morality, so to judge it or to engender it in others is something that is way over their heads."

Table 11.1. Support for Legislating Morality among City Council and School Board Members

	All officials (n = 93)	City Council (n = 51)	School Board (n = 42)
Explicit opposition	30%	35%	24%
Implied opposition	33	37	28
Mixed statements	16	10	24
Implied support	13	12	14
Explicit support	8	6	10

Another 33 percent of urban officials implied through examples and other commentary their reluctance to regulate morality, though they failed to specify such a principle. For example, several city council members in San Jose cited their opposition to Operation Rescue, which sought to block access to abortion clinics; and school board members in most cities advocated more multicultural curricula that taught students to appreciate value systems other than their own. Officials also implied their opposition to social regulations when they discussed their growing appreciation for cultural differences within the community and their need to look beyond their own value systems and the dominant values in their community when resolving community conflict. None of the 63 percent of the officials who have been coded as explicit or implied opponents of legislating morality spoke positively about particular social regulations or expressed sympathy for various justifications for exercising social control over individual choices, except to ensure civil rights.[4]

Sixteen percent of the interviewed officials provided mixed statements about legislating morality. For example, one official claimed at one point in the interview that officials should "live and let live with regard to moral values," but later she claimed that "government should play a greater role than it does in promoting virtue." As another example, a council member in Atlanta claimed that he was both a staunch opponent of gay rights and a strong advocate of the right of women to have abortions. Such commentary may be ideologically inconsistent, but it is not thereby unprincipled. Such mixed statements illustrate that officials often hold a variety of principles and values concerning culture war issues. Sometimes officials understand that these principles are inconsistent, expressing conflicting but valid ethical ideals. For example, a council woman in Pasadena wrestled with the question of no-smoking ordinances. On the one hand, her commitment to "free choice" principles made her reluctant to support a ban on smoking in restaurants. On the other hand, her belief that it was appropriate for public officials to regulate behavior that is harmful to others prompted her support for the ban. In this and a number of other similar cases, a "culture war" took place *within* the official, as well as between competing groups. When officials hold cross-cutting principles, they are, of course, likely to search for compromise solutions, such as having designated smoking and nonsmoking areas.[5]

At other times, officials understand that their principles are inconsistent at an abstract level, but such inconsistencies vanish when faced with concrete issues. The official who opposed gay rights and supported abortion rights saw no inconsistency in his positions. In the first case, the need of officials to support traditional values and marital structures outweighed their commitment to individual freedom. In the second case, legally sanctioned privacy rights outweigh ethical objections to abortion.

Twenty-one percent of our officials indicated, either explicitly or implicitly, their belief that governments should promote certain moral positions and values and control human behavior that is at odds with these values. Most of these indications were implicit, as officials expressed their support of policies to curb particular behaviors. For example, one council woman from Minneapolis supported initiatives to curb youth gangs, because "gangs have destructive moral codes." Another official there supported efforts to make it more difficult for parents to get divorced because he believed that intact family structures were important agents of moral instruction for children. Only 8 percent of officials expressed a principle claiming that it was indeed proper for government to legislate morality. Statements to this effect—such as "governments and public schools should curb the immorality of some people"; "public officials should focus on the commonalties in values among people, not their differences, and they should promote these commonalties"; and "our policies and programs need to reflect the dominant moral values of people in this community"—were somewhat more evident among school board members than city council members. Perhaps school board members are more supportive of legislating morality than city council members because they perceive schools as places of moral instruction and because they believe the young are more appropriate targets of moral guidance by public institutions than are adults whose capacities for autonomous moral judgment are presumed to be more fully developed.

Although urban officials are generally reluctant to legislate morality, a number of justifications for imposing social controls on individual choices were often offered in the interviews, sometimes by "social libertarians" who normally oppose such controls. These justifications are themselves various types of moral principles, as they declare that certain virtues should be promoted by local governments and certain vices should be discouraged and/or punished. Table 11.2 lists these principles, and indicates the number of officials who, in their unprompted comments, expressed support or opposition. Table 11.2 also indicates in parentheses the number of officials who expressly indicated that they were highly active in specific culture war issues in which these principles were at stake. Table 11.3

Table 11.2. Response to Justifications for Legislating Morality

	Support	Oppose
Promote moral standards of religion	6	19 (1)
Promote virtues revealed by natural law	16	3
Promote conformity to public opinion	16 (2)	48
Pursue values as determined by the democratic will	2	2
Protect people from self-inflicted harm (paternalism)	6	8
Control behavior for utilitarian purposes	8 (1)	2
Prevent harm to others	10 (2)	0
Ensure equal rights	22 (5)	3
Protect legal rights	12	3

Note: Numbers indicate officials who commented on justifications for legislating morality in such a way as to show either opposition or support.

Numbers in parentheses indicate the number of officials who actively supported or opposed policies in which these justifications were invoked.

lists the kinds of culture war issues that were discussed as applications of these principles; it also indicates the number of officials who supported and opposed various social controls on these issues.

Religion

The sacred texts of Jews, Christians, and Muslims contain numerous prohibitions on individual freedoms, and religious leaders and church doctrine provide additional moral strictures giving citizens and officials firm beliefs about human virtues and vices. Occasionally, urban officials hope to further their religious convictions by supporting policies consistent with them. One school board member asserted that "God forbids contraception and abortion," and she concluded that sex education classes must therefore avoid any endorsement of "safe sex," and abortions must be prohibited. Another official voted for the removal from public and school libraries of books that Christian conservatives regarded as sacrilegious. Somewhat more frequently, urban officials simply supported policies to facilitate the capacity of various religions to influence moral and spiritual life. They asserted that schools should permit silent or nondenominational prayers and that religious organizations should be allowed access to public buildings. One official claimed that various religious symbols can be displayed in public places, at least as long as other religions have equal opportunities to display their symbols and express their convictions.

Nevertheless, officials are much more opposed to regulating morality on the basis of religion than they are supportive of it. Most opponents simply asserted the principle of maintaining a wall between state and church. Those who called for such a separation do not necessarily believe that the moralities of the churches are unimportant, but they claimed that various religious communities (not the broader political community) should promote religiously defined virtues and restrict religiously defined vices. However, some officials questioned the moralities of the church. For example, one official in Providence claimed that "a noble Catholic Priest led the opposition against a gay rights ordinance, prompting me to articulate what I thought about the separation of church and state doctrine." Even in communities dominated by one religion, there was little sentiment for legislating morality on the basis of religious authority. Several officials in Salt Lake City expressed pride in their state having an especially strong constitutional prohibition against Mormon interference in state affairs, and they claimed "it would be wrong to use the moral criteria of the Mormon Church as a basis for public policy." Some officials in Green Bay agreed that "Catholic norms should not govern Green Bay." In short, culture wars are sometimes ignited by those who believe public policies should reflect religious convictions or should promote religious virtues, but urban officials are unlikely to instigate such wars. When they must adjudicate such conflicts, they are generally predisposed to avoid favoring a particularly religious viewpoint through public policy.

Table 11.3. Response of Urban Officials to Social Issues

	Support	Oppose
Promote moral standards of religion		
Prohibit abortion	1	6
Limit sex education	1	6
Remove sacrilegious books from libraries	1	4
Permit prayers in schools or at public meetings	3	2
Provide religious groups access to public building	1	1
Permit religious symbols on public property	1	0
Limit gay rights	1	20
Promote virtues revealed by natural law		
Teach "fundamental" virtues in school	14	3
Penalize unethical conduct in school (e.g., plagiarism)	5	0
Promote conformity to public opinion		
Prohibit suggestive and obscene dress in school	3	1
Limit or regulate pornography	1	3
Prohibit prostitution	0	2
Emphasize abstinence in sex education classes	2	6
Limit gay rights	2	20
Establish "English only" policies	4	6
Limit bilingual education	3	12
Limit multicultural curriculum	4	12
Pursue values as determined by the democratic will		
Establish school dress codes	1	0
Extend aid to refugees	1	0
Prohibit abortions	0	6
Limit gay rights	0	20
Protect people from self-inflicted harm (paternalism)		
Prohibit or control gambling	0	3
Discourage teenage gangs	4	0
Prohibit use of recreational drugs	2	0
Use bilingual education to teach English	9	12
Control behavior for utilitarian purposes		
Limit access to abortion clinics	0	1
Limit gay rights	0	1
Ban gang colors in schools	1	0
Prohibit weapons in schools	3	0
Require student community service	1	0
Control cigarette smoking	2	0
Limit sale of pornography	1	0
Prevent harm to others		
Control domestic violence	2	0
Limit divorce	2	0
Prohibit medicinal use of marijuana	0	1
Prohibit abortions	0	3
Ensure equal rights		
Enforce civil rights laws protecting minorities from discrimination	4	0
Enact gay rights ordinance	20	2
Extend employee benefits to all domestic partners	3	2
Protect legal rights		
Uphold free speech rights of "hate groups"	3	0
Uphold free speech of students in school newspapers and graduation speeches	3	0
Permit antiabortion protests and blockades	3	1
Permit abortion	3	0
Permit Native-American casinos	2	0
Permit Native-Americans to spear fish	1	0

Note: Numbers indicate the number of officials who supported the policy on the basis of the indicated principle, and who opposed the policy because they rejected the principle or because they invoked other principles on the issue.

Natural Law

A second justification that is sometimes presented for legislating morality is that behavior should conform to certain universal ethical principles. The concept of natural law—the idea that there are generally recognized principles of right conduct that can be understood through rational contemplation of the requirements of natural forces and processes—is one of the oldest and most common expressions of this belief. Although allegiance to the concept of natural law is less prominent in contemporary American society than among the Stoics of ancient Greece and Rome, scholars as diverse as Mortimer Adler (1981) and James Q. Wilson (1994) maintain that there are certain moral sentiments that are universal, natural, and subject to rational agreement. Many urban officials agree. According to a council member from Pasadena, "There are some objective standards, defined by ethical philosophy, that officials must take into account when they pursue and distribute values." Although this official did not specify these standards, he maintained that they may be different from existing values in the community. Rather than articulate a natural law principle, other officials specified various human virtues and vices that they regard as universal and self-evident truths. Among the virtues that officials claimed they should promote are: respecting authority and obeying the law, being considerate of and caring toward others, being good teammates and showing good sportsmanship, respecting and taking care of property, resolving differences peacefully and with civility, coming to the aid of those in distress and need, and being a productive and dependable worker. For the most part, the officials specifying such virtues were school board members, and they held that public schools should be engaged in more than "value clarification" (being aware of the values behind one's moral choices and respecting the choices of others that emphasize different values than one's own). They generally agreed that schools "should only discuss but not advocate certain value choices—such as going to church and abstaining from alcohol," but they usually maintained that schools should unabashedly teach "the fundamentals," the kind of virtues promoted by William Bennett (1993) in his *Book of Virtues*. Beyond having instructors who teach and model these virtues, school board members offered no public policies to reward virtue, but they thought that policies had to be adopted to punish certain vices. Lying, stealing, cheating (including plagiarism), and being disruptive should be punished. Several officials noted that hearings involving the suspension and expulsion of students for such offenses were a distasteful part of their job, but none questioned the propriety of punishing certain behaviors that violated what they regarded as universal ethical standards.

As shown in Table 11.2, only three officials denied the possibility of any universal ethical principles. Illustrative of such moral skepticism were the comments of a school board member in Seattle: "The Board went back and forth on teaching morality. Whenever someone proposed that we should teach morality, the debate would end when someone asked 'Whose morality?' Even the Golden

Rule is controversial. There is no moral consensus in Seattle and 'teaching moral-ity' only makes sense in situations of consensus."

In summary, urban officials often believe that there are certain *basic* univer-sal ethical principles that should be reflected in policy. Promoting virtue and con-trolling vice is much more acceptable when these virtues and vices are based on natural law rather than divine law, perhaps because the virtues identified by natu-ral law are more basic and less controversial than those identified by religious authorities. Nevertheless, culture wars do break out over the promotion of such basic virtues as respecting authority, being considerate of others, and working hard—not because there are outspoken opponents of these particular virtues but because some people believe that there is no scientific or logical defense of them. Opponents of legislating morality believe that officials are subjectively imposing their own values, and this, ironically, is morally wrong.

Public Opinion

A third justification for legislating morality discussed by urban officials is that dominant community values, or public opinion, must be respected. Unlike per-sons who believe that legislative controls should reflect divine and natural laws, persons expressing this principle accept that values are indeed subjective and that there is no scientific or logical basis for certain values. But they agree with David Hume, Edmund Burke, and other traditional conservatives that a widespread con-sensus on moral sentiments is helpful and perhaps essential for achieving the so-cial cohesion that makes communities stable and prosperous. Some contemporary communitarians like Alisdair MacIntyre (1981) maintain that people require some shared conception of human virtue and goodness, and that this is best found in the traditional moral values that prevail in particular communities and give the inhabitants of these communities a historical and social identity. Given the im-portance of traditional values for social cohesion and personal identity, the con-clusion that governments ought to create laws and policies reflecting dominant community values is easily reached.

A significant number of urban officials in our sample ($n = 16$) expressed such sentiments. They claimed that there are—and should be—communitywide moral standards that must be transmitted from one generation to the next and that should be respected in policymaking. Officials applied this idea to establish dress codes in schools (such as prohibiting obscene T-shirts), to limit and regulate pornogra-phy and prostitution, to emphasize abstinence in sex education programs, and to oppose gay rights ordinances. Although obscenity and sexual issues were the most common applications of the need to control behavior so that it conforms to domi-nant community values, the movement toward "Official English" laws has also sparked culture wars because of a felt need to ensure communitywide commonal-ties (King, 1997). Four officials volunteered their strong opposition to accommo-dations of non-English speakers. Declaring that "people who enjoy the privilege

of living in America should speak its dominant language" and ridiculing provisions that allow Latinos to take citizenship oaths in Spanish, such officials believe a common language is a minimal requirement for social cohesion.

However, by a three-to-one margin, the officials in our sample reject the principle that citizens should be required to conform to dominant community values.
Many officials simply rejected the existence of such values: Their communities
were too diverse socially and morally for any communitywide consensus to exist
or for any single set of traditional values to be identified. Other officials thought
that dominant community values could be identified but that they were poor guides
to human virtue. According to one official in Atlanta, "Homophobia is a dominant value here, but that doesn't make it right, nor does it give us the right to fence
off gays." In general, dominant community values were seen as often repressive
of individual rights, as John Stuart Mill argued in *On Liberty*. Still other officials
opposed social controls based on dominant community values because they (like
Mill) found possibilities for moral and social progress in diversity. For them, moral
pluralism is not a problem that must be tolerated because of a concern for individual rights; it is an opportunity for people to enlarge their understanding of human
virtue and thus to acquire new skills and capacities that reflect the value systems
of minorities within their communities.

When reacting to the idea of requiring conformity to dominant community
values, many officials (especially school board members) mentioned and supported
multicultural curricula. Normally, such officials denied the argument that multicultural curricula involved legislating morality by requiring consideration of specific cultural values. Instead, they viewed multiculturalism as efforts to dismantle
the existing and implicit social controls that occur when only the accomplishments
and values in the dominant culture are discussed, endorsed, and celebrated. In
general, urban officials agree with the assertion of Will Kymlicka (1995:121) that
"the value of diversity within a culture is that it creates more options for each
individual, and expands her range of choices." In general, culture wars over
multiculturalism were not over the inclusion of non-Western culture and history;
even their opponents conceded the merit of such inclusion. Instead, those whose
principles stressed dominant community values called for multicultural inclusion
only after the essentials of Western civilization had been covered. For them, values
outside of the dominant culture could be tolerated, but only if the values within
the dominant culture were more strongly promoted and reinforced.

Democratic Will

A fourth closely related justification for exercising social control over individual
choice is the need to respect and conform to the democratic will.[6] Populist conceptions of democracy maintain that democratic procedures—and especially the
majority rule often used by democracies—are effective and fair methods of resolving moral differences and thus culture wars. In this view, politics is inevita-

bly concerned with value conflicts. When two sides of a conflict cannot compromise their differences—as illustrated by the pro-life and pro-choice debate on the abortion issue—what could be more fair than to put the issue to a vote? Democracy, it is said, is the most neutral and peaceful method yet devised for resolving such conflicts (Hayek, 1960), and stronger forms of democracy, like holding referenda on such issues, have the additional merit of being egalitarian; everyone's values count equally in determining whose values will be reflected in policy (Cronin, 1989).

Only four of our officials spoke to the democratic-will justification, and they were split in their judgment of it.[7] Its two proponents saw majority rule as a useful method for resolving relatively inconsequential social regulation issues. One issue involved whether to oppose a dress code in a particular school. The parents were divided on the issue, and the official was willing to resolve it by polling parents, and letting the majority rule. The second issue involved whether Austin should give sanctuary to refugees from El Salvador (in opposition to the U.S. Immigration Service's opposition to such programs). In this case, a large majority of the activists on the issue favored giving sanctuary, and the official viewed such support as a decisive expression of the democratic will on the issue. Neither of these issues involved large numbers of people, implicated the core values of the people involved, or threatened fundamental rights. In these circumstances, officials were willing to let democratic majorities resolve issues that were culture skirmishes, but hardly culture wars. However, the two opponents of imposing social controls in the name of the democratic will viewed this principle as inviting Tocqueville's "tyranny of the majority," and they argued that democracy involved protecting minority rights against majority rule (Dahl, 1956). They were unwilling to let the majority will trample over the rights of women to "control their own bodies" on the abortion issue or the rights of homosexuals to be free of discrimination in the areas of employment and housing. On such high-stakes issues, officials may be less likely to support social controls that limit what they regard as fundamental rights in order to conform to the will of the majority.

Paternalism

A fifth justification for legislating morality discussed by urban officials is that individuals require certain controls over their behavior for their own good, "that state coercion (is necessary) to protect individuals from self-inflicted harm" (Feinberg, 1983). Defenses of paternalism are at least as ancient as Aristotelian ethics. According to Aristotle, the real or rational desire of everyone is to develop and exhibit the virtues and goodness of a truly excellent human. Thus, humans really want controls over their irrational desires, desires whose fulfillment would negate their striving for perfection.

The officials interviewed for the urban justice project were slightly more critical than supportive of paternalism. Eight officials doubted their own ability, or the ability of any governing body, to know the real good of their constituents, or they doubted that all constituents shared any conception of the good. For them, "What I think is good for someone may be far different than what that person thinks is good for himself." On several occasions, gambling was offered as an illustration of people taking risks that they could ill afford and being hurt by their choices, but officials claimed that it was "too paternalistic to prohibit gambling." However, six officials supported paternalism in certain instances. Joining gangs and taking drugs were provided as examples of poor choices that youths make, and because youths lacked the maturity and understanding to make competent choices, laws and programs were required to steer the young away from self-destructive acts. Bilingual education was sometimes opposed for similar reasons. Hispanic and Asian youths may prefer to be educated in their native language or the language spoken in their homes, but some officials saw bilingual programs as being harmful in the long run. According to one school board member, "For their good, in order to succeed in this society, it is important to get kids to be effective English speakers as quickly as possible. Bilingual programs should not have respect for ethnicity as their goal; their goal should be to teach English as quickly as possible; they should facilitate assimilation, not ethnic separation." Because the targets of paternalistic policies are often socially disadvantaged, the impulse to help these targets with programs that will be good for them is strong with well-intentioned officials who are committed to social justice, but culture wars break out over these programs when their liberal friends are more strongly committed to the claim of Mill (1978:9) that the good of the individual "is not sufficient warrant" to justify state coercion over individual choices.[8]

Utilitarianism

For many modern political theorists, the utilitarian principle of enacting social controls to promote the greater good of the community is more compelling than paternalism, dominant community values, and the democratic will as a justification for restricting individual choice. While paternalism assumes that individuals misunderstand their own good, while community values can be prejudicial, superstitious, and uninformed in other ways, and while the democratic will can aggregate illegitimate preferences, utilitarianism provides a straightforward method for resolving moral conflicts and culture wars in a rational way (Kymlicka, 1990:35–44). Utilitarianism simply requires officials to look to the consequences of proposed legislation and determine whether these consequences impose more benefit than harm when the real interests of everyone in the community are given equal weight.

As shown in Table 11.2, few officials in our sample spoke explicitly against utilitarianism as an appropriate principle for legislating morality,[9] but those that did felt it is wrong for public officials to adopt policies that provide the greatest good for most citizens but significantly hurt others. Urban officials who opposed utilitarianism implicitly agreed with Rawls (1971:22–27) that utilitarianism can justify laws that infringe on the fundamental rights and interests of individuals.

For the most part, when officials invoked utilitarianism, they did so positively, but in ways that did not come down consistently on one side or the other of culture war issues. Sometimes utilitarian considerations led officials to side against those who sought to establish greater social control. For example, one official in San Jose said he strongly opposed the efforts of Operation Rescue to limit access to abortion; not only did such efforts have harmful effects on women seeking abortion services that outweighed the benefits sought by Operation Rescue activists, but policing their protests cost taxpayers over $1.5 million. More generally, several officials noted that legislating morality had significant costs for cities—such as making their communities targets of economic boycotts by those who opposed their policies and distracting officials from other more pressing problems—and these costs more than offset any benefits that accrued from the social controls they might establish.

On most occasions, utilitarian considerations justified certain controls. School officials claimed that the overall welfare of their students and teachers prompted them to ban gang members from showing and wearing their colors in school and to prohibit students from carrying weapons into school. One school official praised a law that had been passed by the state of Maryland imposing a community service requirement on all citizens; in his judgment, such a regulation would not only develop the moral character of students, but it would generate a lot of energy for alleviating a host of social problems. Some city council members also turned to utilitarian analysis for resolving culture war issues. According to a council woman in Pasadena, "utilitarianism is the only way to adjudicate the rights of smokers and nonsmokers. As a cancer victim, I see the benefits of protecting people from passive smoke as being decisive." And a council member from Orlando used utilitarian reasoning to deal with the issue of adult video stores. In her judgment, any effort to ban pornography would have little impact, but zoning laws could regulate the location of such outlets in ways that were minimally disruptive and could reduce the exposure of youths to these objectionable materials. In short, officials sometimes find utilitarian justifications sufficient for them to support certain social policies that legislate morality, but they do so cautiously, attending to whether utilitarian justifications lead to policies that harm others or deprive them of their fundamental rights.

Preventing Harm to Others

Imposing social controls to prevent harm to others is a justification that few have opposed. In ancient times, Stoics like Cicero regarded the injunction not to harm others as a natural law, and they believed that state laws should reflect the natural law. In modern times, Mill (1978:13) reflected widely accepted liberal principles when he proclaimed that "the only purpose for which power can be rightfully exercised over any member of a civilized community, against his will, is to prevent harm to others." The contemporary principle of nonviolence overlaps strongly with this notion.

Not surprisingly, several officials explicitly expressed the no-harm principle. According to one official, "Where moral values are concerned, the most we can do is to let people have their own beliefs and live their lives as they choose, as long as they don't interfere with others." Somewhat less liberally, another proclaimed, "People can't just do their own thing, especially when it harms others." No official claimed that harmful acts should be uncontrolled, although the many advocates of abortion rights in our study presumably either regarded aborted fetuses as not-yet-living beings whose harm was subject to the principle, or they thought that the no-harm principle could be outweighed by the privacy rights of women. For most officials, the no-harm principle simply justifies criminal laws, and some indicated that they support ensuring that criminal laws extend to protection against domestic violence. Occasionally, officials invoked the no-harm principle as a justification to return to traditional social controls that had become liberalized in recent years. For example, one official called for an end to no-fault divorces, because of "the harmful effects of easy divorce on the children of divorcing parents" (see Whitehead, 1997). Interestingly, the no-harm principle was sometimes invoked as a justification *against* social control. For example, efforts to limit medicinal uses of marijuana were opposed by one official because such controls were thought to cause unnecessary harm to cancer and AIDS patients who benefited from its availability. As another example, several officials thought that prohibitions against abortion resulted in significant psychological harms and physical risks for the women involved. Thus, despite the widespread appeal of the no-harm principle, it is not a principle that always prompts officials to side with those who would legislate morality.

Equal Rights

Another justification for legislating morality is the equal rights principle. The chief defining characteristic of a "right" today is its universal provision to everyone regardless of their income (i.e., ability to purchase the right), social class, race, gender, or other such defining quality (Rawls, 1971; Okun, 1975). Although conflicts over welfare rights are ubiquitous in politics, they are not culture wars. The rights that are relevant to culture wars deal not with the distribution of goods that people desire to live the good life—like money and commodities, education, office, and power—but with the right to pursue one's own conception of the good life. They include rights to think freely about the requirements of the good life and the good community, to advocate and oppose alternative conceptions of the good life and the good community through various modes of social and political action, and to live according to one's chosen lifestyle, as long as one's actions do not harm others. To declare these as equal rights is to say that they ought to be provided universally to all, and to provide them as rights is to prohibit restricting access to them by any group. Culture wars involving equal rights are normally concerned with the inclusion of previously excluded groups to these universal provisions, or with excluding some groups from these provisions, denying that everyone is universally entitled to them and thereby denying their status as universal and equal rights.

As shown in Table 11.2, urban officials often invoked equal rights principles when resolving culture war issues. Most frequently, the equal rights principle was used as the basis for initiating and supporting efforts to end discrimination against minorities and gays. By ensuring that civil rights laws are fully enforced, several officials sought to control discriminatory practices by realtors, bankers, and others; although it might be rational for such actors to discriminate against particular categories of people to protect and pursue their private interests (D'Souza, 1995), most urban officials believed that the social controls on the freedom to discriminate that are provided by civil rights laws are essential to protect the rights of minorities. By enacting gay rights ordinances forbidding employers from discriminating against people on the basis of their sexual orientation, and by pursuing domestic partnership laws extending benefits to the partners of homosexual municipal employees, officials sought to extend to gays the right to pursue their preferred lifestyle. Although our officials seldom reported initiating culture war issues or being entrepreneurs in them, they were most likely to move into these more active roles on such civil rights issues, and they reported that the reason for such activism was their own belief that fundamental rights that existed for other members of the community were being illegitimately denied minorities and gays. Thus, the equal rights principle is not only a powerful idea that prompts officials to side with those who would control discriminatory behavior, but it sometimes prompts officials to become more active participants in culture wars than is normally the case.

Legal Rights

Another kind of rights principle is also commonly invoked on culture war issues, the legal rights principle. Whereas the equal rights principle is used to *support* social control of discriminatory behavior, the legal rights principle is used to *oppose* social control of groups whose actions are thought to be immoral by some but which are nevertheless protected by constitutional provisions, by judicial interpretations of constitutional rights, by statutory and common law, and by prior agreements. The equal rights discussed above are the abstract rights sought by liberals, but legal rights are the specific real rights emphasized by Burke and other conservatives. Although equal rights are granted universally to all, legal rights can be granted universally to all, or they can apply only to designated groups of people.

The legal rights principle was less frequently discussed by urban officials than the equal rights principle, but several officials invoked it to *oppose* efforts to control behavior. Four examples recurred in our interviews. First, three officials in

Kansas City and Austin recalled dealing with the KKK and the issue of hate speech, and each reported supporting the right of the KKK to have a forum to express its views. For them, the First Amendment of the U.S. Constitution granted this right of free speech to all citizens, including members of the KKK. Efforts by victims of racism to control the free speech of the KKK had to be resisted, even if this meant opposing that side of the culture war with virtue on its side. Second, another three officials recalled dealing with issues of free speech in schools. In each case, administrators sought to censure student articles in school newspapers or speeches by valedictorians at commencement exercises, but the school board members reported interceding on behalf of a student's constitutional right to free speech. Third, almost a dozen officials spoke about efforts of pro-life groups to thwart access to abortion clinics, and each opposed these efforts to impose social control. When resolving this issue, these officials seemed to care less about which side had the greater claim to virtue than they cared about the legal rights of each side. They seemed to agree that the Supreme Court had established women's right to abortions in the *Roe v. Wade* decision. They also agreed that members of Operation Rescue and other pro-life groups had constitutional rights to speak, assemble, and otherwise oppose abortion. For the most part, they sought to protect both rights in this culture war through such compromises as requiring the pro-life groups to stay a certain distance from the clinics and forbidding them from harassing abortion clinic personnel in the privacy of their own homes. Fourth, three officials in Green Bay reported dealing with issues involving the rights of Native Americans to spear fish and to run casinos. Although concerns about their "unsportsman methods and catches" and qualms about the virtues of gambling prompted some groups to mobilize against these activities, each official supported these legal rights that were provided to Native Americans in treaties signed years ago. In each of these kinds of culture wars, the legal rights of the groups who were targets of social controls coincided with officials' predisposition to avoid making moral judgments, and thus the freedoms permitted by law remained intact.

In sum, the stories and comments of urban officials who are often called on to resolve local culture wars suggest that they bring a variety of principles about the resolution of these conflicts to bear on them, and that conflicts are resolved in a manner that reflects the principles most strongly held by officials. An adequate theory of local culture wars must therefore be able to predict and explain the principles that particular kinds of officials hold and are likely to apply to particular kinds of cases.

PRELIMINARY FINDINGS AND FUTURE RESEARCH

Drawing on previous theory and research, what factors are expected to influence the moral principles that officials hold and apply to culture war issues? Because public opinion surveys show that there are often significant racial, gender, and class differences in support for school prayer, controls on pornography, and abortion rights (see e.g., Tatalovich and Daynes, 1988), it is expected that such personal characteristics of urban officials will influence their principles regarding culture war issues. If black elites increasingly identify cultural decay and value nihilism as causes of minority suffering in inner cities (see, e.g., West, 1993), black urban officials might be more supportive of various justifications for legislating morality than their white counterparts. If men are more inclined than women to view rules and laws as appropriate instruments for dealing with moral questions (Gilligan, 1982), male officials may be more willing than women to legislate morality. If formal education promotes tolerance of values and moral positions other than one's own (Davis, 1975; but see also Sullivan et al., 1979), highly educated officials may be less willing to legislate morality than are less educated ones. However, there are no compelling reasons for believing that such effects will be strong, because other studies indicate that the warring parties in these conflicts are often composed of strange bedfellows, as when radical feminists joined forces with conservative men to fight pornography in Minneapolis and Indianapolis (Downs, 1989).

The personal characteristic that should best predict the social control principles of urban officials is their (self-defined) ideology. If a willingness to use governmental authority to "re-moralize" society is central to contemporary conservatism but anathema to contemporary liberalism (Krauthammer, 1995), officials who call themselves conservative should be more supportive of legislating morality than self-defined liberal officials. However, the strength of this relationship is unclear, as ideological orientations may better situate officials on distributional (justice) issues than on morality ones (Reeher, 1996).

Various factors in the urban context may also be related, albeit weakly, to the willingness of officials to legislate morality. Big cities may contain the social pluralism that makes agreement on moral questions difficult (Wirth, 1964), reducing support for legislating morality in larger cities. Citizens in more affluent cities may be less preoccupied with issues of economic production and distribution and more concerned with achieving the good life, defined in less material terms (Inglehart, 1990), prompting officials in such cities to be relatively supportive of various justifications for legislating morality. The presence of city management may reduce support for legislating morality, because conflict over social issues and efforts to legislate morality may be seen as undermining the proper function of city government, which is the efficient delivery of city services (Childs, 1955:402).

Such theoretical expectations are plausible, but hardly compelling, reasons for supposing that the urban context influences officials' support for legislating morality. The contextual variable that should be most important in this regard is political culture. One would expect, for example, that officials residing in what Daniel Elazar (1984) calls *individualistic* (I) cultures would be strongly opposed to the social controls that are imposed when officials legislate morality. One would expect that persons living in *moralistic* (M) cultures would be relatively support-ive of legislating morality and some of the principles used to justify such con-trols. One would also expect that persons living in *traditionalist* (T) cultures would be particularly supportive of the idea that it is important for citizens to conform to dominant community values.

To examine these hypotheses, measures of our dependent variables—officials' support for legislating morality in general and for various justifications for social control—were attained for those officials who volunteered stories and comments on culture war issues in this study. The measure of support for legislating moral-ity is the five-point ordinal scale presented in Table 11.1. Support for the various justifications for exercising social control was assessed using a four-point scale: (1) actively oppose imposing social controls on the basis of the principle; (2) oppose controls; (3) support controls; and (4) actively support controls. Officials who failed to comment on these principles and justifications were, of course, coded as miss-ing data. These measures of support for various social control principles were related to measures of officials' personal characteristics and to the contexts in which they reside.[10] As can be seen in Tables 11.1 and 11.2, the sample sizes for analy-ses of some of the justifications are very small.[11] Because of the small and non-random samples, the results provided in Tables 11.4 and 11.5 must be considered exploratory, but they serve the heuristic purpose of providing initial support for the following hypotheses:

- Minority officials may be more willing to legislate morality than white officials. Such a willingness may be due to blacks' greater receptivity to religious justi-fications and equal rights concerns.
- Men and women may not differ in their overall willingness to legislate moral-ity, but male officials may be relatively receptive to natural law justifications for imposing social controls, whereas female officials may be relatively recep-tive to utilitarian justifications.
- The overall willingness of officials to legislate morality may be little affected by the amount of formal education officials have. However, equal rights justi-fications may be most supported by highly educated officials, whereas religious justifications may be more supported by less well-educated officials.
- Liberal officials may be somewhat more opposed to legislating morality than conservative ones. Conservatives are likely to be most receptive to establishing social controls on the basis of universal ethical principles (natural law), whereas liberals are likely to be most supportive of establishing social controls to real-ize their equal rights principles.
- City size should not be expected to have an impact on officials' overall willing-ness to legislate morality. But officials in smaller cities may be relatively re-ceptive to utilitarian arguments for establishing social controls, whereas officials in larger cities may be relatively receptive to preserving the legal rights of indi-viduals in local culture wars.

Table 11.4. Correlates of Officials' Support for Various Principles Applied to Culture War Issues

	Legislate Morals	Religion	Natural Law	Public Opinion	Paternalism	Utilitarian	Prevent Harm	Equal Rights	Legal Rights
City official									
Minority	.17	.31	-.13	.06	-.10	-.14	.00	.31	.08
Female	-.10	-.02	-.29	-.08	-.12	.48	.00	-.05	-.10
Education (years)	.11	-.33	.26	-.25*	.28	.20	.24	.38	.17
Liberal ideology[a]	-.28*	-.21	-.55*	-.30	.01	-.43	.01	.26	-.05
City									
Population[b]	-.01	-.11	-.20	.14	-.16	-.57	-.54	.03	-.25
Median income	-.01	-.10	-.23	-.10	.00	.60	.21	-.28	-.16
City manager[c]	.05	-.03	.33	-.03	-.05	.38	.77*	-.38	-.37

[a]Respondents' self-defined ideologies were coded on a five-point scale: (1) strongly conservative; (2) weakly conservative; (3) middle-of-the-road responses such as "moderate" and "pragmatist"; (4) weakly liberal (including "fiscal conservative and social liberal"); and (5) strongly liberal, progressive, socialist, and radical.
[b]The measures of population size and median income are from the 1990 census as reported in 1993 County and City Extra.
[c]This dummy variable was taken from the 1993 Municipal Yearbook (1993).
* p ≤ .05 level.

213

Table 11.5. Comparison of Urban Cultural Characteristics with Justifications for Legislating Morality

	Political Culture	Mean Support for Legislating Morality	Justifications	
			Weak Support	Strong Support
Atlanta, Ga.	TI	2.75	Paternalism	Utilitarianism
Austin, Tex.	IT	3.00	Equal rights	Public opinion
Baltimore, Md.	I	2.40	Public opinion	Equal rights
Green Bay, Wisc.	M	2.12	Religion	Legal rights
Kansas City, Mo.	IT	2.25	Public opinion	Prevent harm
Minneapolis, Minn.	M	2.67	Religion	Legal rights
Orlando, Fla.	T	2.25	Paternalism	Utilitarianism
Pasadena, Calif.	TI	2.50	Religion	Utilitarianism
Providence, R.I.	IM	2.00	Public opinion	Equal rights
Salt Lake City, Utah	M	2.28	Public opinion	Legal rights
San Jose, Calif.	M	2.00	Paternalism	Natural law
Seattle, Wash.	MI	2.00	Natural law	Equal rights

- Community wealth may have no impact on officials' overall willingness to legislate morality, but officials in wealthy communities may be relatively supportive of utilitarian justifications for legislating morality, whereas officials in poorer communities may be relatively supportive of equal rights principles.
- Professional city management may have no impact on officials' overall willingness to legislate morality, but officials living in cities with city managers are more likely than officials living in unreformed cities to believe that no-harm principles justify imposing social controls, and they are less likely to believe that equal and legal rights principles justify imposing such controls.

In order to examine the impacts of political culture, the subcultures of the twelve cities in our sample were assessed using the map provided by Elazar (1984). The results are reported in Table 11.5. When the cultural characteristics of the cities in which they reside were attributed to city officials and these cultural attributes were related to the principles of officials, a few predictable and theoretically satisfying relationships were evident.[12] Officials in more individualistic cultures were significantly opposed to paternalistic principles ($r = -.46$). Officials in more traditional cultures were significantly opposed to equal rights principles ($r = -.34$). For the most part, however, the political cultures in which officials resided had little significant impact on the principles that they applied to culture war issues. Analyses of variance showed that there was far more variance in officials' support for such principles within cities than there was variance across communities that could be explained by cultural differences. The third column in Table 11.5 illustrates this point. Although there are some differences in the mean support among officials for legislating morality by cultural type of city, these differences are not statistically significant. With the possible exception of Austin, there is somewhat more opposition to than support for legislating morality in each city in our sample. Given the lack of much variance across cities, measures of political culture are not very helpful in accounting for officials' attitudes toward the principles that they see as relevant to the resolution of culture war issues.

Nevertheless, it is premature to ignore political culture as important in developing theories about the occurrence and resolution of culture wars. If particular kinds of culture war issues invoke certain moral principles, if the resolution of culture war issues are strongly influenced by the moral principles that officials hold, and if certain moral principles resonate more strongly in certain cities having particular cultures, then we should be able to predict the outcomes of culture wars from the moral principles that predominate in the local cultures. For example, equal rights principles appear to be particularly strong in Seattle and, as shown in the last cell of Table 11.5, its officials have values that reflect this strong allegiance to equal rights. In culture wars over minority and gays rights in Seattle, it is thus predictable that the advocates of controlling discrimination would and have prevailed.

CONCLUSIONS

This chapter has claimed that local culture wars require officials to reflect on the principle that governments should not legislate morality. Although most officials agree that it is best for them to avoid imposing controls on the freedoms of their citizens to pursue their own good as they define that good, some officials deny the validity of that principle, and most officials hold other competing principles that sometimes seem relevant to culture war issues and outweigh their reluctance to legislate morality. These other principles maintain that social controls over citizens should be enforced for a number of good reasons: religious authorities require it; universal ethical principles should be followed; dominant community values must be respected; it is for the greater good of the greater number; it is important to prevent people from harming others or themselves, and so forth.

The culture wars that break out in cities invoke these principles in quite obvious ways, as shown in Table 11.3. By knowing the principles that are relevant to a culture war issue, and by knowing the distribution of support among officials for that principle, it is possible to provide fairly strong predictions and explanations about how culture wars will be and are resolved. Consider the case of abortion. Opponents of abortion invoke the principle that behavior should conform to religious sentiments, but most officials reject that principle. Proponents of abortion invoke the principle that legal rights must be honored, and most officials support that principle. The result, of course, is that abortion supporters normally win the culture war against their abortion opponents.

This chapter presents the basic concepts and findings for theorizing about the resolution of culture war issues in this way. Of course, predicting and explaining the outcomes of culture wars is not so simple. To develop a fuller theory of the resolution of culture war issues, three difficulties must be overcome.

First, other principles and values than those identified in the simple abortion example can come into play. Future research needs to identify the full range of principles and values that are at stake in various kinds of culture wars, and it should develop methods that facilitate identification of the particular principles and values that are at stake in particular culture war incidents.[13]

Second, we need to know how officials deal with the culture wars that are ignited in their own souls. Many issues invoke in officials conflicting sentiments because they hold more than one moral principle, and these principles can pull them in opposite directions. We need to know which principles officials will give priority when such conflicts arise.

Finally, we need to know the determinants of principles that officials hold and their ordering of conflicting principles. Tables 11.4 and 11.5 suggest that personal and contextual characteristics are not very strong determinants of these matters. Existing conceptions and measurements of political culture provide only minimal assistance in determining allegiance to moral principles. Better theory and research on factors influencing the moral sentiments of officials is necessary before a powerful theory of urban culture wars can be attained.

NOTES

1. The political cultures of these sample cities are indicated in Table 11.5.

2. This procedure may have contributed to an unrepresentative sample in two ways. First, the topic of fairness may have intrigued some types of people more than others. Second, requesting two-hour interviews may have deterred participation among some with hectic schedules.

3. By this definition, affirmative action policies—which involve conflict over the just distribution of job and educational opportunities—are issues of justice rather than virtue and hence are excluded from analyses of culture wars.

4. As will be shown below, almost a quarter of our effective sample expressed strong support for the civil rights of minorities and/or gays, and half of these officials explicitly expressed their opposition to legislating morality. Rather than coding these officials as providing mixed statements about legislating morality, their scores on this variable were based on their expressed statements and their positions on other issues. Although prohibiting discrimination is a social control of what can be regarded as nonvirtuous behavior, it seems to most officials to be a control of a different sort than that sought on other culture war issues. On civil rights issues, prohibiting discrimination is seen as producing a greater gain in social liberty (for those who have been discriminated against) than loss in such liberty for those who discriminate.

5. Here and elsewhere in this chapter, I draw on official comments to suggest that cul-

ture war issues can sometimes be resolved through compromise. Although some researchers like Mooney and Lee (1995:600) have emphasized the "uncompromising clashes over values" that characterize culture wars, my research suggests that antagonists in these wars may emphasize their irreconcilable differences to a much greater extent than officials who must adjudicate these conflicts and may seek middle ground between strongly opposing positions.

6. The dominant-community-values and democratic-will justifications are obviously closely linked, because democratically enacted legislation is a major means of requiring citizens to conform to dominant values. Nevertheless, as Mill argued in *On Liberty* and for purposes of this chapter, these two justifications are clearly distinct. Dominant community values—or public opinion—can control individual choices through social pressures outside of the democratic process, and the democratic will can be shaped by many factors other than the underlying values of the public.

7. The finding that officials speak more to the role of public opinion than the democratic will as a basis for regulating morality is probably an artifact of the term "dominant community values" being explicitly linked to the issue of rewarding virtue in one of the principles that officials were asked to address. Although officials were also asked to assess the fairness of democratic procedures, the principle regarding the fairness of democratic procedures was not linked to issues of resolving conflicts over different conceptions of human virtue. Many officials who opposed legislating morality based on dominant community values may have thought (but not expressed) the idea that the potential coerciveness of dominant community values lies in their being converted to democratic majorities in the legislative process.

8. For other examples of paternalistic policies that sometimes spark culture wars, see Dworkin (1983).

9. In the broader study, urban officials were asked to indicate their support or opposition to utilitarianism. More officials (47 percent) agree with the principle than disagree with it (33 percent), but most of these officials focused on the distributive implications of the principle, rather than its implications for legislating morality. It may be that more opposition to using utilitarian defenses of legislating morality would have been expressed had the focus of the interviews been culture war issues.

10. Data on the personal characteristics of officials were obtained in the interviews, and data on their social context were obtained from standard sources such as the U.S. Census and the *Municipal Yearbook* (1993). See the footnotes to Table 11.4.

11. Correlates of support for the majority-will principle are not provided in Table 11.4 because only four officials provided comments regarding it.

12. The extent to which an official lived in I, M, and T cultures was assessed using four-point scales of each these cultures. For example, to assess the impact of living in a city with an individualist culture, officials living in a city characterized as having only an I-culture were scored as "4." A score of "3" indicated a city with a cultural mix where the I-culture was most prominent; "2" indicates a cultural mix where the I-culture was evident to a secondary degree; and "1," cultural characteristics other than individualistic ones.

13. See Schumaker (1991:71–72) for a method of identifying the principles that are at stake in policy issues in general. The method discussed there is considerably more rigorous than the method used here.

REFERENCES

Adler, Mortimer. 1981. *Six Great Ideas.* New York: Macmillan.

Bennett, William. 1993. *The Book of Virtues.* New York: Simon and Schuster.

Childs, Richard S. 1955. "Civic victories in the United States." *National Municipal Review* 44 (September): 395–409.

Cronin, Thomas. 1989. *Direct Democracy.* Cambridge, Mass.: Harvard University Press.

Dahl, Robert. 1956. *A Preface to Democratic Theory.* Chicago: University of Chicago Press.

Davis, James A. 1975. "Communism, Conformity, Cohorts, and Categories: American Tolerance in 1954 and 1972–3." *American Journal of Sociology* 81 (November): 491–513.

Downs, Donald A. 1989. *The New Politics of Pornography.* Chicago: University of Chicago Press.

D'Souza, Diesh. 1995. *The End of Racism.* New York: Free Press.

Dworkin, Gerald. 1983. "Paternalism." In Rolf Sartorius, ed., *Paternalism.* Minneapolis: University of Minnesota Press.

Elazar, Daniel. 1984. *American Federalism,* 3d ed. New York: Harper and Row.

Feinberg, Joel. 1983. "Legal Paternalism." In Rolf Sartorius, ed., *Paternalism.* Minneapolis: University of Minnesota Press.

Galston, William. 1980. *Justice and the Human Good.* Chicago: University of Chicago Press.

Gilligan, Carol. 1982. *In a Different Voice.* Cambridge, Mass.: Harvard University Press.

Hayek, Fredrich A. 1960. *The Constitution of Liberty.* Chicago: University of Chicago Press.

Inglehart, Ronald. 1990. *Culture Shift in Advanced Industrial Society.* Princeton, N.J.: Princeton University Press.

King, Robert D. 1997. "Should English Be the Law?" *Atlantic Monthly* 279: 10 (April): 55–64.

Krauthammer, Charles. 1995. "A Social Conservative Credo." *Public Interest* 121 (fall): 15–22.

Kymlicka, Will. 1990. *Contemporary Political Philosophy.* New York: Oxford University Press.

———. 1995. *Multicultural Citizenship.* New York: Oxford University Press.

Lieski, Joel. 1993. "Regional subcultures of the United States." *Journal of Politics* 55 (November): 888–913.

MacIntyre, Alister. 1981. *After Virtue.* Notre Dame, Ind.: University of Notre Dame Press.

Mill, John Stuart. 1978. *On Liberty.* Edited by Elizabeth Rapaport. New York: Hackett Books [first published in 1859].

Mooney, Christopher Z., and Mei-Hsein Lee. 1995. "Legislating morality in the American states: The case of pre-Roe abortion regulation reform." *American Journal of Political Science* 39 (August): 599–627.

Okun, Arthur. 1975. *Equality and Efficiency: The Big Trade-Off.* Washington, D.C.: Brookings Institution.

Municipal Yearbook. 1993. Washington, D.C.: International City Management Association.

Rawls, John. 1971. *A Theory of Justice.* Cambridge Mass.: Harvard University Press.

Reeher, Grant. 1996. *Narratives of Justice.* Ann Arbor: University of Michigan Press.

Schank, Roger. 1990. *Tell Me a Story: A New Look at Real and Artificial Memory.* New York: Charles Scribner's Sons.

Schumaker, Paul. 1991. *Critical Pluralism, Democratic Performance, and Community Power.* Lawrence: University Press of Kansas.

Schumaker, Paul, and Marisa Kelly. 1994. "Alternative Principles of Justice and Their Applications in American Cities." Paper presented at the American Political Science Association.

Sullivan, John L., James Piereson, and George E. Marcus. 1979. "An Alternative Conceptualization of Political Tolerance: Illusory Increases 1950s–1970s." *American Political Science Review* 73 (September): 781–94.

Tatalovich, Raymond, and Byron W. Daynes. 1988. *Social Regulatory Policy: Moral Controversies in American Politics.* Boulder, Colo.: Westview Press.

Van Maanen, John. 1979. "The Fact of Fiction in Organizational Ethnography," *Administrative Science Quarterly* 24 (December): 539–50.

West, Cornell. 1993. *Race Matters.* Boston: Beacon Press.

Whitehead, Barbara Defoe. 1997. *The Divorce Culture.* New York: Knopf.

Wilson, James Q. 1994. *The Moral Sense.* New York: Free Press.

Wirth, Louis. 1964. *On Cities and Social Life.* Edited by Albert J. Reiss. Chicago: University of Chicago Press.

12
Conclusion

Elaine B. Sharp

Using a variety of analytical approaches, the chapters in this volume detail a rich diversity of cases of community politics concerning culture war issues and offer a number of important insights and interpretations. The task of this chapter is to synthesize these diverse findings and to offer cumulative interpretations derived from comparative analysis of the cases in the volume. The synthesis is presented in three parts. The first section provides a discussion of the conceptual refinements in the typology of local government roles that emerge from the chapter contributors' efforts to apply the typology to their cases. The second section discusses what these cases suggest concerning the effects of cultural ideals, institutional arrangements, and regime types on the likelihood of each of the roles; and the third section draws out a number of unexpected, interpretive themes suggested by the work of the volume's contributors.

CONCEPTUAL REFINEMENT: RETHINKING THE TYPOLOGY OF GOVERNMENTAL ROLES

In terms of conceptual refinement, the chapters introduce three phenomena—agenda denial, nonresponsiveness, and symbolic responsiveness—that invite us to stretch the limits of what should be included within the various governmental roles initially identified. Although repression is most easily viewed as including overt acts to suppress dissidents (e.g., the billy clubs against the protesters version of repression), Wald, Button, and Rienzo remind us that systematic efforts to prevent activists' claims from ever being considered (i.e., agenda denial) can be interpreted as a form of repression. Alternatively, agenda denial might have been construed as fitting within the evasion category. In fact, a single instance of denying agenda status to activists' claims—by deferring action on a proposal, for example—would probably best be interpreted as evasion. But systematic efforts that continually prevent activists' claims from getting a formal hearing are better construed as a repressive exercise of power. In short, the boundary between evasion and repression is defined, in part, by whether evasion is sustained and systematic.

A number of the chapters suggest the need to define better the boundary between responsiveness and evasion as well, particularly when responsiveness comes in a symbolic form. Symbolic responsiveness involves governmental action that appears to deal with activists' claims, but which primarily involves rhetorical devices or gestures that do not really address the problem or substantively alter the authoritative allocation of values. In their chapter, for example, Haider-Markel and O'Brien point to the adoption of hate crime ordinances that are never enforced as an example of symbolic responsiveness. And Rosenthal describes a variety of symbolic policies—such as painting lavender lines to acknowledge gay pride activities—that are symbolically responsive to gay and lesbian interests without materially altering the status of gays. Symbolic responsiveness thus occupies a peculiar position astride the two categories of evasion and responsiveness: It is a way of responding to claimants without actually responding fully to their demands. From this perspective, it is tempting to include symbolic responsiveness within the evasion category, or even to treat it as a form of nonresponsiveness, as Haider-Markel and O'Brien suggest.

There are two problems with this. At the semantic level, it would seem peculiar to treat symbolic responsiveness as a form of nonresponsiveness. Symbolic responsiveness may be a very low-level, even trivial form of responsiveness, but it is surely not *non*responsiveness. Furthermore, although there is a substantial line of inquiry that views symbolic politics as a way of propping up the legitimacy of the status quo (Edelman, 1964) and thereby evading substantial alterations in power arrangements, the special features of culture war issues are such that their stakes can often be meaningfully symbolic. Antiabortion forces may have the instrumental goal of closing down abortion clinics; but hand-in-hand with that is the symbolic goal of defining abortion as an abhorrent act. Gays may have a variety of instrumental goals involving spousal-equivalent benefits or legal protections from harassment; but along with those is the symbolic goal of having their status acknowledged as legitimate. For these and other culture war claimants, then, symbolic policy may not be trivial at all. This suggests that symbolic responsiveness be treated as a subcategory of responsiveness rather than a form of evasion or nonresponsiveness.

By the same token, there is clearly a need for the initial repertoire of roles to be expanded to include an additional category of *nonresponsiveness*. Such a category is needed to characterize the situation in which local government officials consider the demands of culture war activists and refuse to make policy in accordance with those demands, as, for example, when a community deliberates on a proposed gay rights ordinance but votes it down. Although systematic denial of agenda status qualifies as repression, making a policy decision that does not accede to an activist group's demands surely does not. If it did, any group that did not prevail in policymaking deliberations would be classified as being repressed, and every city council decision would involve responsiveness to some and repression of others. This seems too generous a use of the concept of repression. Nor does nonresponsiveness involve evasion, because it involves a definitive and authoritative decision rather than tactics designed to avoid the controversy that might attend such a decision. In short, just as city governments can be responsive to the demands of activists pressing for changes in the moral status quo, so also can they play a straightforward role of authoritatively denying those demands.

CULTURAL IDEALS, INSTITUTIONS, AND GOVERNMENTAL ROLES IN CULTURE WARS

In their analyses, the various contributors to this volume generate information on at least twenty-five different cities' experiences with various forms of culture war controversy.[1] This set by no means constitutes a random sample; hence, one cannot definitely conclude that the results are representative of cities and culture war controversies across the country. Nor does twenty-five constitute a sufficient number of cases for much in the way of quantitative data analysis. By the same token, this set constitutes an unusual opportunity. Systematic information on the activities of local governments in culture war controversies is, so far, unavailable;[2] and the challenges in gathering such information for a large, random sample of cities are daunting. Although not a random sample, the twenty-five cities incorporated in this volume certainly exhibit a great deal of the diversity in geography, city size, demographics, political culture, and governing institutions that are to be found in the United States. Hence, any emergent patterns from this set of twenty-five cities may be at least suggestive of larger patterns and, therefore, useful in considering the potential of the methods of accounting for variation in governmental role outlined in chapter 1. The appendix contains a listing of the twenty-five cities with information on the governmental, culture war roles exhibited in each, and a categorization of each city's formal governing institutions and type of political subculture, derived from Elazar's (1986) mapping of political subcultures in the United States.[3] The appendix constitutes the data set from which the tables in the following paragraphs are derived.

Table 12.1 summarizes the findings with respect to the formal institutions of local government. The table suggests that reform and unreformed governments do not differ much in their propensity to exhibit most of the roles, but the types have two substantial differences. Hyperactive responsiveness and unintentional instigation are relatively rare roles for local governments in culture wars. Judging by these cases, these roles are rare partly because they are not particularly unusual in reformed settings but are notably absent from unreformed settings. The implications of this are considered below in the discussions of each of these par-

Table 12.1. Percentage (and number) of Cities Exhibiting
Governmental Roles

	City Type	
	Reformed	Unreformed
Evasion	30 (3)	40 (6)
Responsiveness	50 (5)	60 (9)
Hyperactive responsiveness	20 (2)	0 (0)
Entrepreneurial instigation	30 (3)	40 (6)
Repression	40 (4)	40 (6)
Unintentional instigation	40 (4)	0 (0)
Total number of cities	10	15

Note: The reformed category includes three cities with purely reform
institutions plus the seven hybrid cities classified as predominantly
reform because they have a council manager form of government but
some mixture of ward and at-large elections. The unreformed category
includes ten cities with purely unreformed institutions plus five cities
that do not have council-manager government but do have some at-
large representation or a professional chief administrative officer.

ticular roles. The larger message of Table 12.1 is that variation in cities' formal
governing institutions does not appear to make much difference in what role cities play in culture war controversies.

Table 12.2 summarizes the impact of political subculture on communities'
handling of culture war controversies. The analysis is complicated because Elazar's
mapping of the subcultures places many cities in hybrid categories with elements
of more than one subculture. Some noteworthy emergent patterns are highlighted
in the table with boxed areas.

Responsiveness, for example, appears to be linked to the individualistic subculture. Twelve of the fourteen instances of responsiveness occurred in settings
that have at least some element of individualistic culture. This finding is incon-

Table 12.2. Relative Frequency of Governmental Roles, by Political Subculture

	Traditionalistic (n = 5)	Traditionalistic-Individualistic (n = 3)	Individualistic (n = 5)	Moralistic-Individualistic (n = 9)	Moralistic (n = 3)
Evasion	3	1		3	2
Responsiveness	1	1	3	8	1
Hyperactive responsiveness	1			1	
Entrepreneurial instigation	1	1	2	3	
Repression	4		2	2	2
Unintentional instigation	2			1	

sistent with what might have been expected. As noted in chapter 1, the demands of culture war activists initially might have been hypothesized to be inconsistent with the prevailing ethos of individualistic communities, where politics is viewed as a specialized activity for professionals rather than amateurs, where partisan political considerations are paramount, and ideological concerns are dwarfed by a businesslike view of politics (Elazar, 1994:231). But, as a number of the cases suggest, culture war activists in individualistic settings can frame their demands in ways that fit the instrumental and highly partisan view of politics in their sub-culture. Gay and lesbian groups, in particular, have mobilized in ways that fit the pragmatic partisanship of individualistic settings. This theme is discussed further in the section on responsiveness below.

The evidence in Table 12.2 suggests that entrepreneurial instigation is also distinctively present in settings that have at least some element of individualistic culture. Indeed, six of the seven instances of entrepreneurial instigation occurred in such settings. Such a finding is consistent with the logic of individualistic culture, with its utilitarian view of politics and its assumption that professional politicos will jockey for leadership in a political marketplace.

Although the pattern is less conclusive, Table 12.2 also suggests that repression is more likely in purely traditionalistic or purely moralistic cultures. Repression was exhibited in four of the five traditionalistic communities and two of the three moralistic communities. These two settings account for six of the nine observed instances of repression. With respect to traditionalistic settings, these results are consistent with hypothesized expectations (see chap. 1). Traditionalistic cultures feature both an intolerance for political activism from those who do not have formal roles in politics and an emphasis on maintenance of the status quo, both of which offer strong grounds for repression. With respect to moralistic settings, the results are *not* consistent with hypothesized expectations. In fact, because discussion of what constitutes appropriate conduct for the greater good of the community is a normal part of politics in moralistic settings, repression of those who advance such issues was hypothesized to be least likely there. The discussion of repression below offers some considerations that help to interpret this unexpected result.

The analysis needs to go beyond the findings in Tables 12.1 and 12.2 for a number of reasons. Although Table 12.1 suggests disappointing results with respect to the direct impact of formal institutions on adoption of various governmental roles, this does not mean that such institutions are completely unimportant in understanding how these controversies unfold. As Wald, Button, and Rienzo suggest, they are perhaps better understood as mediating institutions, shaping the strategies that activists use in attempting to reach their goals and the incentive structures of governing elites in distinctive ways that are best understood in the context of the other elements of the local political culture. In addition, although the analysis in Table 12.1 is limited to the formal institutions of government, the informal arrangements that constitute governing regimes need to be considered as well, as argued in chapter 1. Although information on regimes is presented by only some of the chapter contributors, thus precluding a quantitative assessment like that in Table 12.1, it is important to tease out what we can from the case information. Finally, even though Table 12.2 provides a systematic assessment of the role of culture in terms of Elazar's cultural types, other conceptualizations of cultural dynamics are represented in the chapters, and these also need to be woven into the analysis, with a focus on each of the governmental roles.[4]

Evasion

Much evidence in this volume supports the notion that evasion is the default role for local government. On the one hand, Schumaker demonstrates that individual officials are generally predisposed to believe that they should not legislate morality. A variety of principles override that one, but getting a collection of governing elites to agree on such a principle or building a coalition of decision makers willing to take the same sort of action based on differing principles is required.

The chapters also illustrate the diversity of both methods and motivations for evasion. In Tulsa and Raleigh, officials who opposed unduly controversial issues evaded them by shunting them off to special commissions and then ignoring the recommendations of those commissions. In Greenville, officials fearful of abortion-clinic controversy invoked federal laws and mandates as a way of evading responsibility for taking a position on the issue, whereas Topeka officials' fears of litigation, coupled with their belief that ignoring a strident activist would be the most effective form of neutralization, led to evasion in the form of a no-arrest policy. In Albany, officials switched the focus away from a controversial issue by taking symbolic action instead on a different issue involving gays, and in Buffalo, the lack of gay political power during a particular period allowed officials to function with complete indifference to gay concerns. On the other hand, evasion is an important strategy not only when officials simply wish to avoid controversy, but also when officials sympathetic to the claims of challengers of the status quo deem that the timing is not right and decide on strategic grounds to defer action. Wald, Button, and Rienzo suggest that this is why a proposed gay rights ordinance in Philadelphia languished in committee in the mid-1970s.

In sum, evasion is a low-cost strategy in the terms that Susan Clarke adapts from Cobb and Ross (1997). It is usable in a variety of institutional settings, appealing both to the strategic calculations of officials in more partisan, politicized settings and the impulses of reform government officials to depoliticize governance. It can be legitimized by the ideals of traditionalistic cultures where threats to the existing social order are disdained and by the ideals of individualistic cultures, which view some claimants as being too politically weak to matter. Evasion can even be justified in moralistic cultures, which might otherwise be relatively susceptible to communal debate about morality issues, if the activities of challengers of the status quo can be framed as unwarranted calls for personal attention or otherwise illegitimate threats to the moral order.

As noted earlier in this chapter, when sustained long enough, evasion becomes a repressive strategy, and repression is far from low-cost. As so many of the chapters show, although evasion is a low-cost, default strategy in the short run, it may not be sustainable in the long run. It often gives way to either responsive or repressive stances.

Responsiveness

In various ways, the contributors to this volume suggest that responsiveness to challengers of the status quo is a problematic role for local governments. Schumaker's analysis, for example, suggests that many of the principles that can justify efforts to legislate morality entail responsiveness to the status quo rather than to its challengers. Conformity to dominant public opinion and to the democratic will, along with the protection of institutionalized legal rights, would presumably favor status quo interests; nor is it likely that culture war activists would be privileged by decision making based on the paternalistic principle. In addition, the chapters by Haider-Markel and O'Brien and Button, Wald, and Rienzo show that, local officials may create a backlash when they are responsive to challengers of the status quo. Officials wary of any unintentional instigation of even more conflict over morality issues may be constrained from responding to the demands of activists. In addition, responsiveness is one of the more collective governmental roles, at least for actions that are more than symbolic. Although the multiplicity of governing institutions means that there is some capacity for activists to get responsiveness in one quarter but not in another, substantial demands, such as those for passage of a gay rights or hate crime ordinance, or official sanctioning and funding for a needle exchange, require agreement of a majority of council members and implementation by the administration.

As we have seen, responsiveness does seem to be more likely in individualistic cultures where politics is viewed instrumentally and pragmatically rather than morally. This pattern is unexpected and illogical if culture war controversies are viewed *solely* as debates about the appropriate moral standards of the community, because individualistic cultures supposedly eschew such moralistic concerns. Indeed, culture war issues do feature moralistic concerns: It is the element that makes this phenomenon distinctive. As DeLeon notes, however, morality and other issues are not treated as separate spheres in San Francisco's progressive regime, because its governing coalition incorporates identity groups that bring a morality and cultural agenda to city decision making as a whole. Similarly, Kirp and Bayer's analysis suggests that needle exchange is differentially affected by racial politics depending on the status of African American interests in the governing regime and the extent of their morality concerns about needle exchange. More generally, the cases in this volume suggest that, under certain circumstances, culture wars can and do take on some of the features of politics as usual. In particular, when the identity groups that are key activists mobilize politically and press their claims through electoral coalition building, culture wars can become much like interest-group politics. Among our cases, such an approach is most pronounced for gay and lesbian identity groups. Such groups have been able to take advantage of political partisanship and fragmentation in a number of cities. Indeed, the clear theme of Rosenthal's chapter is that the gay and lesbian communities in his four New York state cases have made progress in getting more responsiveness, if only of the symbolic sort, "by taking advantage of the highly partisan politics" in those settings. In most of the cases presented in this volume, gays and lesbians function as a group seeking inclusion in a governing regime or at least demanding specific governing responses as a constituency group. In 61 percent of the cases involving gay and lesbian issues, the responsiveness role is exhibited, whereas it appears in fewer than half (48 percent) of the cases where gay and lesbian issues are not involved.

But the identity groups and activists involved in culture war controversies are not necessarily electorally mobilized in the fashion of these gay and lesbian organizations nor necessarily even interested in inclusion in the governing regime. In his discussion of direct action movements, Sturgeon notes that such groups often have quite different goals: "The nature of the direct action movement's structures and practices is different from that of more mainstream groups. It has a different aim and a different assessment of power and its operation. Its aim is not inclusion but the articulation of an oppositional political theory" (Sturgeon, 1995:43). In short, although activists in culture wars sometimes use strategies designed to achieve incorporation into the political regime, at other times and places their goal is to accomplish broader, societal change using city government as a venue to get the attention of the rest of society. In the terms that Clarke, DeLeon, and Woliver borrow from Tarrow (1994:6), local government is sometimes not the real target of activists' demands, but the "*fulcrum* of claims against others." Just as the characteristics of a governing regime may shape what a social movement does (Swidler, 1995:37), so also does this variation in activist groups' goals and tactics shape the likelihood that local government will be responsive.

Entrepreneurial Instigation

Entrepreneurial instigation has two faces, depending on the motivation of the individual entrepreneur. On the one hand, individuals might take on leadership roles in sparking attention to culture war issues out of deep-seated moral convictions or personal commitment to ideals. Consistent with Schumaker's treatment of the moral principles that officials bring to culture war issues, we might designate this the principled version of entrepreneurial instigation. On the other hand, the entrepreneurship concept also implies that instigators of culture war controversies may

be political opportunists who recognize the potential for political credit and career building that can accrue to those who take a visible stance on the right side of
a morality issue. We might designate this the opportunistic version of entrepreneurial instigation. This is not to say that individuals cannot have both motivations; presumably some do. These two faces of entrepreneurial instigation have
important implications for theory. If this role is typically occupied by individuals
largely motivated by individual political ambition, then theories of entrepreneurship keyed to political incentives (Schneider and Teske, 1992) make the most sense;
but such theories would not be as relevant for understanding the principled version of entrepreneurial instigation.

Instances of entrepreneurial instigation are relatively few here, but a review
suggests that the opportunistic version and the principled version are nearly evenly
represented. In Raleigh, for example, a city council member took the lead in
mobilizing a variety of liberal groups to press for gay rights legislation. It is important to note that her leadership occurred after gays, who had already begun
lobbying on behalf of such legislation, "recognized they needed an advocate on
the city council to take the lead in promoting the legislation" (Button et al., 1997)
and organized to get this individual elected. By contrast, there is no evidence of
the opportunistic version of entrepreneurial instigation in Santa Cruz, where a task
force created by the school board to respond to a need for preliminary information gathering ultimately took a aggressive stand and served as an entrepreneurial
instigator as it pursued additional efforts "to identify and address sexual orientation issues" (Rienzo et al., 1996) and tried to educate school administrators on the
topic. Similarly, in Iowa City, a school teacher, reacting to antigay comments,
exhibits the principled version of entrepreneurial instigation, outing himself to
coworkers, organizing off-campus meetings with gay and lesbian teachers and
students, drawing up an agenda for change, and presenting it to the appropriate
school governing body.[5] In Buffalo, Councilman Arthur is depicted as a classic
example of the opportunistic version of entrepreneurial instigation as he took
actions to mobilize support for gays and lesbians in his fight to unseat Mayor
Griffin. In Chicago, Alderman Bernard Hansen served as an entrepreneurial instigator to get a city hate crime ordinance that included sexual orientation, when
at least some political capital was to be gained. "Hansen chose to announce the
proposal against a backdrop of supportive aldermen, minority groups, and lesbian and gay activists," and few groups appeared in opposition. In Oklahoma City,
Councilman Mark Schwartz's entrepreneurial instigation of a hate crime ordinance
may initially have been keyed to personal beliefs, but it appears ultimately to have
involved at least some political capital formation, because the incorporation of
sexual orientation in his proposed ordinance occurred only after local gay groups
"convinced Schwartz to include the clause by reminding him of their role in his
election." There were numerous instances of entrepreneurial instigation in the case
of needle exchanges. Some involved politicos; in other cases, needle exchanges
were propelled by charismatic figures outside of government who found entre-

preneurial partners within the public health sector, motivated by professional norms and humanitarian concerns.

The existence of these two versions of entrepreneurial instigation helps to explain why a community's form of governing institutions is not a better predictor of the emergence of this role. Unreformed settings may offer incentives for the emergence of opportunistic as well as principled leadership on culture war issues. Although reformed settings offer fewer incentives for the opportunistic version, entrepreneurs of morality issues nevertheless can emerge in those settings as well, more likely exhibiting the principled version of entrepreneurial instigation.

Although the type of governing institutions may shape the form that entrepreneurial instigation takes, the broader subculture is more important in conditioning whether entrepreneurial instigation occurs at all. As shown in Table 12.2 entrepreneurial instigation is far more common in communities with at least some element of the individualistic subculture, suggesting that, whether principled or opportunistic, entrepreneurial instigation flourishes only where prevailing cultural norms include the assumption that the political process is an open marketplace that many individuals and groups can properly use to advance their interests.

Repression

Repression, as Susan Clarke notes, is surely a high-cost strategy for local governments in culture wars. It is high-cost in that it may unintentionally instigate further conflict and controversy, inadvertently have negative effects on constituencies that are not the immediate target (Clarke), have financial and legal repercussions for the city (Musser), and may play adversely vis-à-vis community leaders' desires to project a favorable city image. Given these constraints, it is notable that repression is nevertheless one of the more common roles observed in these cases. And the cases are suggestive of the ways that city officials overcome these constraints.

As noted, repression does not appear to be directly conditioned by the character of governing institutions: Repressive responses to abortion protesters are evident in Denver, with its mayor-centered form of government, and in Greenville and Columbia, with their council-manager forms of government. It is evident in the actions of city government regarding gays in both reform-government Cincinnati and in unreformed Philadelphia, Albany, and Syracuse, as well as in the actions of the predominantly unreformed government of Topeka as it dealt with strident antigay protest. In short, the formal structures of government do not appear to limit the emergence of a repressive response. As the analysis of Table 12.2 suggested, repression may be slightly more prevalent in traditionalistic and moralistic settings than in individualistic ones. Presumably, the pluralistic politics of individualistic settings may slightly diminish the emergence of repression because of the greater tolerance of diverse claims on the political system in those settings.

Beyond this, the cases suggest a number of important conditions that facilitate repression. One clear message from the cases is that repression is more readily possible if city officials can frame the actions of activists in ways that portray them as outsiders. In this respect, the ideational element of political culture appears to be much more important than institutional arrangements for governance. Officials functioning in quite different formal structures of governance were able to repress abortion activists by drawing contrasts between acceptable levels of protest that were presumed to characterize local, antiabortion forces, and unacceptable forms of protest that were attributed to "nut cases" or outside forces descending on the city at the bidding of some distant Operation Rescue office.

As noted above, the goals and strategies of culture war activists may have a great deal to do with the likelihood that city officials will be responsive. Direct-action groups that eschew political incorporation in favor of articulating broader, oppositional theories are less likely to generate responsive reactions. By the same logic, they may be more likely to generate repressive reactions. In essence, such groups define themselves as outsiders vis-à-vis local political customs and social norms. By so doing, they provide officials with much of the raw material that is needed to legitimate a repressive response.

Beyond these culturally based insights concerning the facilitators of repression, the cases introduce some important insights concerning the ways in which the repressive response is shaped by officials' reactions to other cities' experiences with strident protest, by federal and state policies that can either hinder or facilitate repression, and by the threats that strident protest can pose for economic development imperatives. These will be explored more fully in the final section on unexpected themes.

Hyperactive Responsiveness and Unintentional Instigation

The evidence from the twenty-five cases in this volume suggests that hyperactive responsiveness and unintentional instigation are relatively rare roles for local governments. Only two instances of the former and four of the latter were detected. With respect to hyperactive responsiveness, such a finding is perhaps not surprising, for hyperactive responsiveness by definition entails action that is favorable to challengers of the status quo and taken in *unusual* haste, with evidence of a short-circuiting of normal methods of deliberation, and even with disregard for constitutional issues that might be involved. In short, hyperactive responsiveness is conceptualized as an unusual or extreme sort of role; hence rarity is to be expected. The types of culture war issues represented in this volume may also contribute to the small number of instances of hyperactive responsiveness that were observed. Hyperactive responsiveness is presumably more likely for morality issues that are more clearly one-sided, like the cases of women's rights and pornography regulation examined by Donald Downs (1989). From Downs's point of view, hyperactive responsiveness involves a dynamic in which governing officials are in a rush to be in the right on a morality issue; and when concerns about pornography, prostitution, and the like arise, they would presumably be more likely to evoke this one-sided rush to judgment than do more divisive issues like abortion.

The two cases of hyperactive responsiveness examined by this volume's contributors do not, therefore, allow for much elaboration on the relative importance of various aspects of political culture to the emergence of hyperactive responsiveness. A comparison of the two cases, however, suggests that hyperactive responsiveness to morality-based issues involving gays is by no means confined to areas with liberal political cultures and progressive political regimes that are hospitable to those activist groups. Santa Cruz may be a "lesbian mecca," but Springfield, located in one of the most conservative regions of a far from progressive state, lies at quite the opposite pole in terms of political culture and regime type. What the two communities have in common is their formal governing institutions—reformed institutions that, on theoretical grounds, would be expected to be more prone to hyperactive responsiveness because that role entails co-optation of the state apparatus by an activist group. Such co-optation, according to social movements theory (McCarthy and Wolfson, 1992:282), is most likely to be found where there are fewer linkages between governing institutions and the community. Diminished linkages, such as the replacement of district elections with at-large elections, mean that there is less potential for countervailing interests to oppose the co-optation of the state apparatus by a particular group (Sharp, 1997:272). Thus, in Springfield, Missouri, a newly formed citizen group opposed to hate crime quickly co-opted the mayor and three council members; and in Santa Cruz, the apparatus of local government was even more dramatically co-opted when a local political action committee was able to get an openly gay mayor and a more progressive set of council candidates elected.

In short, hyperactive responsiveness appears to be facilitated in settings where formal governing structures allow the local state to be quickly bowled over by the power of a moral argument. In both cases of hyperactive responsiveness, the consequence of being quickly overwhelmed is the unintentional instigation of controversy as oppositional forces eventually react to what they perceive to be extremist action by local government. There are too few cases here to be definitive, but the logical linkage between hyperactive responsiveness and unintentional instigation of controversy is evident in both cases of hyperactive responsiveness.

If hyperactive responsiveness is an extreme role in support of culture war activists, repression is an extreme role on the nonsupportive side. A similar logic suggests that unintentional instigation can be sparked by repression; that is, repression may fan the flames of resentment on the part of those targeted for repression, giving them the ammunition for much higher levels of political activation than they had before they were subject to repressive acts. This is precisely what occurred in the other two instances of unintentional instigation reported in this volume, where either cancellations of park reservations for gay events or police crackdowns on gays in parks led to heightened levels of gay political activation and controversy over gay rights issues.

UNEXPECTED THEMES

Consistent with the emphasis in chapter 1 on cultural theory, social movements, and institutional arrangements, the preceding section explored what the cases presented in this volume suggest about the relevance of those phenomena for understanding local governmental roles in culture war controversies. The contributors to this volume generate the added bonus of additional insights concerning this phenomenon. This section acknowledges these important interpretations, involving the existence of multiple roles and the intergovernmental context for local culture wars.

Multiple and Interacting Roles

A crucial observation that can be gleaned from many of the chapters is that it is not necessarily possible or appropriate to identify a single role that local government plays in a culture war controversy. Rather, even for a single city at a single point in time, it is possible to observe more than one of the roles. There are at least three reasons for this. First, it can be a strategic advantage for city officials to simultaneously maintain two, quite different postures toward culture war activists. With regard to abortion protesters in particular, city officials appear to find it advantageous to combine repressive responses with either evasion (as in Woliver's South Carolina cases) or modest levels of responsiveness (as in Clarke's Denver case). In this culture wars variant of the "good cop–bad cop" routine, each role enhances the other. An invitation to a dissident group to join police officials in reviewing protest containment policy is presumably more compelling when it is backed by evidence that officials are willing to arrest and prosecute aggressively protesters who exceed the limits of locally acceptable behavior. The use of repressive responses is less likely to instigate heightened controversy unintentionally if it is coupled with a variety of evasive tactics that make repression appear to be only the routine administration of mandates from the federal government. These insights suggest that theorizing about the roles that local government plays in culture war controversies might need to be more ambitious than identification of factors that account for variation in the emergence of a single role; it may require that we tease out the explanatory factors that generate strategically important combinations of roles.

There is a second reason that we sometimes observe more than one governmental role in the same culture war controversy. Cities are not monolithic entities; each has a constellation of elites and governing institutions (e.g., mayor, city council, public health department, school board) and, as Haider-Markel and O'Brien aptly note, these governing elites and institutions may well be divided in their stance with respect to a particular culture war issue. It is true that, for a particular governing institution, many of the governmental roles explored in this volume cannot be adopted when elites are divided, or at least are much more difficult when elites are divided because they involve *collective* action on the part of the authorities.

Collective action of a particular kind on the part of a city council or a school board does not preclude quite different actions on the part of other elements of the local state. In their review of the Philadelphia case, for example, Button, Wald, and Rienzo note that in 1991 the police department engaged in overtly repressive action against gays at the same time that the council and mayor were committed to an evasion strategy. In their comments about needle exchange in Philadelphia, Kirp and Bayer note that even while the rest of city government was evading official endorsement of a needle exchange program, the public health director, with the support of the mayor, stated that he would take unilateral action for clean needle distribution, even at the risk of arrest.

The fact that cities have many governing institutions and sometimes have divided elites can be a strategic advantage for challengers of the status quo, an observation that is a staple of research on social movements, protest, and regime change. It provides activists with multiple access points for advancing their demands and allows for "venue-shopping," that is, the choice of an institutional target that may be either more receptive or more vulnerable to activists' demands. Thus, in a given city, quite different "roles of government" may be exhibited in the same culture war because activists are taking advantage of the multiple venues that exist for pressing their claims. It also suggests that the degree of fragmentation of local governing regimes will be a critical factor in shaping whether or not multiple roles are evident.

Finally, multiple roles may be acted out as a culture war controversy in a particular setting evolves over time. Button, Wald, and Rienzo explicitly take such a dynamic approach, and several other chapters implicitly explore change over time as well. From a theoretical perspective, the dynamic approach is most appealing if it identifies characteristic sequences, that is, patterns of uptake of the various roles that are repeatedly observable. As noted above, two such characteristic sequences are evident: a sequence in which unintentional instigation of controversy and culture war activism is sparked by hyperactive responsiveness, and a sequence in which repression sparks unintentional instigation. Apart from this, however, the sequences of roles identified by the chapter authors are quite diverse, without the replication and patterning that would be of greatest interest.

Intergovernmental Perspectives

Although this volume represents an explicit attempt to examine the dynamics of culture wars in local settings, a number of the chapters illustrate the intergovernmental dynamics that shape local culture wars in important ways. Local governments are embedded in networks of horizontal relationships (with other local governments) and vertical relationships (with the state and federal governments). Scholars of urban politics have generated a considerable literature investigating the cooperative and the competitive sides of these relationships with respect to phenomena other than culture wars, such as the competition among cities for economic development; the cooperative arrangements by which localities engage in joint service delivery or constitute information networks for policy innovation; conflictual relationships between federal, state, and local governments over mandates; and the cooperative elements of federal and state grant programs to localities. There are subtle but important differences in the character of these intergovernmental dynamics with respect to culture war issues.

VERTICAL RELATIONSHIPS. Abortion-related court rulings and federal legislation such as the Freedom of Access to Clinic Entrances Act (FACE) are, in one sense, examples of mandates. It would be a mistake to conceptualize these as constraints on local government autonomy and to expect that they represent a point of conflict between subnational governments and the federal government, as is typical of the mandating literature. Rather, as Woliver's and Clarke's chapters make clear, these "mandates" function as welcome tools that local governments can use to ease the job of normalizing strident conflict. Local officials can engage in levels of repression that are deemed appropriate to community circumstances and evade pressures to take a substantive stand on the merits of abortion, with federal law and policy serving as a cover for their actions. Communities thus may differ dramatically from each other in the aggressiveness with which abortion protesters are handled by law enforcement authorities; but federal mandates give each local government the ability to avoid undue costs of repression by carrying out that repression under the banner of required enforcement of federal law. Similarly, state drug paraphernalia laws make it easier for local officials to evade the controversial issue of needle exchange.

On the other hand, officials at the state or federal level can exert pressures that make it more difficult for local officials to repress local activists, to evade culture war issues, or to be responsive to challengers of the status quo. Rosenthal, for example, illustrates how the Cuomo administration entered directly into the politics of gay and lesbian incorporation in Syracuse, putting pressure on local officials to respond to a proposed antidiscrimination ordinance. By contrast, Kirp and Bayer note a number of cities in which local officials' desires to move ahead with needle exchange programs were thwarted by gubernatorial and congressional opposition.

On the other hand, the existence of a complex federal system does allow for strategic maneuvering within the constraints of higher-level interference or opposition. When federal or state governments have been less than fully responsive to the demands of culture war activists, those activists frequently turn to local governments for recourse, as Haider-Markel and O'Brien found in their investigation of hate crime policy. Indeed, the federal system provides an opportunity for venue shopping, and Kirp and Bayer argue that this has allowed some county and municipal health officials to push ahead with needle exchange programs despite opposition from state and federal authorities.

HORIZONTAL RELATIONSHIPS. With respect to interlocal relations, culture wars are powerfully shaped by the dynamics of intergovernmental competition for economic development that were initially highlighted by Peterson (1981). Extending this logic, Pagano and Bowman (1997:47) point to the central importance of image in economic development politics. In order to realize their developmental goals, "local officials attempt to project a favorable and distinct image of the city." Economic development thus involves more than the strategic use of particular business incentive programs or capital improvements; it "is also very importantly an effort at image creation or preservation" (Pagano and Bowman, 1997:44).

A favorable city image can be threatened by high crime rates; high taxes or other policies that constitute an unfriendly business climate; a decaying downtown; or a lost professional sports franchise. As the contributors to this volume make clear, a city's image can also be threatened by culture war incidents. At least, community leaders perceive that such incidents are a threat to city image; and because of these perceptions, city governments' handling of culture wars is caught up in the imperatives of economic development politics. Thus, for example, Rick Musser's chapter documents how the city of Topeka's movement toward repression of a strident and disruptive homophobic activist was hastened when the actions of that individual most clearly threatened the city's image and impinged on economic development prospects. Similarly, in their assessment of the repression of antiabortion activists in Denver and Greenville, both Susan Clarke and Laura Woliver note threats to city image and concerns about bad publicity.

Thus, although culture war issues constitute a distinctive domain of urban politics, that domain is not autonomous from the other domains. Just as economic development imperatives limit action within the redistributional arena (Peterson, 1981), so also is there a connection between the economic development arena and what cities do with respect to culture wars. This logic can be extended to help understand the circumstances under which we are most likely to observe city government roles like evasion and repression that are hostile to culture war dissidents. Presumably, such roles are more likely in cities that are most preoccupied with their image, either because they are what Pagano and Bowman (1997:38) call "cities with uncertain orbits"—cities with a "weakened economic base" such that "city officials encounter difficulty in influencing the local economy"—or because they are "cities with expanding orbits"—cities where "the economic base is strong" and "city officials want their city to move up to the next orbit and compete beyond the region." By contrast, "cities with self-contained orbits," where the economic base is strong but officials are not aspiring to compete economically with cities at a higher level, are presumably less preoccupied with image and consequently less motivated to evade and repress culture war activists. Furthermore, DeLeon's analysis suggests the addition of yet another kind of city to the list, the world-class, corporate centers that are already both economically strong and competitive at the highest levels of the urban hierarchy. DeLeon's analysis suggests that a city in this category, such as San Francisco, is not only relatively immune to the need for repression of culture war dissidents, but may itself play a role as a dissident city in the national hierarchy of cities, adopting radical stances on culture war issues in order to provide leadership for similar action in other locales.

There is more to the interlocal aspect of culture wars than economic competitiveness among cities, important as that is. Cities are also joined in communication networks, borrowing ideas, and learning from each others' experiences. This insight has long been a staple for understanding the diffusion of a variety of policy innovations (Bingham, 1976). In the context of culture wars, we see the same dynamic, as cities learn from other cities that have been innovation leaders in needle exchange or gay rights and adapt their efforts to control antiabortion protesters in the light of what has happened in other cities.

CONCLUSION

Morality policies and the culture war controversies that they entail are arguably among the most divisive and explosive of episodes for local government. In the light of all that has been learned from these chapters, is it appropriate to conclude that morality politics is a truly distinctive domain, sharing few if any of the features of urban politics as usual? As inviting as it may be to give an unqualified response to this "big picture" question, the most appropriate response is probably mixed. Morality politics shares certain important features of urban politics as usual, and it exhibits some important differences.

With respect to similarities, we find that the competitive dynamics of economic development that shape other aspects of local government decision making also shape decisions in culture war controversies and that the cross-jurisdictional comparisons, policy learning, and diffusion of innovations that characterize other programmatic functions of local government also come into play with respect to these morality issues. We also find that the peculiar combination of conflict and cooperation, constraints and facilitation that characterizes inter-governmental relationships in our federal system applies to culture war phenomena. Just as political entrepreneurship is important in the developmental domain of local governance, so also is it an important role for local officials in culture war controversies. The important role that lower-level bureaucrats play in defining policy outcomes of other types is mirrored in the importance of lower-level public health, school, and law enforcement authorities in dealing with needle exchanges, gay issues, and abortion conflict. Just as there has been mixed and somewhat inconclusive evidence concerning the impact of the formal institutions of governance on policy outcomes of other kinds, so also do we find that when culture war issues are at stake, these formal institutions subtly shape the way that governmental roles are defined rather than having a definitive and direct impact on the emergence of the roles.

There are important differences between the morality politics of culture war controversies and politics as usual in American cities. Although organized interests are evident—many of them are the same sorts of interests that can be found in other arenas of urban politics—culture wars feature a somewhat more complex ensemble of interests, including not only identity groups based on race and ethnicity but identity groups based on sexuality, religion, public health, and other interests that are seldom featured in the analysis of urban politics.

The motivations, constraints, and opportunities that shape public officials' actions are also distinctive. Officials dealing with the allocation of street-surfacing funds, the siting of landfills, the negotiation of wage contracts with police and firefighters, and the issuance of tax abatements for development projects presumably bring to bear a number of the moral principles articulated in Schumaker's chapter, along with classic considerations of a straightforward political calculus. But, both because of their own beliefs about these issues and the fact that the issues evoke deep-seated moral beliefs on the part of many citizens, the principled, or ideological aspects of local officials' handling of culture war controversies are of greater interest than they have been in analysis of other aspects of urban governance. By the same token, the raw materials that officials have at their disposal for defining issues and for generating solutions are different from the material benefits that are the usual staples of urban politics. Because the legitimation of particular ways of life and the official sanctioning of morally contentious modes of conduct is at stake, officials are both uniquely constrained by the political culture of the community and empowered to use a variety of cultural ideals as they frame issues. They are also dealing in a realm in which symbolic policy outcomes are far from unusual, and far from trivial.

Finally, just as issue salience is important in understanding policymaking processes more generally, the development of culture war controversies is in part a function of issue salience. The difference is that these issues always carry with them the potential for explosively high levels of issue salience and for extraordinarily divisive and even violent forms of conflict within the community. Given these considerations, fear is a notable element in public officials' dealings with culture war issues. No city wants to be "another Wichita" or "another Pensacola," yet free speech rights and other constitutional issues are important constraints on officials' handling of these issues.

Given these distinctive features, then, culture war controversy rightly constitutes a fourth arena of local politics, alongside the allocational, developmental, and redistributional arenas. Much is yet to be learned about the patterns of politics and policymaking in this arena, but the cases and analyses presented in this volume make a persuasive case for the importance of that arena of local politics and offer a starting point for further inquiry.

Appendix. The Twenty-Five City Data Set

City	Governing Institutions	Cultural Setting	Governmental Roles					
			Evasion	Responsive	Hyperactive Responsiveness	Entrepreneurial Instigation	Repression	Unintentional Instigation
Springfield, Mo.	mixed reform	T			X			X
Tulsa, Okla.	unreformed	TI	X					
Albuquerque, N.M.	unreformed	TI		X				
Louisville, Ky.	unreformed	I		X				
Wichita, Kans.	mixed reform	I		X				
Chicago, Ill.	unreformed	I				X		
Oklahoma City, Okla.	mixed reform	TI				X		
Denver, Colo.	mixed unreform	M		X			X	
Topeka, Kans.	mixed unreform	M	X				X	
Greenville, S.C.	mixed reform	T	X				X	
Columbia, S.C.	mixed reform	T	X				X	
Rochester, N.Y.	unreformed	MI	X	X				
Albany, N.Y.	unreformed	MI	X	X			X	
Buffalo, N.Y.	unreformed	MI		X		X		
Syracuse, N.Y.	unreformed	MI					X	
San Francisco, Calif.	unreformed	MI	X					
Raleigh, N.C.	mixed reform	T		X		X	X	X
Cincinnati, Ohio	reformed	T		X		X	X	X
Philadelphia, Pa.	unreformed	MI	X			X		
Santa Cruz, Calif.	reformed	MI		X	X			X
Iowa City, Iowa	reformed	MI		X				
New York, N.Y.	unreformed	I		X		X	X	
Baltimore, Md.	unreformed	I					X	
Tacoma, Wash.	mixed reform	MI		X		X		
Portland, Oreg.	unreformed	M	X					

NOTES

1. Although the Kirp and Bayer chapter mentions needle exchange activists or developments in a substantial number of cities, for purposes of this analysis there was adequate information for comparative analysis on only some of the cities. In particular, New York, Philadelphia, Baltimore, Tacoma, and Portland were incorporated into the comparative analysis. Philadelphia also serves as a case in Wald, Button, and Rienzo's chapters; governmental roles that were evidenced either in the needle exchange analysis or in the gay rights analysis were recorded for Philadelphia and used in the twenty-five-city analysis presented in this chapter.

2. The exceptions, of course, are the larger data sets assembled by Button, Rienzo, and Wald (1997) on city adoptions of gay rights ordinances and by Haider-Markel (1998) on city adoption of hate crime ordinances. In addition to being focused on single culture war issues, however, these larger data sets typically do not have detailed information on local officials' actions other than the official outcomes of policymaking processes—for example, whether a gay rights ordinance was adopted—and hence they do not allow for an examination of the full range of local governmental roles.

3. The governmental roles for each city are those designated by chapter contributors, but in some cases (Denver, Rochester, Albany, Buffalo, and Syracuse), this involved the editor's interpretation of the chapter author's evidence. For the cases discussed by Kirp and Bayer, the editor was fully responsible for interpretation of the case vis-à-vis governmental roles exhibited. Categorization of each city by cultural setting was accomplished using Elazar's (1994:177) mapping. Categorization of each city's formal governing institutions was taken from the chapters, if presented; when information on formal government structures was not present in the chapter, the information was obtained from checks with such cities' web sites.

4. The analysis covers only the roles initially identified and therefore consistently considered by the chapter contributors. Hence, the nonresponsiveness role is not explicitly discussed.

5. This instance is not shown in the appendix because, in order to maintain consistency in tabulating results vis-à-vis type of city governing institution, that table charts only the roles exhibited in chapters dealing with city government. This instance was drawn from the chapter dealing with schools.

REFERENCES

Bingham, Richard. 1976. *The Adoption of Innovation by Local Government.* Lexington, Mass.: Heath.

Button, J. W., B. A. Rienzo, and K. D. Wald. 1997. *Private Lives, Public Conflicts: Battles Over Gay Rights in American Communities.* Washington, D.C.: Congressional Quarterly Press.

Cobb, Roger W., and Marc H. Ross. 1997. *Cultural Strategies of Agenda Denial.* Lawrence: University Press of Kansas.

Downs, Donald. 1989. *The New Politics of Pornography.* Chicago: University of Chicago Press.

Edelman, Murray. 1964. *The Symbolic Uses of Politics.* Urbana: University of Illinois Press.

Elazar, Daniel J. 1986. "Marketplace and Commonwealth and the Three Political Cultures." In Marilyn Gittell, ed., *State Politics and the New Federalism*. New York: Longman, pp. 172–79.

———. 1994. *The American Mosaic: The Impact of Space, Time, and Culture on American Politics*. Boulder, Colo.: Westview Press.

Haider-Markel, Donald. 1998. "The Politics of Social Regulatory Policy: State and Federal Hate Crime Policy and Implementation Effort." *Political Research Quarterly* 51(1): 69–88.

McCarthy, John D., and Mark Wolfson. 1992. "Consensus Movements, Conflict Movements, and the Co-optation of Civic and State Infrastructure." In Aldon Morris and Carol McClurg Mueller, eds., *Frontiers in Social Movement Theory*. New Haven, Conn.: Yale University Press, pp. 273–97.

Pagano, Michael A., and Ann O'M. Bowman. 1997. *Cityscapes and Capital*. Baltimore: Johns Hopkins University Press.

Peterson, Paul. 1981. *City Limits*. Chicago: University of Chicago Press.

Rienzo, B. A., J. Button, and K. D. Wald. 1996. "The Politics of School-Based Programs That Address Sexual Orientation." *Journal of School Health* 66:33–40.

Schneider, Mark, and Paul Teske. 1992. "Toward a Theory of the Political Entrepreneur: Evidence from Local Government." *American Political Science Review* 86 (September): 737–47.

Sharp, Elaine B. 1997. "A Comparative Anatomy of Urban Social Conflict." *Political Research Quarterly* 50 (June): 261–80.

Sturgeon, Noel. 1995. "Theorizing Movements: Direct Action and Direct Theory." In Marcy Darnovsky, Barbara Epstein, and Richard Flacks, eds., *Cultural Politics and Social Movements*. Philadelphia: Temple University Press, pp. 35–54.

Swidler, Ann. 1995. "Cultural Power and Social Movements." In Hank Johnston and Bert Klandermans, eds., *Social Movements and Culture*. Minneapolis: University of Minnesota Press, pp. 25–40.

Tarrow, S. 1994. *Power in Movement: Social Movements, Collective Action and Politics*. Cambridge: Cambridge University Press.

Contributors

RONALD BAYER is a professor in the School of Public Health at Columbia University School of Public Health. He has been examining ethical and policy issues raised by the AIDS epidemic since 1982, with articles appearing in the *New England Journal of Medicine,* the *Journal of the American Medical Association, The Lancet,* the *American Journal of Public Health,* and the *Millbank Quarterly.* Since 1981 he has authored two books—*Homosexuality and American Psychiatry: The Politics of Diagnosis* (Basic Books, 1981) and *Private Acts, Social Consequences: AIDS and the Politics of Public Health* (Free Press, 1989), the latter cited among the notable books of the year by the *New York Times.* Bayer co-edited (with David Kirp) *AIDS in the Industrialized Democracies: Passions, Politics and Policies* (Rutgers University Press, 1991) and (with Gerald Oppenheimer) *Confronting Drug Policy: Illicit Drugs in a Free Society* (Cambridge University Press, 1993). In 1995, Bayer's work was recognized by the National Institute of Mental Health when he was awarded a five-year Senior Scientist Award.

JAMES W. BUTTON is a professor of political science at the University of Florida. His work on minorities in city politics has appeared in numerous journals and edited volumes. His book *Blacks and Social Change* (Princeton University Press, 1989; paper edition 1992), winner of the V. O. Key Award, has been influential in the urban subfield. He has, in coauthorship with Ken Wald and Barbara Rienzo, published several articles on gay rights and city politics and is coauthor of *Private Lives, Public Conflicts: Battles Over Gay Rights in American Communities* (Congressional Quarterly Press, 1997).

SUSAN E. CLARKE is a professor of political science at the University of Colorado and a past president of the American Political Science Association's organized section on Urban Politics. While she has authored or coauthored numerous books and articles in the urban politics field including *The Work of Cities* (University of Minnesota Press, 1998), her work linking gender issues to urban analysis makes her an important participant in this volume. In particular, her chapter on "Gender, Place and Citizenship" (in *Gender and Urban Research,* Sage, 1994) and her chapter "Women Redefining Local Politics (in *Theories of Urban Politics,* Sage, 1994), along with her lead article on "Sex, Fear, and Urban Politics" in the Urban Politics section newsletter make her an important agenda setter for expanding urban research to the sorts of issues of relevance for this volume.

RICHARD DeLEON is a professor of political science at San Francisco State University. He is best known in the urban field for his work on the politics of San Francisco, including an *Urban Affairs Quarterly* article on San Francisco's progressive politics as an "anti-regime" and his book *Left Coast City* (University Press of Kansas, 1992), winner of the best book award given by Urban Politics section of the American Political Science Association.

DONALD P. HAIDER-MARKEL is a postdoctoral associate in the Department of Political Science at the University of Kansas. He has authored and coauthored several articles on gay and lesbian politics, abortion, hate crimes, and citizen militia groups, some of which have appeared in the *Journal of Politics, Political Research Quarterly, Social Science Quarterly,* and *Demography.* He is currently working on a book examining gay and lesbian politics at the state and national level and is continuing to research the role of "outsider" groups in the policy process.

DAVID L. KIRP is a professor at the Goldman School of Public Policy at the University of California-Berkeley and a member of the Board of Directors of the ACLU's Northern California chapter. He writes regularly on a variety of social policy issues and is a regular contributor to a host of scholarly and general circulation publications, including *P/S*, the *New York Times,* and the *Nation.* His recent books include *Our Town: Race, Housing, and the Soul of Suburbia* and *Learning by Heart: AIDS and the Schoolchildren of America's Communities.*

RICK MUSSER is the Clyde Reed Teaching Professor at the University of Kansas School of Journalism and Mass Communications and director of the journalism program's graduate studies. He was vice president of American City Business Journals, a chain of more than thirty business weeklies, and has published numerous articles as a reporter for magazines and newspapers.

SEAN P. O'BRIEN is a doctoral candidate in political science at the University of Wisconsin-Milwaukee where he specializes in terrorism and political violence. His articles on these subjects have appeared in the *Journal of Conflict Resolution, Social Science Quarterly,* and *Political Research Quarterly.*

BARBARA A. RIENZO is a professor in the Department of Health Science Education at the University of Florida. She has published numerous articles and chapters on sexuality education and school health programs. She is coauthor, with James Button and Kenneth Wald, of numerous articles and *Private Lives, Public Conflicts: Battles Over Gay Rights in American Communities* (Congressional Quarterly Press, 1997).

DONALD B. ROSENTHAL is a professor of political science at the State University of New York at Buffalo. Professor Rosenthal has authored, coauthored, or edited seven books as well as contributing numerous articles and chapters in urban politics. Among his publications is *The Politics of Community Conflict,* published in 1969, which treated the culture wars set off by proposals to fluoridate municipal water supplies. His recent work includes an article in *Urban Affairs Review* on gay and lesbian politics and an article in *Polity* on AIDS politics. Professor Rosenthal is currently engaged in editing a collection of original pieces on AIDS politics and policy for a journal symposium and a related book.

PAUL SCHUMAKER is a professor of political science at the University of Kansas whose work spans the fields of urban politics and political theory. In his 1991 book *Critical Pluralism, Democratic Performance, and Community Power* (University Press of Kansas), Schumaker showed how local officials in a small community have been responsive to demands to regulate morality despite the dominance of more liberal values opposing such regulation within the culture. He has also published numerous articles on community conflicts and local politics, including recent articles on community power analysis (in *Urban Affairs Quarterly*), and articles on gender cleavages and local policy issues (in the *American Journal of Political Science* and *Social Science Quarterly*).

ELAINE B. SHARP is a professor of political science at the University of Kansas and a past president of the American Political Science Association's organized section on Urban Politics. Her published work in urban politics includes two books, *Urban Politics and Administration* (Longman's, 1990) and *Citizen Demand-Making in the Urban Context* (University of Alabama, 1986), along with numerous articles and chapters, the most relevant of which are "Culture Wars and City Politics: Local Government's Role in Social Conflicts" (published by *Urban Affairs Review* in 1996) and "A Comparative Anatomy of Urban Social Conflict" (published in *Political Research Quarterly* in 1997).

KENNETH D. WALD is a professor of political science at the University of Florida. He is a specialist on religion and politics and has published a variety of articles in that area as well as his influential book *Religion and Politics in the United States* (Congressional Quarterly Press, 3rd edition, 1997). He is currently collaborating with James Button and Barbara Rienzo on a line of research involving gay rights in local politics and is a co-author with Button and Rienzo of *Private Lives, Public Conflicts: Battles Over Gay Rights in American Communities* (Congressional Quarterly Press, 1997).

LAURA R. WOLIVER is an associate professor of Government and International Studies at the University of South Carolina. She is the author of a book featuring several case studies of community controversy over moral issues (*From Outrage to Action: The Politics of Grass Roots Dissent,* University of Illinois Press, 1993) and her work on abortion politics, police conduct and black civil rights, and other issues of social controversy has been published in *Policy Studies Journal,* the *Western Political Quarterly, Women & Politics,* and edited volumes published by Routledge, Columbia University Press, Rowman and Littlefield, and others.

Index